# The Investor's Guide to Closed-End Funds
## The Herzfeld Hedge

**Thomas J. Herzfeld**

**McGraw-Hill Book Company**  New York  St. Louis  San Francisco
Auckland  Bogotá  Düsseldorf  Johannesburg  London  Madrid  Mexico  Montreal
New Delhi  Panama  Paris  São Paulo  Singapore  Sydney  Tokyo  Toronto

*Author's Note:* Because there is no such thing as a foolproof stock market strategy, none of the concepts discussed in this book should in any possible way be considered a guarantee of profits. As for the profitable examples cited here, all of them must be considered as theoretical trades for the purposes of illustration only. In no way are they to be regarded as an accurate "track record." Finally, it must be constantly kept in mind that any and all investments in the stock market involve risks and that no one, no matter how qualified, can offer any guarantees of success.

Library of Congress Cataloging in Publication Data

Herzfeld, Thomas J
  The investor's guide to closed-end funds.

  Includes index.
  1. Investment trusts.   I.  Title.
HG4530.H4        332.6′327        79-13714

1234567890   KPKP   89876543210

The editors for this book were Kiril Sokoloff and Celia Knight, the designer was Elliot Epstein, and the production supervisor was Thomas G. Kowalczyk. It was set in Electra by University Graphics, Inc.

Printed and bound by The Kingsport Press.

To My Loving Wife
**Rutli**
and to
**Britt** and **Erik**

# Contents

# List of Figures and Tables

# Preface

The risk-reward relationship in trading closed-end funds represents the best opportunity the stock market has to offer the individual as well as the institutional investor.

That is most definitely a hard-nosed statement, especially in the light of the stock market's behavior in recent years, but I make it with no excuses for the past and no apologies for the future. I also firmly believe that my statement applies to the conservative investor as well as to the aggressive one.

It must be emphasized that my belief in the potential for gain in trading closed-end funds—by knowledgeable investors professionally guided—did not come to me in a mystical flash. Nor is it the result of one of Wall Street's never-ending succession of "tips."

Rather, I came to closed-end funds slowly and laboriously, and I did not begin to recommend them to my clients until I had completed thousands of hours of study and research. My studies, it should be noted, were under no circumstances limited to closed-end funds. They covered every area of investment included in that amorphous term "Wall Street."

To understand this, let's briefly look at the more or less standard education of registered representatives or customers' men. Generally speaking, Wall Street trainees listen to lectures and attend seminars presided over by business school faculty members, and, quite naturally, they hear presentations from the heads of various departments at the brokerage house where they are training.

In addition to being given a formal introduction to the basic world of common stocks and bonds, trainees have a curriculum which includes option writing, puts and calls, commodities, mergers and acquisitions, and municipal bonds. They also hear a lot about investment trusts, particularly of the open-end type commonly known as mutual funds.

About closed-end funds, however, hardly a word is spoken. They seem not to exist, and if they do, it is in a financial limbo, in a world apart.

In addition to having their personal favorites, brokerage house instructors also understandably preach the "party line." They recommend that trainees work closely with their firm's research department and that they rely heavily on the department's advice when discussing stock purchases with clients.

In the 1950s and 1960s, trainees who became brokers, more often than not, followed this advice and did rather well. Why not? Just about all Wall Street research departments in those heady days were enamored with the so-called glamour stocks. And these stocks meant profits for happy clients and healthy incomes for their brokers.

Then, as the saying goes, something happened. For reasons which have been endlessly analyzed and debated, the go-go years ended, and the market started sliding downward, smashing the Dow Jones Industrial Average as well as hosts of individual stocks. No group, it is safe to say, was smashed harder than the so-called "glamours." Stocks which had been selling in the $150 to $200 range—and which a lot of "experts" claimed would go even higher—emerged in the wreckage of the 1970s selling for $5 or $10 a share, or less. Some glamour stocks which had been endorsed by research departments as the IBMs and Xeroxes of the future for all intents and purposes disappeared, as did the personal fortunes and emotional well-being of all too many investors. For better or worse and to the chagrin of many investors to whom they had once been fair-haired boys, many brokers had to try to write off the debacle while continuing to struggle with the recommendations of their research departments.

I readily admit that a few years passed before I fully realized that most brokerage houses do not have the answers to the needs and aspirations of a large percentage of investors. This failure, it must be stated, most definitely applies to mutual funds, many of which, like the glamour issues, had their day in Wall Street's sun and then faded into a dull, plodding oblivion.

And so, although not completely disillusioned with Wall Street's conventional thinking, I struck out more or less on my own, searching for areas in which investors might realize solid gains with the least possible risk. Eventually, I entered that limbo to which closed-end funds or *closed-end investment trusts* (CEITs) had for so many years been consigned. In time, as this book will show, I was devoting all of my working energy to closed-end fund research and trading. I readily admit that I virtually ignored all other sectors of the stock market, refusing to heed friends and associates who insisted that I get out of the area which they, in varying degrees, swore held no future for the broker or the investor.

The fact is that I accelerated my research as I began to recognize distinct trading patterns in closed-end funds. More importantly, I also learned that these patterns were quite predictable.

I began keeping daily charts on some 40 different funds, tracking their performances, their yields, net asset values, dividend policies, management philosophies, the composition of their portfolios, and, most importantly, their discounts. I also kept track of the behavior of these funds in up and down markets, as well as who traded in them, both on and off the stock exchange floors.

Gradually, this accumulation of research began to pay off in the only fashion which counts—in real profits. Closed-end funds might be overlooked and ignored by the Wall Street herd, but not by intelligent investors.

In my investigation into CEITs, one of the astounding things I discovered early on is that no single book was devoted to the subject. Indeed, published material of any sort on the subject was sparse. The most I could ever locate was a few casual pages in various texts devoted to the general stock market. Brokerage houses which publish material on funds concentrate on open-end mutual funds that generate hefty sales commissions.

A handful of advisory services do show, on occasion, a modicum of interest in CEITs, but it is the sort which more often than not surfaces briefly and then fades completely, for months if not years. When this interest does appear on the Wall Street stage, closed-end funds quite naturally rally. However, there is no denying that since the 1930s, there has been a pitiable amount of interest in them for any sustained length of time. As a result—and as we shall explain in detail—closed-end funds in general have tended to trade at widening discounts from their net asset value.

Here I must make a personal confession. After I had established my basic trading strategies for CEITs about 1970–1971, for the next 5 years or so I was as secretive as possible about my work. I had discovered a better mousetrap, and I was not about to share it casually. I was going to make the most of it, for my customers and myself personally. And, in full modesty, I can say that I did.

In 1976 I decided it was time to reveal some—I repeat, some—of my ideas to the general investing public. My reasons, as any honest Wall Street trader should admit, were not based on charity. I realized that by exposing my ideas in an occasional newspaper article or research report, I could do two things: assist investors to try to make money in what had been a "foreign" area of the stock market and demonstrate to investors the advantages of doing their trading through my firm. The idea worked. On the one hand, I was giving away some ideas, but, on the other hand, my firm and I were making more money in the form of commissions from those who accepted my theories and wanted to put them to use.

I also came to understand that by sharing my knowledge of closed-end funds, I had added a positive stimulus to them: the more individuals trading in closed-end funds, the more liquidity there is for everyone. (I admit to being curious about the long-term impact of this, the first book published on closed-end funds, their trading, and arbitrage.)

Before getting into specific details, I believe the title of this book merits explanation. "The Herzfeld Hedge" is the name I originally gave to an arbitrage strategy which involved establishing a long position in a closed-end fund and a short position in the listed options whose underlying stocks were in that fund's portfolio. I expanded that strategy and came to recognize that most of my work in closed-end funds involved a form of hedging or arbitrage. The title of this book, *The Investor's Guide to Closed-End Funds: The Herzfeld Hedge*, seemed to be the only suitable one to describe the aggregate of my trading strategies.

Different types of traders can and will, I am convinced, find a variety of applications for the Herzfeld Hedge. The subject of trading closed-end funds is not limited to investors with a single goal. On the one hand, an aggressive trader can use margin in buying dual-purpose funds and achieve leverage of up to 6 to 1. On the other hand, a conservative investor looking for income might trade in bond funds yielding 10 percent; and by the timely rotating of one fund into another in order to catch dividends and small profits, he might realize from 15 to 20 percent total return without any more risk than he would have incurred in buying a portfolio of investment grade bonds.

Some aggressive stock market traders have told me trading closed-end funds is dull. Later we'll describe in detail how shortsighted this kind of thinking is. For now, it should be noted that in the past few years several funds have more than doubled in value. The highly aggressive investor who bought one of the more volatile funds, including the dual-purpose vehicles, could have realized gains ranging from 3 to 1 to 6 to 1, and, if he was an in-and-out trader, even better gains.

I intend this book to show how closed-end funds can be used by both individual and institutional investors seeking income, capital gains, arbitrage, and yes, even takeover candidates. I will go into every aspect of closed-end fund trading, hoping to show the individual reader, regardless of his specific investment objectives, the true potential for gain presented by closed-end fund trading.

This book, then, is an attempt to "go public" on what has been a relatively private subject. But regardless of the research and experience on which it is based, it will succeed only if it helps investors do the all-important: make money.

*Thomas J. Herzfeld*

*Note:* For illustration purposes the author sometimes refers to the hypothetical investor as "he." In such situations masculine pronouns are used to make the text easy to understand, not set standards as to the sex, or even the number, of parties involved.

# Acknowledgments

I am deeply indebted to my personal editor, Bernard J. Swartz, without whose hard work and dedication this book would not have been possible. Mr. Swartz has that rare ability to translate the jargon of Wall Street into the kind of simple, straightforward language which is easily understandable to both the sophisticated and the ordinary investor.

I am also indebted to my friends and colleagues who contributed their expertise, time, and suggestions to this book. The following is only a partial list of those to whom I am very grateful.

Harry Altman, Richard B. Cohen, Bruce Dorfman, Robert F. Drach (options), Robert Fisher (open ending), Arthur N. Franke, CPA, Samuel Friedman, Farrell C. Glasser, Esq. (securities law), Keith Gollust, Armand Gottlieb (utility analyst), Maurice Gottlieb (utility analyst), Simon Grow, Henry W. Hays (portfolio management), Bennett B. Herzfeld, CFP, Leonard L. Herzfeld, Esq., Leonard Itkin, Patrick M. Joyce, Benjamin Jacobson, Harvey A. Karter, Michael C. Kalnick, Esq., Alexander Lamont (trading), Jay B. Lesselbaum, Elton Meltzer, Judd S. Meltzer, Roger Miller, Thomas Murphy, Barbara Neilson, Richard Phalon, George Palmer, CPA, James Sutton Regan, Robert S. Rosen, Anthony Ramondi, Steven G. Rabinovitz (fixed income securities), Leonard A. Salamon, Louis A. Scherer, Martin Spector (gold stocks), Donald B. Shafto, Esq., Isaac Schlesinger, Ira Sochet, Herbert Spooner, Warren Weiss, Ann White, Ronald Yellin (statistics), Robert Zelinka (bond market strategist).

A general word of thanks is due to my colleagues at Bishop, Rosen & Co., Inc., whose names I have not mentioned but whose assistance and contributions were invaluable.

All charts were prepared on two-cycle, semilogarithmic TEKNI-PLAT charting paper, supplied by John Magee Inc., Boston, MA. The daily price and volume information were also provided by the Magee staff. The charts were rendered by Susan MacFarlane.

*TJH*

# A History and Description
# of Closed-End Funds

Closed-end funds have been in existence at least since one was formally created in Belgium by King William I of the Netherlands in
1822.[1] Today, more than a century and a half later, there are more
than 60 such closed-end funds [closed-end investment trusts (CEITS)
or publicly traded funds] in the United States alone. As a group, they
have a market value of well over $6 billion.

It is most ironic, however, that most executives of financial institutions, professional traders, and stock brokers, to say nothing of individual investors, are rarely able to name even five closed-end funds.
Indeed, many Wall Street experts to whom I have spoken cannot
name a single one.

This should give the reader an idea of how little interest exists in
Wall Street in the group—except for a small, curious handful who are
determined not to follow the mob but who prefer instead to search
thoroughly and conscientiously for profit-making opportunities.

Before getting into a brief history of closed-end funds, it is essential
that the student and potential investor understand precisely what they
are. One of the best ways to define a closed-end fund is to state what
it most definitely is not . . . and that is this: a closed-end fund is not a
mutual fund, which, by its very nature, is open-ended, continually
offering new shares for sale to the investing public. In addition to being
much more well known than closed-end funds—thanks to millions
spent in sales promotion—mutual funds also operate differently.
Their purchase price, for example, is the net asset value per share
(NAV)—meaning the total net assets of the fund divided by the number of its outstanding shares, plus a sales charge which can run as high
as 8 percent. In the case of the so-called no-load funds—those without
a sales commission—shares are generally bought and redeemed at
their net asset value.

Closed-end funds, on the other hand, do not continue to sell shares

endlessly, as the mutual funds strive to do. Closed-end funds issue—
and this is essential to understand—a fixed amount of stock. In this
respect, they are just like any industrial firm or utility which, with the
exception of splits or additional offerings of stock, essentially always
has the same number of shares outstanding. Closed-end fund shares
trade in the open market exactly like common stocks of any publicly
traded company.

In an effort to emphasize this trading similarity, the Association of
Closed-End Funds recommended in 1977 changing the name of the
group to *publicly traded funds*.

There is only one way to buy or sell shares in a closed-end fund—in
the open market. This is another factor that differentiates the closed-
end fund from the mutual fund. An investor purchases a mutual fund
from the fund itself through its sales agents, and when the investor
sells his shares, they are redeemed by the fund. The only method of
trading in closed-end funds, either on the buy or sell side, is in the
open market—on the stock exchanges or in the over-the-counter markets. Shares in closed-end funds, it must be remembered constantly,
are not redeemed at their net asset value, as are shares in open-end
funds. Rather, they are bought and sold at the price the general market places on them. And that price could be at net asset value, above
it, or, as is more usually the case, below it, meaning at discounts.

Historically, with variations, the primary objective of closed-end
funds—diversification—has essentially stayed the same. Even the
trust created by William I of the Netherlands was designed to provide
a means of capital diversification (as well as a way to invest in foreign
government loans). The concept, that of spreading risk through diversification, was further developed by the British.

The London Financial Association and the International Financial
Society, both formed in 1863, were apparently the first British investment trusts.[2] They were of the closed-end type, and they were
designed to provide the comparatively small investor with the advantages of spreading his risk over a number of different stocks. The development of British investment trust companies was enhanced by the
passage of the Joint Stock Companies Acts of 1862 and 1867. Under
them, British investors could share in the profits of an enterprise with
their liability limited to the size of their individual investment.

Robert Fleming, generally regarded as the "father of investment
trusts," after a visit to the United States, foresaw this country's need
for capital for railroads as well as other industries. As a result, in 1873,

hc helped to form the first association in Scotland for investment in United States rail bonds.[3] These bonds had to be "carefully selected and widely distributed, and where the investments would not exceed one-tenth of the capital in any one security."[4]

In 1909, Fleming formed Robert Fleming and Company to carry on a general financial business. It has been estimated that because of interlocking directorships or more direct relationships, the Fleming company exerted an influence on the investment policies of some 56 trusts with aggregate resources of £114 million.

The first major challenge to the British investment trusts came in 1890 with the Baring crisis, named for the key role played in it by the highly prosperous financial organization, the House of Baring. The firm had granted a large amount of capital to the Argentine Republic, undertaking the loans and guaranteeing the interest. With the default of the Argentine government, a general financial crisis, if not panic, was touched off. Baring was believed to be on the brink of suspending payments, with liabilities amounting to some £21 million. Fortunately, the Bank of England, along with some leading financial institutions, took over the liabilities and averted further, if not total, disaster. However, because of the losses suffered by British investment trusts during the crisis, trust managers tended to become more conservative.

From about 1900 until World War I, British investment trusts increasingly invested in American securities, especially in the stocks and bonds of railways. During the war, from 1914 to 1918, "British trusts sold a large proportion of their American investments, or in lieu of sale, deposited them with the British government for the purposes of financial mobilization, obtaining in return a Government income guarantee."[5] Actually, until the 1950s, all British trusts were of the closed-end type. The majority of the trusts today, like their predecessors, are characterized by conservative management practices.

The first investment trust in the United States was the Boston Personal Property Trust. It was created in 1893 and "it met every definition of a closed-end general management company,"[6] being closely modeled after its conservative British counterparts. Boston Personal Property Trust was converted to an open-end fund in 1967. It was not until 1904 that the United States had its first closed-end fund which was entitled to employ leverage. This company, originally known as Railway and Light Securities, in 1954 changed its name to the Colonial Fund, Inc., and 2 years later converted into an open-end fund.

During the 1920s, closed-end funds experienced what can best be described as phenomenal growth in the United States. Among the hundreds of companies which were formed and thrived in the seemingly endless boom of the decade were Adams Express, International Securities Trust of America, and Tri-Continental Corporation, which in 1978 was the largest closed-end fund in the nation, with assets of close to half a billion dollars.

The Securities and Exchange Commission (SEC) estimated that by the end of 1929, of the public's investment of over $7 billion in companies studied by the agency, the overwhelming amount was in closed-end companies and what should strictly be called holding companies. "There was a mere $140 million in open-end companies, $163 million in fixed trusts and very minor amounts in other types," the SEC said.[7]

When the stock market crashed on Black Thursday, October 24, 1929, among the biggest losers were holders of shares in highly leveraged closed-end funds. In fact, the fate of leveraged closed-end funds was drastically worse than the fate of nonleveraged companies. According to the SEC, "By the end of 1937, the average dollar which had been invested in July 1929 in the index of leverage investment company stocks was worth 5 cents, while the nonleverage dollar was worth 48 cents."[8]

The massive numbers of investors who had holdings in investment companies had taken a fierce beating. Many sold out at whatever price they could get. Amid the general devastation, however, there were those who saw opportunities for profits. With investment company securities selling far below their asset values, if control of such companies could be gained, the companies themselves could be dissolved or consolidated profitably. Mindful of this, organizations like Floyd Odlum's Atlas Corporation and the Equity Corporation began scooping up voting stock of floundering companies. Then the absorbing companies purchased senior securities of the target institutions at prices far below their possible liquidation values. Control was then obtained by an offer of securities of Odlum's company in exchange for the company being taken over. Once control was obtained, the "raided" company was either dissolved or consolidated.

It is safe to say that closed-end investment companies never regained the elevated status they enjoyed in the 1920s before the Crash. It is true that shortly after the Great Depression itself, there was a brief rise in interest in fixed unit investment trusts, perhaps because investors believed their rigid nature provided more security.

But since the Depression, the overwhelming growth in investment trusts has been concentrated in open-end mutual funds.

Today, the basic guideline in the United States for both closed-end and mutual funds is the Investment Company Act of 1940. In many respects, it is a detailed code designed to provide individual investors in investment trusts with the kind of protection sorely lacking before the Great Depression. For example, the overly leveraged companies which fared so poorly during the Depression have been prohibited. Similarly, the capital structure and dividend policies of the funds are now strictly regulated. The funds may not issue any debt which is not adequately covered by their assets, and they are not permitted to pay dividends from profits realized on the sale of securities without disclosing the source of such distributions.

Another provision protects existing stockholders from new issues of stock at a price below current net asset value. Such transactions are closely scrutinized by the SEC.

Since the passage of the Investment Company Act there has been minimal growth in closed-end investment companies in the United States. A major reason is that their common stocks have been selling at discounts from net asset value for a lengthy period. When such companies attempt to issue new shares, they find themselves, therefore, in a very difficult position. If they were to issue shares at a discount from net asset value, they would be diluting the holdings of existing stockholders—something which might be prevented by the SEC. On the other hand, if they were to issue shares at a premium, they would find it next to impossible to market those shares in an environment where most closed-end funds are selling at a discount.

Despite the debacle of the Depression, despite regulations and the appeal—to say nothing of the hucksterism associated with mutual funds, good and bad—the American investor of today has a wide variety of potentially profitable closed-end funds in which to invest. Some of these funds invest only in common stocks, others only in preferred stocks or bonds. Some portfolios are diversified, reflecting a broad spectrum of American industry; others are concentrated in a single industry.

It is safe to say that for the vast majority of investors, closed-end funds generally remain a mystery. Certainly these funds, like all other investment vehicles, are not to be entered into lightly. Potential investors must be aware of their special language and qualities and, most of all, must have an understanding of how closed-end funds should and should not be traded in the all-important quest for profits.

## NOTES

[1]Stuart B. Mead, *Mutual Funds: A Guide for the Lay Investor*, D. H. Mark Publications, 1972, p. 3.

[2]Theodore J. Grayson, *Investment Trusts, Their Origin, Development and Operation*, New York, John Wiley & Sons, Inc., 1928, p. 14.

[3]Hugh Bullock, *The Story of Investment Companies*, New York, Columbia University Press, 1959, p. 5.

[4]Ibid.

[5]Grayson, op. cit., p. 18.

[6]Bullock, op. cit., p. 15.

[7]Bullock, op. cit., p. 46.

[8]*Report of the Securities and Exchange Commission, Investment Trusts and Investment Companies*, part III, chap. 1, p. 4.

# The Discount and the Other Variables of Closed-End Fund Trading and Analysis

## 2

Trading in closed-end funds requires a full-scale understanding of the discount and its causes and effects, as well as an evaluation of an assortment of other variables which affect closed-end funds. Unfortunately, the degree of importance of the variables is not constant for the different types of funds (stock funds, bond funds, etc.). Also, the variables continually shift in relative importance to each other under various trading conditions. There is no method to establish a practical mathematical formula that can adjust under all conditions for the shifting variables.

In later chapters, emphasis is devoted to specific variables which have particularly sharp impact on the type of fund being discussed. For now a single general example—expenses—should be sufficient. Expenses are of considerable importance in evaluating a bond fund but of minor consequence in a stock fund. In a bond fund yield is the paramount objective. Therefore, expenses bear directly on a fund's ability to attain its stated objective. On the other hand, expenses do not bear directly on a stock fund's ability to obtain capital gains; that is a function of management's ability to pick the right stocks.

## THE DISCOUNT

The discount from net asset value (NAV) per share is the most significant variable in all types of closed-end fund trading, regardless of the fact that funds may differ in scores of other aspects. The discount by definition is the difference by which the price of a fund is lower than its net asset value per share. Net asset value per share is the market value of the securities owned by a fund plus cash, etc., minus liabilities divided by the number of shares outstanding.

A fund selling at a premium, which is rare in closed-end funds, is one which is selling at a price higher than its NAV. The following table gives an example of the discount and the premium.

| | | |
|---|---|---|
| NAV | $10.00 | $10.00 |
| Price | 8.00 | 12.00 |
| | $2.00 Discount or 20% | $2.00 Premium or 20% |

## REASONS FOR THE DISCOUNT

Despite the many attempts and studies that have been made, I have never seen a complete and accurate explanation of why closed-end funds sell at discounts. I divide the reasons for the discount into two categories—those which apply to all funds, as a group, and those which apply to specific funds.

### Reasons Applying to All Funds

1. Lack of sponsorship. Most stock brokerage firms tend to avoid recommending closed-end funds, primarily because other forms of investment trusts, such as mutual funds and fixed unit investment trusts, generate higher sales compensation. If this sounds harsh, it is primarily a criticism of the management of the brokerage firms, not their registered representatives. In most firms, the registered representative is encouraged to sell (and some times restricted to recommending) his firm's research recommendations. If the firm says he should sell fixed unit investment trusts or mutual funds instead of closed-end funds, he readily complies, especially if he gets paid twice as much or more for doing so. A customer buying $10 of NAV of a mutual fund ordinarily pays an 8 percent sales charge or $10.80. A customer buying a closed-end fund with a NAV of $10, besides getting the shares at a discount from NAV, that is, at $8 or $9 a share, pays only a regular New York Stock Exchange commission, which since May 1975 has been negotiable. His cost would be about 20 to 25 cents a share versus about 80 cents in the mutual fund. Fixed unit investment trusts usually have sales charges of about 3 percent. Ironically, since fixed unit investment trusts are offered at a "net price," the customer often thinks he is saving the commission, when actually he is paying a higher (built-in) commission.

2. Relatively poor yield. If an investor buys a portfolio of stocks on his own, the yield he receives will be the total dividends divided by the

cost of the portfolio. If an investor buys a portfolio of stock by taking a position in a closed-end fund, the yield will be reduced by the extent to which the expenses of the fund cut into its income. A fund drifting to a 10 percent discount may be compensating for 10 percent of operating expenses.

3. New issues. Occasionally, for no apparent reason, a certain type of closed-end fund will begin to sell at larger discounts. This may be caused by brokers liquidating existing closed-end fund issues in order to obtain capital to switch their customers into a new issue. For example, in the winter of 1977–1978 a new "junk bond" fund was coming to market. Junk bonds are by definition lower-quality, higher-yielding bonds. The managers of several brokerage offices encouraged their salesmen to switch customers out of closed-end bond funds, then yielding 9 to 9¼ percent, into the new junk bond fund with an estimated yield of 9½ to 10 percent. This switching into the new issue caused discounts to widen on closed-end bond funds.

In my opinion, incidentally, this was a very poor recommendation. The 9 to 9¼ percent yield then available in closed-end bond funds was highly attractive. Most closed-end bond funds have at least 50 percent of their portfolios invested in bonds rated single A or better and sell at a discount from their NAV. The new junk bond fund was being brought out at a premium from NAV and had almost no investment grade bonds in its portfolio.

4. Domino theory. If one or two funds go to a discount, investors tend to shy away from those funds not selling at a discount. Eventually the lack of demand for the funds without the discount virtually forces those funds to gravitate to a discount. The domino theory, then, is the old law of supply and demand in action in the fund market.

5. Fear of a larger discount. Investors are naturally reluctant to buy a fund at a narrow discount if that fund has a historical pattern of selling at a wider discount. The fear of the discount's being wider when an investor wants to sell adds fuel to the discount widening.

A sure way to avoid a widening discount would be to buy an open-end fund, which by definition is redeemable at NAV.

If closed-end funds made annual tenders for their shares, this would solve the entire discount problem. I will discuss this concept in later chapters.

6. Tax selling. Discounts almost always widen toward the end of the calendar year. In an effort to offset a realized capital gain in another security, an investor will sell a fund he is holding at a loss. Quite often

the maneuver is unwise because the funds tend to rebound in January and the investor loses more by selling the fund than he gains in the tax savings.

### Reasons Applying to Specific Funds

1. Capital gains tax liabilities. This is a frequently mentioned reason which is not fully understood. Some of the older funds, as well as those which have been highly profitable, might very likely be holding positions which they purchased at prices substantially lower than their current market value. For example, a fund might own IBM at a fraction of its current market price. To qualify for favored tax treatment, a fund is required to distribute to its shareholders at least 90 percent of any net realized capital gain (as well as dividend income). This means that if such a fund sold its IBM, thus realizing a substantial capital gain, the individual shareholder would be liable for his proportionate share of the capital gains tax—even if he only owned the fund for one day! Therefore, if an investor buys a fund with large unrealized capital gains, he is buying a potential tax liability. This is indeed a valid reason for a fund to sell at a discount.

However, my studies have not been able to establish an obvious correlation between discounts and unrealized capital gains. I can only conclude that the reason for this is that some of the funds with large capital gains tax liabilities are also the funds with superior performance. One variable is therefore offsetting the other.

2. Poor performance. Of course, if good performance is a reason for no discount, poor performance is certainly a reason for a wide discount. If a stock fund consistently underperforms the Dow Jones Industrial Average, investors are obviously going to shy away from it in the kind of growing numbers which will quite naturally cause it to move to continually larger discounts.

3. High management fees and fund expenses. Very little discussion is needed on this point. It is self-evident that if the assets of a fund are drained by large expenses, it will and should sell at a sharp discount.

4. Illiquid portfolios. Funds with high concentrations of illiquid holdings, that is, private placements or stocks with investment restrictions, more often than not sell at large discounts. The reasons for this are quite simple: positions which are not readily marketable reduce the potential performance of the fund. Also, it makes those funds less desirable as takeover or open-ending candidates (see Chapter 10 on open ending).

## ADVANTAGES OF THE DISCOUNT

Now that we have given the warnings about discounts and their causes, let's move to the positive side—to the main advantages to the investor in buying closed-end funds selling at discounts from their NAV.

1. Leverage. When it comes to leverage, CEITS are of unique value to the investor. In all other forms of investing when leverage is used, the investor pays for the leverage. The reverse is true with closed- end funds where the investor receives leverage and, in addition, is being paid for it.

If an investor buys 1000 shares of a $10 stock, a $10,000 investment, he only needs to put up $5000, with the remainder provided by the broker in the form of margin. He would, therefore, be investing $5000 to control the market value of $10,000 worth of stock. As for the $5000 balance in his account, he would be charged monthly interest. In other words, in this case the investor is paying interest for the use of the leverage.

If the same investor bought 1000 shares of a CEIT with a NAV of $10 per share, at a 50 percent discount from NAV, or $5, he would also be getting $10,000 worth of securities and investing only $5000. However, he would be receiving the dividends and capital gains potential on the entire $10,000 worth of securities without incurring any interest expense. A CEIT is therefore, as previously mentioned, unique with respect to leverage and the absence of cost for the use of that leverage.

2. Higher yield. This is a matter of simple arithmetic. If a CEIT's dividend is 50 cents per year and the fund is selling at its NAV of $10 a share, the yield would be 5 percent. However, if the CEIT is selling at a 20 percent discount at $8 a share, the 50 cent dividend would then result in a 6¼ percent yield.

3. Larger capital gains potential. CEITs bought at excessive discounts in declining markets tend to have narrowing discounts when the market turns higher. This causes a two-pronged force on the price of the CEIT: as the stock market moves higher, the CEIT's portfolio and thus its NAV move higher. This combination of a narrowing discount and a rising stock market creates a dramatic effect on the price of the CEIT.

4. Protection in declining markets. Odd as it may seem, initially, CEITs purchased at excessively wide discounts may provide the inves-

**FIGURE 2.1**
**Example of Discount and Premium**

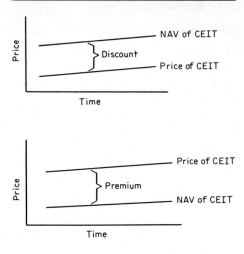

tor with a cushion in a declining market. As a CEIT's portfolio declines in market value and its NAV decreases, the CEIT's discount may begin to "normalize," or narrow, absorbing the erosion in the fund's portfolio.

Figure 2.1 is a chart of two CEITs, one trading at a discount and the other at premium. (Chapter 3 provides a detailed analysis of closed-end fund charting.)

## VARIABLES AND OTHER CONSIDERATIONS AFFECTING CLOSED-END FUNDS

Broadly speaking, there are two categories of variables which influence the price of CEITs: those which generally relate to specific funds and those which apply to the overall stock market and economy.

### *Variables Relating to Specific Funds*

1. Capital gains tax liability. This factor was discussed earlier as a reason for a discount. It bears repeating that a very large capital gains tax liability is a pressure for a higher discount.

2. Loss carry-forward. CEITs with loss carry-forwards merit positive consideration. This is quite simply because the loss carry-forward rules

out any problem of capital gains tax liabilities. It also gives the fund added appeal as a merger target.

3. Past performance. The ability of a fund's management to consistently outperform the indexes is a reason for a fund to sell at a narrower discount than funds with poor performance.

4. Volatility. From a trading point of view, it is recommended that a trader look for funds which are relatively volatile, that do some "swinging." Adams Express, for example, is significantly less volatile than either Madison Fund or National Aviation and Technology. For example, a fund selling at $10 a share should not be considered for trading unless it had at least a 2- or 3-point range in the previous year.

5. Leverage. In rising markets, funds with highly leveraged capital structures have much more appeal than those without. Conversely, in declining markets, the buying of funds with leveraged capital structures should be avoided. (A leveraged capital structure means that the fund has a large proportion of preferred stock and/or debt in relation to its common stock.) Dual-purpose funds usually provide the highest leverage—2 to 1—in their capital structure in the closed-end fund group.

6. Yield. If it were possible for all other variables to be equal, then the investor should seek funds offering the greatest yield. Yield will usually depend on the type of stocks in a fund's portfolio as well as the fund's discount and its operating expenses.

7. Management fees and expenses. As funds with high yields are attractive, so too are funds with low management fees and expenses. Tri-Continental Corporation is a good illustration of a fund whose operating expenses are relatively low; General American Investors and U.S. & Foreign Securities have been on the comparatively high side.

8. Where the funds trade. It is advantageous to trade funds listed on the New York Stock Exchange as opposed to the American Stock Exchange and especially the over-the-counter (OTC) market. This is primarily because funds traded on the Big Board tend to have deeper, more liquid markets. Also, when it comes to funds which trade OTC, the investor has the spread between the bid and the asked price working against him. He is buying on the asked side and selling on the bid. On the other hand, with funds traded on an exchange, the investor has a better opportunity buy on the bid and sell on the offer.

9. Relative liquidity. Funds with illiquid portfolios should be avoided, especially for short-term trading, unless the investor is quite

certain that the discount more than compensates for this basic disadvantage.

10. Depth of the market. A CEIT trader quickly learns which funds can be readily traded in any appreciable size and which cannot. As a general rule, the more largely capitalized CEITs can be traded in larger sizes at prices at or close to their last sale. An exception to this rule is a fund in which a single shareholder owns a large percentage of the stock.

11. Portfolio composition. One must continually evaluate which industry groups are the strongest. Careful attention should be given to being invested in funds whose portfolios have large concentrations in currently strong industry groups. For example, if oil and gas stocks are strong, Petroleum and Resources Corporation would most likely be a strong performer.

As a second example, we can compare Madison Fund (MAD) and Lehman Fund (LEM) in the 1977–1978 period. During that time, blue chip stocks were sliding and secondary stocks were strong. MAD held the latter group and did very well, whereas LEM held blue chip stocks and consequently had a disappointing performance by comparison.

12. Reputation of management. Wide discounts in some funds often represent the investment community's appraisal of a fund's management. Some officers and directors of CEITs have actually been censured by the Securities and Exchange Commission. Others, who have not been formally censured, have nevertheless established poor reputations for themselves. The prime question one should ask is, "Are the officers and directors acting in the best interests of the shareholders?" Poor management reputation could prevent a fund's discount from narrowing to any appreciable degree. Many of the funds do, however, have capable, dedicated management. Farrell C. Glasser, a leading securities attorney, has done extensive studies on the various conflicts of interest existing in investment companies. (For an interesting examination of this subject, see Farrell C. Glasser, "Attorney's Conflicts of Interest in the Investment Company Industry," *University of Michigan Journal of Law Reform*, Fall 1972.)

13. Dividend reinvestment program. If the fund has such a program, its performance should be evaluated. Here the principal question is, "Do the reinvesting shareholders usually pay the relatively lowest or highest price for their new shares during the reinvestment period?" Some funds have an extremely poor record in this area, with reinvesting shareholders continually paying the highest prices every

quarter. I have done extensive studies of this subject, but it is beyond the scope of this book.

Other funds may issue new shares at the current market price, which, if it is below NAV, will dilute the NAV of the fund. This practice, in my opinion, is unfair to the shareholders who do not reinvest their dividends.

14. Options. In recent years, some stock funds have begun to write covered options on stocks in their portfolios. This may increase yield but at the expense of decreasing capital gains potential. If an investor is seeking income, he should buy a bond fund. One fund gave up option writing after a brief try, because it lost a considerable amount of money with the experiment.

15. Special objectives. Two funds which usually sell at premiums are ASA and Petroleum and Resources Corporation (PEO). They sell at premiums, in my opinion, primarily because they have special objectives. ASA is the only CEIT on the NYSE which specializes in South African gold mining companies. PEO, as its name indicates, specializes in the petroleum industry (it diversified slightly and changed its name in 1977). The funds' premiums may be a reflection of their unique objectives. Conversely, a fund whose investment objective is the same as 10 other funds will tend to sell at a relatively larger discount.

16. Quality. Funds which have high-grade portfolios should and usually do sell at relatively narrow discounts. This means that unless one of the other variables is far out of line, a CEIT with a very high-grade portfolio which is trading at a large discount represents an unusually good buying opportunity.

17. Dividend payment schedule. Depending on the policy of the fund, dividends may be paid monthly, quarterly, or semiannually. Monthly dividends mean that the trader has the advantage of possibly catching a dividend on a short-term trade. On the other hand, if a fund pays an infrequent, but large, dividend or capital gains distribution, anticipation of such a payout usually touches off extra buying in the CEIT. As a result, the fund's price may tend to be more volatile at that time.

18. Dividend policy. According to the tax laws, to qualify under the conduit theory, which is designed to eliminate double taxation of dividends to investment trust shareholders, a fund must distribute at least 90 percent of its dividends and capital gains. However, some funds have adopted the strategy of making large distributions whether or not

the capital gains are earned. This may be misleading to shareholders. It appears that they are getting a higher yield, but actually they are only getting their own money back.

19. Takeover and open-end candidates. Funds with poor performance, relatively high expenses, and liquid portfolios may well be candidates for a takeover or for conversion to an open-end fund. The trader is advised to be on the lookout for such funds. When a CEIT is converted to an open-end fund, it may be redeemed at NAV. This would in most cases mean an instant profit. Chapter 10 is devoted to this highly important variable.

20. Historical discount. This variable is continually evaluated. The essence of my work involves trading at established deviations from a moving average of the fund's discount.

21. Maturity. This variable applies only to bond funds, which are discussed in Chapter 5. Basically (assuming a normal yield curve), the longer the average maturity of a fund's portfolio, the deeper the discount should be; the shorter the maturity of the bonds in the portfolio, the narrower the discount should be. It is paradoxical that the opposite is usually true.

22. Hedging opportunities. Funds which can be easily hedged are more desirable than other funds for trading purposes. There are two basic forms of hedges: fund versus fund and fund versus naked options—the Herzfeld Hedge. Chapter 9 is devoted to this subject. Funds which can be easily hedged are those whose portfolios contain stocks on which options are traded on an option exchange or funds which have similar portfolio composition to other funds.

23. Convertibility. This variable applies to funds with convertible bonds. Such bonds are convertible into the common stocks of their respective issues. Convertible bonds either have low interest rates and are selling close to their conversion price or high interest rates and less interesting convertibility features. A thorough discussion of this concept appears in Chapter 6 on convertible bond funds.

24. Termination. This applies usually to dual-purpose funds and is discussed in detail in Chapter 8. Briefly, a dual-purpose fund at a fixed date is either liquidated or converted to an open-end fund. The termination date is vital because the discount will always be zero on that date.

**External Variables Affecting Closed-End Funds.** By my definition, the external variables are those which have no direct impact on CEIT's

**FIGURE 2.2**
**The Three Phases of Bull and Bear Markets**

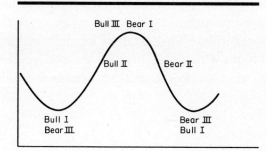

individually or collectively. And yet, because they are "facts" of the economics of investing, their impact on the funds' prices is more often than not of crucial importance. They include:

1. Market direction. In bull markets, one should buy undervalued funds, that is, ones at wide discounts. In bear markets, one should sell short overvalued funds—those at narrow discounts or premiums. In the first and second stage of a bull market, bid aggressively. By explanation, each bull and bear market has three *emotional* phases. Phase I of a bull market begins, as Figure 2.2 shows, at Phase III (the final phase) of a bear market. The public is panicky and dumping stocks. Professionals are buying and covering short positions. Closed-end fund discounts are often extremely wide in this phase. In Phase II of a bull market, which the public considers a rally in a bear market, the professionals are still buying. In Phase III of the bull market or Phase I of the bear market, the public begins to buy wildly, and the professional is selling and establishing short positions. Closed-end funds have very narrow discounts or perhaps even premiums. In Phase II of the bear market, which the public calls a correction in a bull market, the professional is still selling short. In Phase III of the bear market, which is Phase I of the bull market, the professional is covering short positions and buying, while the public is selling out.

2. Interest rates. Rising interest rates usually mean a generally lower stock market, while declining interest rates usually point to a rising market. Interest rates have an even more direct effect on closed-end bond funds because not only are the prices of the bond funds caught in the general stock market weakness, but also their NAVs are falling due to declining bond prices.

3. Net mutual fund redemptions and sales. There is an extremely

high coefficient of correlation here. When mutual fund redemptions are high, discounts tend to be wide. During periods of net mutual fund sales, discounts are narrow.

4. The Herzfeld Index. This external variable was invented by the author. It is an index which measures the general trends of closed-end fund discounts as a group. It will be discussed in depth in later chapters.

# Charting

## 3

The finest book I have read on stock market charting is *Technical Analysis of Stock Trends* by Robert D. Edwards and John Magee (John Magee, Springfield, Mass., 1966). If it were not for the fact that closed-end funds are in a world of their own, I might omit this chapter and refer the reader to that book. However, closed-end fund charting requires a special dimension, resulting in special charts. This chapter, therefore, concentrates on my specially devised closed-end fund charts as opposed to those which are traditionally employed by stock market chartists.

## TRADITIONAL STOCK MARKET CHARTS

Most traditional stock market charts which are published on a daily basis include the following standard information: the stock's price, its volume, the relevant time period, and dividend and stock split data. As for the stock's price, it is usually represented by a vertical line showing the high, low, and close for the day being reported. Figure 3.1 is an example of a price line.

The second ingredient is the price scale, which is invariably on the left side. A chart combining price and time scale is presented in Figure 3.2.

Volume is shown on the bottom of the chart, usually either in hundreds or thousands of shares, depending on the activity in the stock (see Figure 3.3).

As displayed in Figure 3.4, the time period involved generally runs along the bottom of the chart. Depending on need, it can be shown on a daily, weekly, monthly, yearly, etc., basis.

Dividends are often noted at the bottom of the chart with the ex dividend date indicated. Figure 3.5 shows a stock which was ex dividend 25 cents on February 15.

**FIGURE 3.1**
**High, Low, and Close of a Stock on a Given Day**

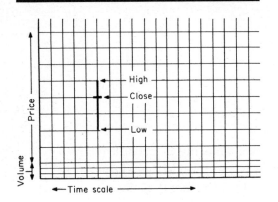

**FIGURE 3.2**
**Price and Time Scales**

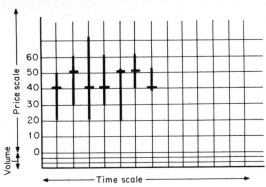

Figure 3.6 and Table 3.1 represent a hypothetical traditional stock and contain the factors cited above.

**FIGURE 3.3**
**Volume Scale**

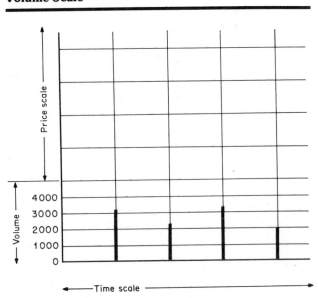

**FIGURE 3.4**
**Time Scale Marked Off at Monthly Intervals**

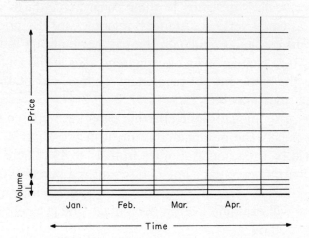

**FIGURE 3.5**
**Time Scale Indicating Ex Dividend Date**

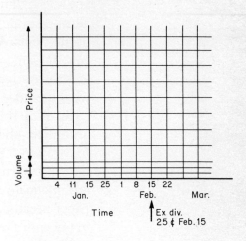

**FIGURE 3.6**
**Graph Representing Behavior of Hypothetical Stock**

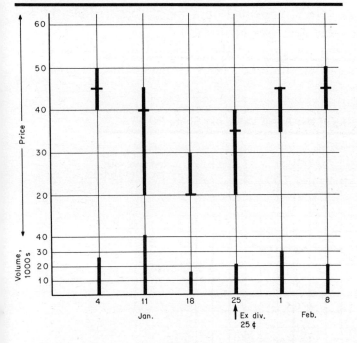

**TABLE 3.1**
**Behavior of Stock in Figure 3.6**

| Week | High | Low | Close | Volume |
|------|------|-----|-------|--------|
| Jan. 4 | 50 | 40 | 45 | 25,000 |
| Jan. 11 | 45 | 20 | 40 | 40,000 |
| Jan. 18 | 30 | 20 | 20 | 15,000 |
| Jan. 25 | 40 | 20 | 35 | 20,000 |
| Feb. 1 | 45 | 35 | 45 | 30,000 |
| Feb. 8 | 50 | 40 | 45 | 20,000 |

ex div. 25¢ week of Jan. 25

## HERZFELD CLOSED-END FUND CHARTS

The paper used in my charts is TEKNIPLAT, manufactured by John
Magee, Inc. This paper's most important feature is that it has a ratio
or semilogarithmic scale. According to the manufacturer, "the paper

shows percentage advances or declines" of what is being charted "in their true relation, even though the (stocks) may be selling at different levels. . . . The price scale is designed to show equal percentages of advance or decline as equal vertical distances, regardless of the price of the stock. A certain vertical distance on the paper will always indicate the same percentage change and a moving trend at a certain angle will always indicate the same rate of percentage change, no matter what the price of the stock may be."

By using this type of semilogarithmic charting paper, as opposed to arithmetic charting paper, the distance consumed on the chart in a move from 6 to 7 will be the same as a move from 12 to 14. There is no feasible way to chart a percentage line (a discount is a percent) on arithmetically scaled paper. This must be done on semilogarithmic paper because, as we will examine later, a percentage line is essential to my entire trading method.

My charts, in addition to the traditional information on price, volume, time frame, and dividends, include the following: net asset value per share, my buy line, my sell line, an index, and a leading indicator.

The net asset value (NAV) is plotted on a weekly basis, while the price of the fund is plotted daily (see Figure 3.7).

The distance between the price of the fund and the NAV is, of course, the discount—when the fund's NAV is higher than its price.

**FIGURE 3.7**
**Weekly Plotting of Net Asset Value per Share (NAV)**

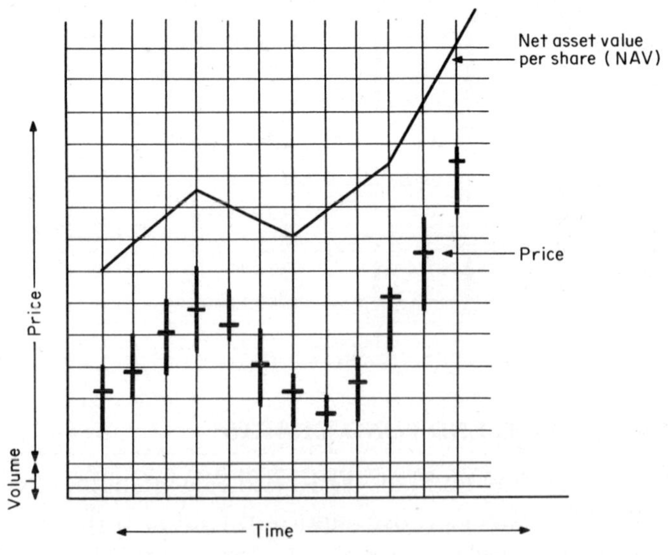

**FIGURE 3.8**
**Discount (*a*) and Premium (*b*) in Relation to NAV**

**23**
Charting

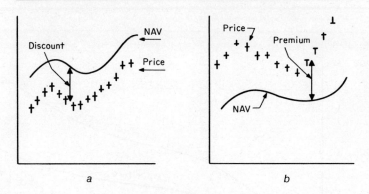

a                                          b

The distance between the NAV and the price of the fund is the premium, if the price is higher than its NAV (see Figure 3.8).

The suggested buy line, which is intentionally oversimplified here, is a mathematically established percentage deviation greater than the (moving) average discount, or premium, of the fund. The sell line, oversimplified, is an established percentage deviation smaller than the (moving) average discount or premium of the fund (see Figure 3.9).

Comparing the percentage performance of a NAV to an established index can be highly useful. For example, in a stock fund, the Dow

**FIGURE 3.9**
**Suggested Buy and Sell Lines**

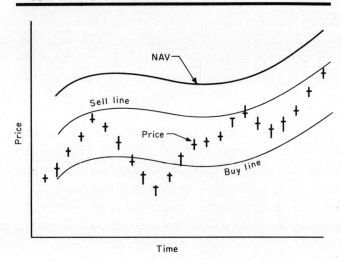

**FIGURE 3.10**

**Chart Showing Relationship between NAV of a Stock Fund and Dow Jones Industrial Average**

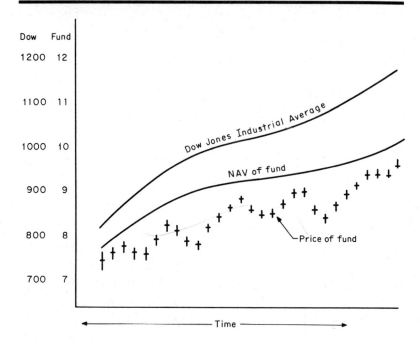

Jones industrial index is a valuable benchmark. In the case of a bond fund, the Dow 20-bond average provides an excellent comparison of performances (see Figure 3.10).

An index is not essential to all charts, but one should be included in at least every chart for each group of funds. I recommend placing the charts of all funds with similar objectives on a wall, one under the other, with the index included on the top. By standing back a few feet from the charts, one can easily see how all of the funds in a particular group are performing in relation to each other and in relation to the index included in the top chart.

Because the NAV of funds is published only on a weekly basis, it is essential to employ a separate daily indicator. Through interpolation, this indicator can project the NAV of a fund for the coming week. For utility funds, as an example, I employ the Dow Jones Utility Average. In Figure 3.11, a hypothetical one, the utility average was on the upswing during the first week of April. Based on that leading indicator, we can easily and accurately conclude that the NAV also will be higher.

**FIGURE 3.11**
**Projecting Next Week's NAV of a Utility Fund by**
**Interpolating the Dow Jones Utility Average**

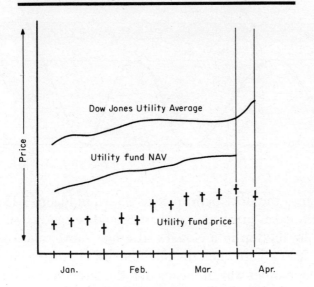

## A NOTE FOR EXPERIENCED CHARTISTS

In discussing charts for closed-end funds, I feel like the golf pro who makes videotapes of his students' lessons. After examining these tapes, the pro inevitably advises the pupil to forget all he knows about golf and start over, from the beginning. Such advice, on the golf course, is the beginning of wisdom.

When it comes to trading closed-end funds, wisdom begins in the same way. The investor using standard charting concepts is destined for disaster. Speaking from personal experience, I can confidently say that what looks like a "breakout" is more likely, in fact, to be a top. And what looks like a "breakdown" usually turns out to be a painful bottom. For example, Figure 3.12 shows a stock in a horizontal chan-

**FIGURE 3.12**
**Stock in Horizontal Channel**

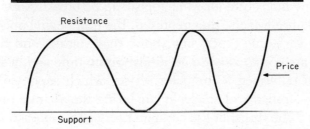

**FIGURE 3.13**
**Stock in "Breakout"**

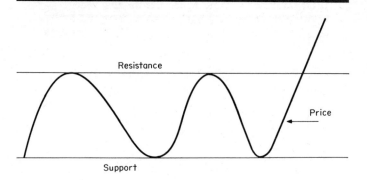

nel. However, if the stock performed as shown in Figure 3.13, it would usually be termed a "breakout" by chartists and be aggressively bought. This is usually the top in a closed-end fund's move, and the fund is therefore a "sale"—just when the traditionalist chartists would be buying. To put it another way, it means that the discount is too narrow—a sure sale signal.

Examples abound of erroneous breakout signals when traditional charting approaches are applied to CEITs. The fundamental weakness is that traditional chartists usually interpret abnormal current strength as an indicator of what they consider probable future strength. It is ironic that an unusual show of strength in a CEIT is generally the end of a move, not a forecast of a future move.

One can think of what takes place when a rubber band is being stretched. The price of a closed-end fund in relation to its net asset value is like that rubber band. When the fund moves sharply higher and begins to look like a breakout situation, the fund is in reality becoming overpriced in relation to its NAV. The rubber band—like the fund—must return to a relaxed position if it is not to snap.

It must also be kept in mind that what might look like a breakout on an ordinary chart of a CEIT may simply be the result of a large order being filled. After the order is executed, the fund tends to sell off again. The opposite holds true for what appears to be breakdowns; for skilled closed-end fund traders, they represent the best buying opportunities.

In a similar vein, experience shows that volume and tick studies cannot be applied to closed-end funds. Some time ago, a major brokerage firm published a computer service which supposedly showed the relative strengths of stocks by analyzing the volume on plus and minus ticks. The thrust of the computer service's approach was to buy stocks with large up tick volume and sell those with a high minus tick volume.

I did not follow the guidelines of the service. Instead, in trading closed-end funds, I did exactly the opposite, buying funds with the largest minus tick volume and selling those with the highest plus tick volume. As for the results, they were surprisingly good. Why? Simply because strong up tick volume meant the discounts were becoming too narrow, and strong minus tick volume meant they were becoming too wide.

This anecdote is a way of reemphasizing that when it comes to closed-end funds, take a professional's advice: forget everything you know—or think you know—about the game and start over, from the beginning.

There is probably no better starting point than the subject of the next chapter. It deals with the trading of stock funds.

# Trading Closed-End Stock Funds

**4**

Here is a capsulized list of the principal closed-end stock funds traded in the United States:

| Name | Trades on | Symbol | Shares in millions |
|---|---|---|---|
| The Adams Express Company | NYSE | ADX | 14.5 |
| Carriers and General Corporation | NYSE | CGR | 1.3 |
| Central Securities Corporation | ASE | CET | 5 |
| General American Investors Co., Inc. | NYSE | GAM | 8.3 |
| The Lehman Corporation | NYSE | LEM | 32.6 |
| Madison Fund, Inc. | NYSE | MAD | 22.9 |
| Niagara Share Corporation | NYSE | NGS | 7.2 |
| Source Capital, Inc. | OTC | SORC | 6 |
| Tri-Continental Corporation | NYSE | TY | 23.7 |
| U.S. & Foreign Securities Corporation | NYSE | UFO | 5.3 |

## ADVANTAGES OF CLOSED-END STOCK FUNDS AS LONG-TERM INVESTMENTS

For a variety of reasons, a large number of investors are not inclined to be traders. Usually, trading goes against their nature. Without trying to "convert" such individuals, I would like to note the general advantages of investing in closed-end stock funds for the long-term. Among the major advantages are:

1. Diversification. With such funds, the investor is buying a diversified portfolio of stocks through a single transaction. Some portfolios are speculative; others consist of blue chip stocks. The kind of fund an investor purchases should depend on his own financial position, the degree of risk he wishes to undertake, and, of course, the kind of

advice he receives and heeds. The prime objective of diversification is the spreading of risk. History has demonstrated that it is extremely unlikely that a fund's entire portfolio could fall out of bed—crumble—overnight. With the ownership of an individual stock, on the other hand, an investor may be vulnerable to a bad earnings report or some other form of negative news which could send the price down sharply.

2. Professional management. A group of professional managers is working in behalf of the investor in a closed-end fund. The managers constantly monitor the portfolio, making buys and sells when they believe the timing is opportune to strengthen the fund's portfolio.

3. The discount. Here is an advantage uniquely enjoyed by investors in closed-end funds. With rare exceptions, they buy an entire portfolio at a discount from its market value.

## A BASIC TRADING APPROACH FOR BEGINNERS

Trading closed-end funds need not be especially complicated. The approach I'm about to outline is relatively simple. I used it for many years before developing more refined techniques. The performance attained in using the basic approach is not, it should be noted, significantly different from performance attained in using more sophisticated methods. The primary advantage of the basic approach is that it requires less research time.

The beginner's first step should be the construction of a chart of a specific closed-end stock fund. That chart should show the fund's net asset value and its price. Although Figure 4.1 is made on a daily basis, a fund can be charted weekly, eliminating much tedious work.

The next step is to determine the average of the three widest discounts and the three narrowest discounts at which the fund traded over the previous year. For example, if a fund's three widest discounts in a year were 30, 32, and 34 percent, the average of these three discounts would be 32 percent. And if its three narrowest discounts over the course of the same year were 20, 21, and 22 percent, the average discount of the three would be 21 percent.

Once these two average percentage discounts have been established, they should be plotted on the chart. These percentage discount lines become the buy and sell parameters for trading the fund. In this example, the buy line would be at a 32 percent discount, and the sell line would be at a 21 percent discount.

The plotting of a percentage discount on a closed-end fund chart is

FIGURE 4.1
Fund without Buy and Sell Lines

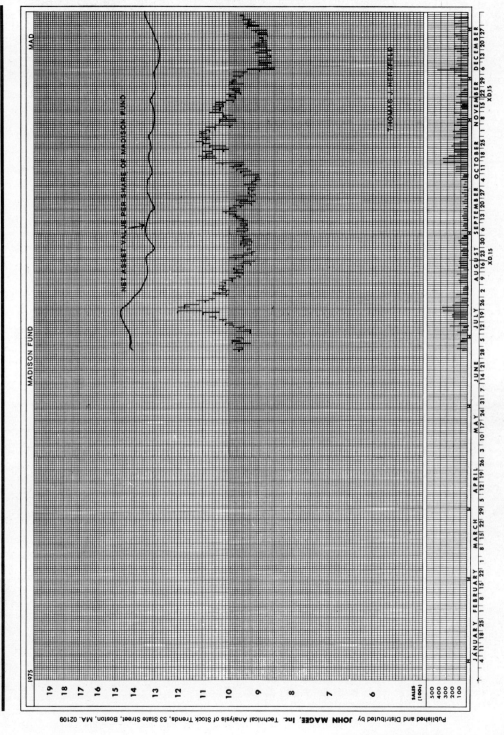

**FIGURE 4.1**
**Fund without Buy and Sell Lines** *(Cont.)*

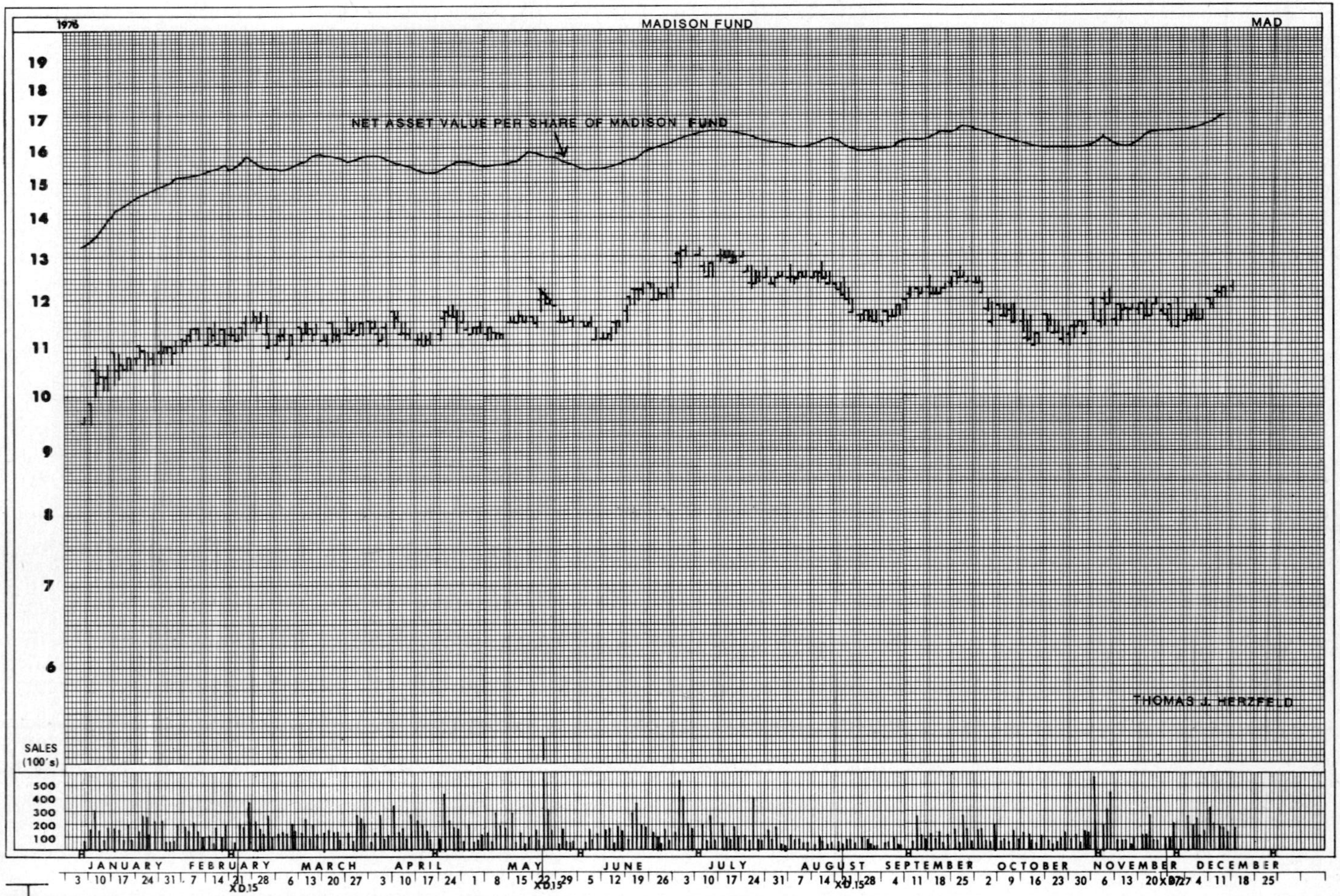

MADISON FUND

MAD

NET ASSET VALUE PER SHARE OF MADISON FUND

THOMAS J. HERZFELD

very simple if semilogarithmic paper is used (as discussed in Chapter 3 on charting). A specific percentage discount from net asset value *will always be the same distance from the net asset value line on the chart, regardless of price*. To repeat, this is the single most important advantage to be gained from using semilogarithmic paper.

To see how this method works, we will examine Figure 4.2 on the Madison Fund (MAD) during the second half of 1975 and all of 1976. For the period being charted, the average of Madison's three widest discount points was 32 percent, and the average of the three narrowest points came to a 20 percent discount. Then, every week when Madison Fund's net asset value was published, a 20 percent and a 32 percent deviation from that discount were plotted. (Figure 4.2 is a daily chart, but a weekly one would suffice.)

What would have happened if an investor had traded Madison Fund based on this basic charting method? In July 1975, at Point A, he would have been a buyer in the 9¼–9½ range. He would have received a sell signal 3 weeks later, at Point B, when the stock went to the 11¾–12 area, or to a 20 percent discount from net asset value. This very sharp, short-term move in the stock, if the investor had followed the basic method, would have generated a profit before commissions of approximately 2½ points.

The next buy signal came in the first week of October at Point C, when the stock again declined to a 32 percent discount and sold at $9 a share.

Then just two weeks later, in the week of October 18, the stock rallied, not only to the sought-after 20 percent discount, but to 18 percent when Madison went through 11. However, the trader would have been a seller at 10½, when the stock hit a discount of 20 percent, producing a precommission profit of 1½. (In the advanced method, which will be discussed later, the trader may have been a seller when the discount was at a more profitable 18 percent discount.)

Aggressive traders would not only have been selling when the fund reached the sell line, they would also have established short positions. Such traders would have bought at Point A, sold at B, sold short at B, covered at C, gone long at C, sold at D, and gone short again at D.

The next buy point occurred in the beginning of December at Point E, when Madison Fund declined to a 32 percent discount, selling at 8½. Within 5 weeks at Point F in the beginning of January 1976, the fund rallied again to 10¾ and was selling at a 20 percent discount, where it would have been sold. (A precautionary note is necessary. It

**FIGURE 4.2**
**Madison Fund with Buy and Sell Lines**

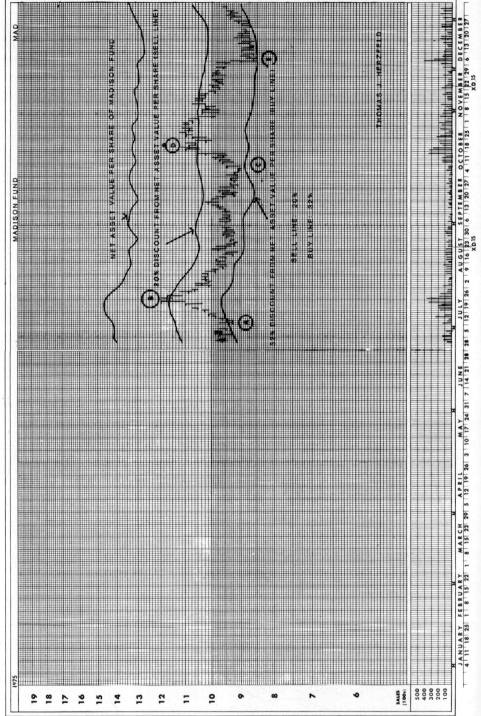

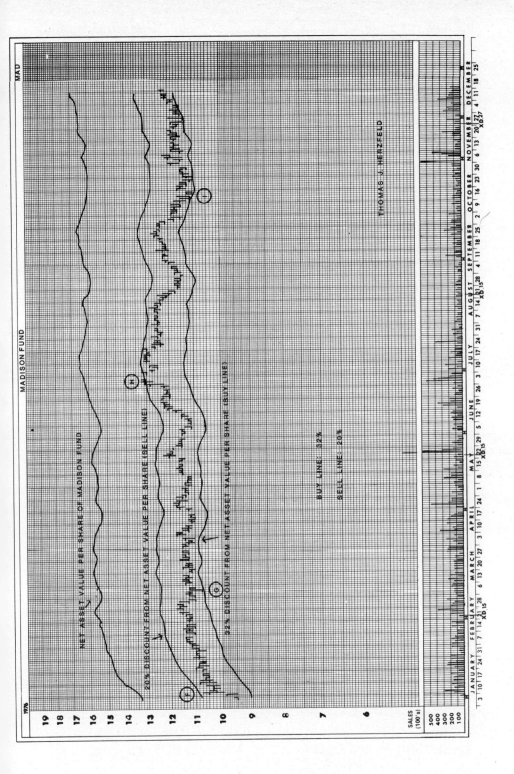

MADISON FUND

MAD

1976

NET ASSET VALUE PER SHARE OF MADISON FUND

20% DISCOUNT FROM NET ASSET VALUE PER SHARE (SELL LINE)

32% DISCOUNT FROM NET ASSET VALUE PER SHARE (BUY LINE)

BUY LINE: 32%

SELL LINE: 20%

THOMAS J. HERZFELD

JANUARY | FEBRUARY | MARCH | APRIL | MAY | JUNE | JULY | AUGUST | SEPTEMBER | OCTOBER | NOVEMBER | DECEMBER

SALES (100's)

35

does not pay to hold out for the last ⅛ of a point when trading any closed-end fund. Let someone else get that last bit. Madison only momentarily touched that 20 percent line in the January rally. Therefore, allowing someone else to reap the last ⅛ would have been very wise here.)

At the beginning of March 1976, at Point G, Madison Fund again sold—momentarily—at a 32 percent discount. The price was 10¾ and by the end of June, at Point *H*, the discount had narrowed to 20 percent (actually 19 percent before the move was completed, when the stock traded in the 13 area). The next buy signal came in the beginning of October, Point *I*, when Madison again sold at a 32 percent discount which was then $11 per share.

This example of the Madison Fund should demonstrate that seeking substantial profits by trading closed-end funds is not an overly complicated process. It should also serve to confirm something which I have believed for many years—*that there is significantly more potential profit to be derived from trading a fund, or most stocks for that matter, than in long-term investing.*

From the period of July 1975 to December 1976, Madison Fund moved from 9½ to 12 and a fraction, representing a potential capital gain of almost 3 points for an investor who had bought and held it during that period. However, if in the same period, an investor had traded in Madison Fund, using the "simple method," buying as well as selling short, his total profit could have been an amazing 16 points. And if this same investor had traded on margin, his return in that period could have been a profit of 213 percent on an annualized basis. (These examples should not be regarded as the type of profits which should typically be expected from trading in closed-end funds. In applying my basic method to the Madison Fund, I admittedly used the best example I could find. When asked my opinion on what percentage return a trader in closed-end funds can expect in a year, I am compelled to avoid giving a direct reply. This is because too many variables are involved. The objective for accounts I manage is a 20 to 30 percent profit a year. Obviously, there are no guarantees such an objective will be attained.)

Figure 4.3 for Lehman Corporation (LEM) in 1975–1976 provides us with another good example of the basic method in action. In the beginning of 1975, LEM was selling at a narrow discount. Our sell line was established at 13 percent and a multiple sell (sell short) signal was given at Points $A_1$ and $A_2$ in February–March of 1975. The price at $A_1$

## FIGURE 4.3
Lehman Fund

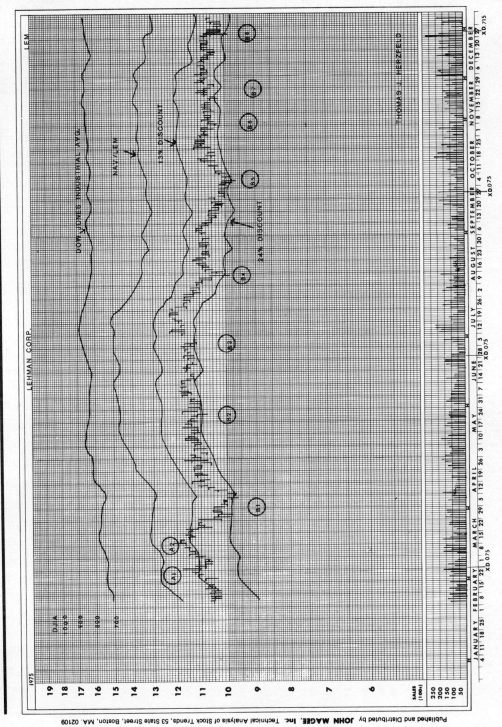

**FIGURE 4.3**
Lehman Fund  *(Cont.)*

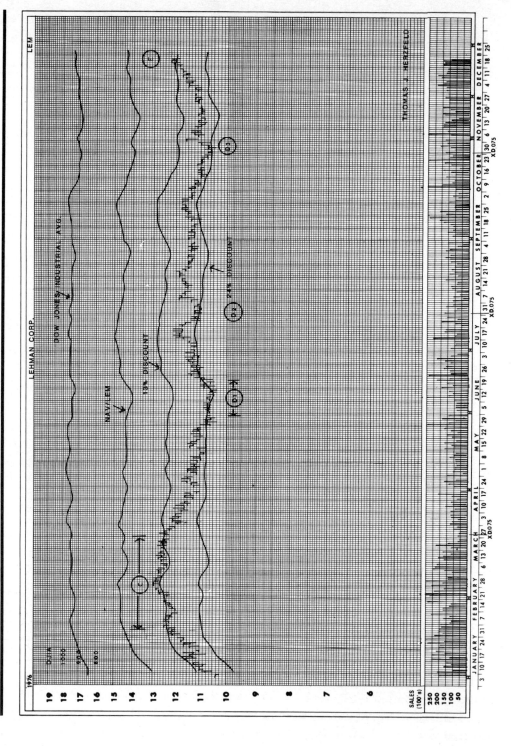

38

and $A_2$ was approximately $11\frac{1}{2}$, and the NAV was about 13. A short sale at points $A_1$ and $A_2$ could have been covered in the beginning of April at Point $B_1$, about \$10 at a 24 percent discount. From the entire period of April through December of 1975, LEM was selling at wide discounts, and multiple buy signals were given at Points $B_1$ through $B_8$, at prices ranging from $9\frac{3}{4}$ to $11\frac{1}{4}$. Long positions established during the April–December 1975 period could have been sold profitably at Point C in February–March 1976. The NAV rose to about 15 and the discount narrowed to 13 percent, resulting in a price for LEM in the 13 area. Short positions established at Point C could have been covered three months later at Point $D_1$ in June 1976 in the $10\frac{5}{8}$ area when the discount again widened to 24 percent. Stock bought at $D_1$ and $D_2$ could have been sold at Point E at $12\frac{1}{4}$ with a 13 percent discount. The basic method as shown here would not have been less profitable than the advanced method and at the same time would have required a lot less work. However, LEM's discount did in fact narrow in 1977, and several buying opportunities would have been missed if no adjustments had been made for that shift. On the other hand, LEM again was trading back at a 24 percent discount by June 1978 and was, therefore, on my buy list.

For a final example of the basic method, which is what most of the readers of this book should use, let's look at Figure 4.4, which shows Tri-Continental Corporation (TY) between November 1975 and January 1977. Our buy and sell lines were established at 26 percent and 15 percent, respectively. Point A in November 1975 gave a sell signal at 20, when TY sold at a 15 percent discount from its NAV of about 23.50. A short sale at Point A could have been covered at Point B in December 1975 at about 17, when it reached a 26 percent discount. From Point B in December, TY rallied to 21, when it reached Point C In January 1976. The volatility in TY faded during the rest of 1976, and the stock traded at relatively wide discounts, giving multiple buy signals at Points $D_1$, $D_2$, and $D_3$ at prices between 19 and 20. Point E provided the final sell signal for this period at 22 in January 1977.

***Drawbacks of the Basic Trading Approach.*** What are the drawbacks to the basic method? The most significant one is that it does not adjust to long-term continuous narrowing and widening of the discount. For example, consider MAD again throughout 1977 when its discount was in a generally narrowing trend. The widest discounts during that year, as shown in Figure 4.5, occurred in March (Point A), in

**40**

FIGURE 4.4
Tri-Continental Corporation

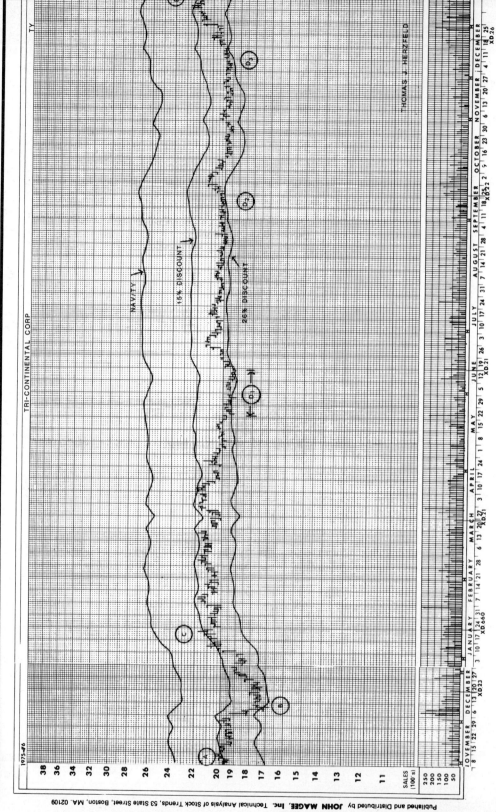

TEKNIPLAT Chart Paper

Published and Distributed by JOHN MAGEE, Inc. Technical Analysis of Stock Trends, 53 State Street, Boston, MA. 02109

**FIGURE 4.5**
**Madison Fund**

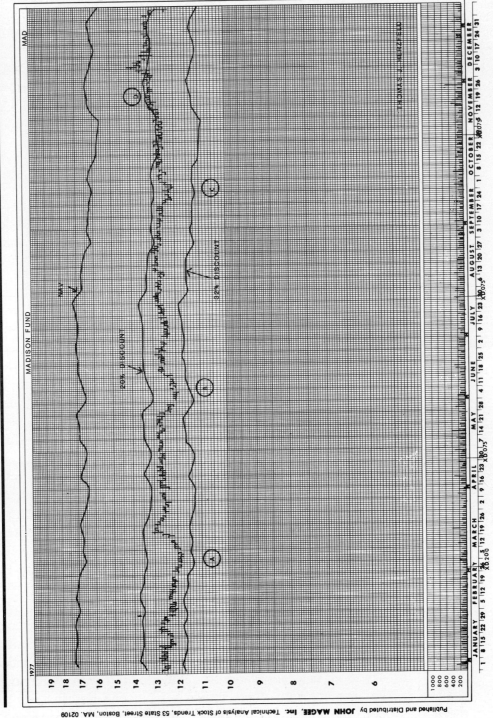

41

June (Point *B*), and in September–October (Point *C*), with an average of approximately 29 percent. As a result, one who was committed to my original method and was waiting for a 32 percent discount to buy would have missed all three purchase opportunities.

The next major flaw in the basic method, as applied to MAD, is that its follower would have been a short seller in December 1977 (Point *D*) when the fund was selling for $13 a share or at a 20 percent discount. Just two weeks later, the stock was selling at $14 a share or a 14 percent discount.

## THE ADVANCED APPROACH

It is reasonably safe to say, therefore, that the basic approach will work for at least a one-year period with most funds. However, because it will not adjust for long-term shifts in the discount, there was obviously a need to develop a more advanced approach which would.

The one which I developed for trading closed-end stock funds is based partly on an improved chart which I currently use in my chart service (see Figure 4.6). The first step here is to construct, on semilogarithmic paper, a daily chart plotting a fund's net asset value, price, volume, and dividend. A moving average of the discount should also be established. This moving average can cover a 12-month, 6-month, or 3-month period, though I have found that for short-term trading a 3- or 6-month moving average is preferable.

The next step is to establish the volatility of the fund. This is based on the fund's yearly range as a percentage of its price.

Then comes the key ingredient—the plotting of buy and sell lines based at specific established deviations from the moving average of the discount. The average deviation for most funds is about 5 percent. The correct deviation to trade at is based on the percentage of the fund's range for the previous year. In most cases, the correct deviation to trade at is 10 percent of the range for the previous year. For MAD in 1977, the established deviation was 3.3 percent (10 percent of its 32.9 percent range which was 3¾ points).

The end result for a typical fund is that if the moving average of the discount is 25 percent, we would be a buyer at a 30 percent discount and a seller at a 20 percent discount—at 5 percent deviations. The deviation, naturally, varies from fund to fund; with some funds, it may be 3 percent; with others, it may be 6 percent. But whatever the deviation, the concept of trading on it from a moving average eliminates

FIGURE 4.6
Madison Fund, Advanced Method

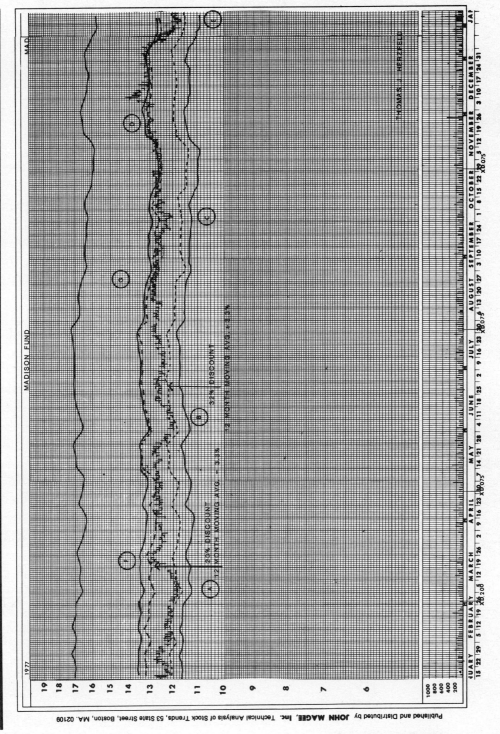

Published and Distributed by JOHN MAGEE, Inc. Technical Analysis of Stock Trends, 53 State Street, Boston, MA. 02109

the number one drawback of the basic method—the lack of adjustment for long-term discount shifts.

Figure 4.6 shows MAD for the same period as Figure 4.5, but with buy and sell lines plotted according to the advanced method. The buy line was plotted at a 3.3 percent deviation greater than the 12-month moving average of its discount. The sell line is plotted at a 3.3 percent deviation smaller than MAD's 12-month moving average of its discount. It should now be apparent that the major flaw in the basic method is thus overcome. The basic method used in Figure 4.5 missed the buy opportunities at Points A, B, and C. However, the advanced method which compensated for the narrowing discount gave the correct buy signals at A, B, and C as well as accurate sell signals at Points F, G, and D.

The advanced method is best suited for those who work with computers in as much as nonelectronic computing of moving averages and establishing the proper trading deviations from those moving averages for all 60 funds can be very time-consuming.

I must emphasize again that the basic method should give satisfactory results with much less effort. There are only a handful of readers of this book who should consider using the advanced method.

After constructing a chart with buy and sell lines plotted, the balance of the decision-making process in the trading of closed-end stock funds becomes somewhat subjective, calling for a degree of investor judgment instead of trading based solely on mechanical methods. Here, buy and sell lines are adjusted based on some of the variables discussed in Chapter 2.

However, even after adjusting for all possible variables, the net effect ordinarily should not change a fund's buy or sell price by more than $\frac{1}{4}$ to $\frac{3}{8}$ of a point. (An exception to this rule occurs in a fund which is the subject of an open-ending attempt.) Following are the variables which bear particular watching:

1. The Herzfeld Index. The index is an average of all closed-end funds as a group. If, for example, that average is 20, it is simply telling us that the average discount for the closed-end group is 20 percent. The formula I use to compute the index is an average of moving averages. If that average narrows substantially at any given time, I become more aggressive in bidding for stocks. Conversely, when the index is widening, I drop my bid down $\frac{1}{8}$ or $\frac{1}{4}$, even though my mechanical method is giving me a buy signal at a higher price.

My charts are always before me tacked on the walls of my office, by groups in vertical rows. This enables me to see quickly how the funds in a group are performing in relation to each other without having to refer to the Herzfeld Index. For instance, Fund A may be on its buy line, thus giving a buy signal. However, Funds B, C, and D may also be on their buy lines. In this case, I would drop my bid for those funds by $\frac{1}{8}$ or $\frac{1}{4}$ of a point below their buy lines to adjust for the general weakness in the group.

2. Performance of the net asset value. If Funds A, B, C, and D are all on their buy lines and I anticipate a rally, I would buy the fund which historically has the best performance, bidding a little more aggressively for it than for other funds.

3. Liquidity. If I intend to trade in any size, I would avoid initiating trading positions in inactive funds, such as Adams Express or U.S. & Foreign Securities. I would look to the relatively more active funds like Lehman, Madison, and Tri-Continental.

4. Leverage. When looking to buy when feeling bullish on the market, I look more closely for funds with highly leveraged capital structures. In a nervous market, on the other hand, the highly leveraged funds are to be avoided.

5. Volatility. If all other factors are equal and if the general sentiment appears bullish, I seek out the more volatile funds and bid a bit more aggressively for them.

6. The currently strong groups. This is a variable with deep significance. As an example, if chemical and electronic stocks are strong and several of the funds concentrating in them are on buy lines, I would bid more strongly for them than for funds whose portfolios are weakly represented in the chemical and electronic industries.

7. Quality. In rising markets, funds of comparatively lower quality often show better performance than those with top-grade portfolios. This phenomenon usually depends on the particular phase of a bull or bear market.

8. Hedging possibilities. Funds can be hedged against each other or against other trading vehicles, such as options. The Herzfeld Hedge (which is discussed in detail in Chapter 9) is a concept involving the selling of naked options on stocks which are in closed-end fund portfolios. I personally prefer concentrating my buying in funds holding stocks which have options that are traded on an options exchange. Sometimes when it becomes difficult to sell a large position in a fund, we may want to sell short a fund with a similar portfolio. If funds have unusual portfolios, setting up these hedges, which are actually substi-

tute sales, becomes difficult. This is certainly the case with the Japan Fund, simply because there are no other funds with large amounts of Japanese securities. (Niagara Share Corporation can be regarded as somewhat of an exception, because it does hold a representation of Japanese issues.) Then there are closed-end stock funds like U.S. & Foreign Securities and Tri-Continental; their portfolios are relatively similar, and they could be hedged against each other.

9. Overall market performance. I use the Dow Jones Industrial Average as the leading daily indicator for the net asset value of the closed-end stock funds which I chart. The net asset values themselves are published on Saturdays. Then, by Tuesday or Wednesday of the following week, if the Dow should show a sharp rise, through interpolation, I can accurately project the extent to which the next week's net asset value of a particular fund will be higher. Consequently, my bidding would become more aggressive.

## TRADING TECHNIQUES

I am convinced, as I mentioned earlier, that closed-end fund trading should be for small profits with high turnover. A trader who can continually move in and out of funds, both buying and selling short, taking small profits, will have a total return at year-end that is much higher than he would have realized by holding any fund as a long-term investment.

With regard to bidding and offering, I suggest the following procedures. If a buy signal appears at $10, first I might adjust to $9\frac{7}{8}$ or $10\frac{1}{8}$ based on the variables. Assuming my total objective is to accumulate 5000 or 6000 shares, I initially buy only 1000 at that point ($10). Then I bid for 2000 shares at $9\frac{7}{8}$ and 3000 at $9\frac{3}{4}$. With more expensive stocks, I may bid at $\frac{1}{4}$ of a point intervals rather than $\frac{1}{8}$ of a point intervals. The theory is to increase the size as we lower the price. This is an extremely dangerous strategy in buying common stocks because the stock may never reverse its downward movement, leaving the investor with a large loss from which there is no recovery. However, with a high degree of certainty it can be said that a closed-end fund will make a reversal when the discount becomes wide enough. If our method is correct, it will make that turn at a point extremely close to our projection. Even if we fail to pinpoint the exact $\frac{1}{8}$ of a point where that turn is ultimately made, at the very least when the reversal occurs, our average price will be near the reversal point—because we increased the size of our holdings at successively lower prices.

Dividends are also a factor in determining trading techniques. If a fund is about to go ex dividend and it is not necessary to pay up to get that dividend, then it is definitely recommended that the investor try to buy a fund in which he can catch that dividend. If a fund has a sharp rise before a dividend, it usually should be regarded as a sale. Experience shows that more often than not, a stock falls off at least more than the amount of its dividend.

As for leverage, there is no reason why closed-end funds should not be traded on margin, especially in bull markets. In neutral or declining markets, one might not want to use margin, preferring to play a less than aggressive role. The proper way to adjust to such markets is to avoid trading solely on the long side and make short sales to establish a hedge position instead.

Quite often, a fund at an excessive discount will not decline in a down market, while a fund at a narrow discount will decline sharply in a similar situation. The fund at the narrow discount will decline on a percentage basis which is greater than that of the fund at the excessive discount. There, setting up the hedge position—being short in funds at narrow discounts and long in those at large discounts—often works to good advantage. (This is discussed in more detail in Chapter 9.)

# Trading Closed-End Bond Funds

**5**

Throughout my career, I have always put a great deal of emphasis on trading closed-end bond funds. This is primarily because the risks involved are in many cases lower than those of stock funds, while the rewards in many instances can be as high. The bond funds I recommend trading are listed in Table 5.1.

## ADVANTAGES AND DISADVANTAGES OF BOND FUNDS

As with any kind of investment, bond funds have their advantages and their disadvantages. Short-term considerations aside for the moment, a long-term investor in bond funds enjoys several advantages. First, by investing in a bond fund instead of individual bonds, the investor automatically derives the advantages of owning a portion of a diversified portfolio of investment grade bonds—usually consisting of from 30 to 60 bonds selected and managed by professional bond specialists.

Another plus of bond funds is that they pay, depending on the fund, quarterly or monthly dividends, while individual bonds make interest payments semiannually.

Most bond funds trade at discounts from their net asset value per share. This means that the purchaser of a fund can buy an entire diversified bond portfolio at a discount from its true market value. Because of this, the yield is usually higher than what could be obtained through direct purchase of the underlying bonds.

Yet another advantage of bond funds is that they provide opportunities for trading—probably more trading opportunities than are available in individual bonds.

There are two main disadvantages inherent in the bond fund concept. The first is the management fee and the overall expenses of operating the fund which usually will consume about 10 percent of a fund's income. The second concerns the discount. While one should

**49**

**TABLE 5.1**
**Recommended Bond Funds**

| Name | Trades on | Symbol |
|---|---|---|
| American General Bond Fund | NYSE | AGB |
| Bunker Hill Income | NYSE | BHL |
| CNA Income Shares | NYSE | CNN |
| Current Income Shares | NYSE | CUR |
| Drexel Bond-Debenture Trading Fund | NYSE | DBF |
| Excelsior Income Shares | NYSE | EIS |
| Fort Dearborn Income Securities | NYSE | FTD |
| Hatteras Income Securities | NYSE | HAT |
| INA Investment Securities | NYSE | IIS |
| Intercapital Income Securities | NYSE | ICB |
| John Hancock Investors | NYSE | JHI |
| John Hancock Income Securities | NYSE | JHS |
| Lincoln National Direct Placement Fund | NYSE | LND |
| Mass Mutual Corporate Investors | NYSE | MCI |
| Mass Mutual Income Investors | NYSE | MIV |
| Montgomery Street Income Securities | NYSE | MTS |
| Mutual of Omaha Interest Shares | NYSE | MUO |
| Pacific American Income Shares | NYSE | PAI |
| Paul Revere Investors | OTC | PREV |
| RET Income Fund $4.38 cm Pref* | ASE | RET Pr |
| SG Securities $1.70 cm Pref* | ASE | SGO Pr |
| St. Paul Securities | NYSE | SPI |
| State Mutual Securities | NYSE | SMS |
| Transamerica Income Shares | NYSE | TAI |
| USLIFE Income Fund | NYSE | UIF |
| Vestaur Securities | NYSE | VES |

*Technically not a bond fund although approximately 75 percent of its assets are invested in bonds. (See discussion of the stocks in Chapter 7 on specialty funds.)

always try to purchase at a substantially wide discount, there is absolutely no guarantee that when the fund is sold, the discount will not be wider than when it was purchased. Of course, it could be smaller, as we shall see.

## VARIABLES AFFECTING BOND FUNDS

Apart from the above advantages and disadvantages, a number of variables must be weighed before any decision to buy a bond fund is made. Among those variables are:

1. What is the bond fund's discount from its net asset value? As in all forms of closed-end fund trading, this is a crucial variable. During

1977, the average discount was about 5 percent for bond funds as a group from the NAV, although discounts did tend to get larger in December because of traditional tax selling. In 1978, the average discount was over 8 percent. What is essential in reaching a buy decision is determining the "normal" discount of each particular fund on a moving average basis. Assuming other bond fund variables fall into place, a fund should only be purchased when it is selling at a discount substantially larger than its average discount. Conversely, a fund should be sold when it is trading at a much narrower discount than its average.

2. What is the expense ratio? What are the management fees in relation to the income generated by the fund's portfolio? For instance, of the 26 some bond funds which I trade, the average expenses of the fund are about 10 percent of income. If a fund's expense cost is 10 percent or higher, the fund cannot be truly regarded as a sound buy—unless it is selling at a discount of at least 10 percent to compensate for the above average expense ratio. An exception to this "10 percent rule" occurs in the case of bond funds which employ leverage (or borrowed money) in their trading. The interest expenses for the borrowed money should be deducted from the total expenses of the fund before computing the expense ratio. The reason for this is that interest expenses should be considered a trading cost of the fund, not an operating expense. Examples of funds with relatively higher expense ratios are Drexel Bond-Debenture Trading Fund and INA Investment Securities (before adjusting for interest expenses). Some of the bond funds with lower expense ratios are John Hancock Income Securities, John Hancock Investors, Montgomery Street, and American General Bond Fund.

A final note on expenses. The investor should be wary of "free" in-house services supplied by the investment adviser. Such services often tend to result in higher management fees. Other funds which choose to purchase these services on the outside do not have to incorporate the cost for in-house services into the management fee. A serious bond fund trader should, therefore, carefully study the fund's advisory contract and the breakdown of its various operating expenses.

3. Where is the fund traded? Because of the depth of market, etc., assuming all other factors are equal, a fund traded on the New York Stock Exchange would usually be preferred to one traded on the American Stock Exchange. And an Amex fund, in turn, would be preferred to one traded on the over-the-counter market.

4. What is the quality of the fund's portfolio? Several funds have

relatively low quality portfolios, with an emphasis on single-A or triple-B bonds. Others stress triple-A or double-A holdings. The average percentage of a bond fund's portfolio as a group, with A or better grade investments, is between 54 and 58 percent. A good example of a higher quality portfolio is Fort Dearborn Income Securities which in 1977 was 100 percent invested in bonds rated single A or better. At the other end of the quality scale are funds such as John Hancock Investors, with only about 24 percent of its portfolio in bonds rated single A or better, and USLIFE Income Fund, about 23 percent of whose assets are in bonds rated single A or better.

5. What is the average maturity of the fund's portfolio? If other variables are equal, I recommend trying to buy funds whose overall holdings are of relatively shorter maturities. This indicates that the fund's NAV should be comparatively stable to the other funds' NAV during periods of rising interest rates, when bond prices are declining.

(Changes in maturity and quality could be used by the management of a closed-end bond fund to cause a fund's market value to rise. This is not to say or even imply that such strategies are used; let's simply consider them as an academic exercise. A management so disposed could lower the quality of a fund's portfolio and/or buy longer maturities, since most investors don't closely compare portfolios; they simply look at the funds' yield. Assume that five different funds of equal quality are all selling for $10 per share and paying 90-cent dividends—or a 9 percent yield. Then one of the funds might be tempted to buy lower quality bonds and lengthen maturities. This could very well serve to increase the dividend to 95 cents, causing the price of the fund to rise to 10½. At a price of 10½, the fund would still be yielding 9 percent, remaining in line with the 9 percent yield of bond funds as a group. In a situation like this, the price of the fund might even go higher than 10½, simply because an "uninformed public" might believe that a higher dividend is a result of management's doing an above-average job when, in fact, the dividend increase was a result of a more speculative investment posture.)

6. What is the degree of liquidity of a bond fund's portfolio? Several bond funds have portfolios which are relatively or even highly illiquid, primarily because they are heavily invested in privately placed bonds. Such bond funds usually sell at higher discounts than ones with relatively liquid portfolios. The reason for this, of course, is that if a declining bond market is forecast, it is comparatively more difficult for fund managers to move into a cash position from privately placed bonds; they are not readily marketable. On the other hand, it must be noted

that bond funds with a large percentage of privately placed securities usually have a higher yield than those with liquid portfolios. The result of this combination of factors is a bond fund selling at a larger discount and offering a much higher yield than many funds with relatively liquid holdings. This does not mean, however, that the shares of such a fund trading on a stock exchange are illiquid. They are indeed liquid, thereby giving the investor an opportunity to purchase an illiquid but high-yielding portfolio while enjoying the liquidity of a NYSE-listed common stock. Generally speaking, a closed-end bond fund holding private placements will perform as well as a fund with liquid and readily marketable securities. This is illustrated in Figure 5.1 showing the Drexel Bond Fund which also includes the NAV of Mass Mutual Corporate Investors. Over the past few years, the net asset values of the two funds performed at approximately the same level. Drexel has a liquid portfolio while Mass Mutual has a large percentage of private placements.

7. How does the fund pay its dividend? Those funds which pay monthly dividends are generally regarded as more attractive by investors, even though the yield—because of processing and mailing expenses—may be a touch lower than those which pay on a quarterly basis. The investor enticed by the monthly check should be advised that there is no guarantee that the practice will continue. The trend lately—to reduce fund expenses—has been toward quarterly payouts. When such a conversion takes place, the discount on the fund tends to widen a bit.

8. What is the size of the fund? If a fund has a very small capitalization, for instance 2 million shares or less, I would not feel comfortable trading more than 3000 to 4000 share positions. However, if it is capitalized with between 5 and 10 million shares, a position of 10,000 to 15,000 shares would not be excessive. In this regard, one should also determine whether or not the fund is actively traded. If a single individual or institution has an extremely large position in a fund, therefore causing the float to be thin, one should, of course, avoid taking large trading positions.

9. Does the fund utilize leverage? That is, does it borrow in order to make investments? If we believe that interest rates are going to decline, then there is an advantage to buying a fund utilizing leverage. This is because in a general bond market rally, the fund using leverage will tend to outperform one which does not use that technique. Naturally, when the opposite situation obtains, when interest rates are rising and the bond market is falling, one should avoid funds utilizing leverage.

## FIGURE 5.1
Drexel Bond-Debenture Trading Fund

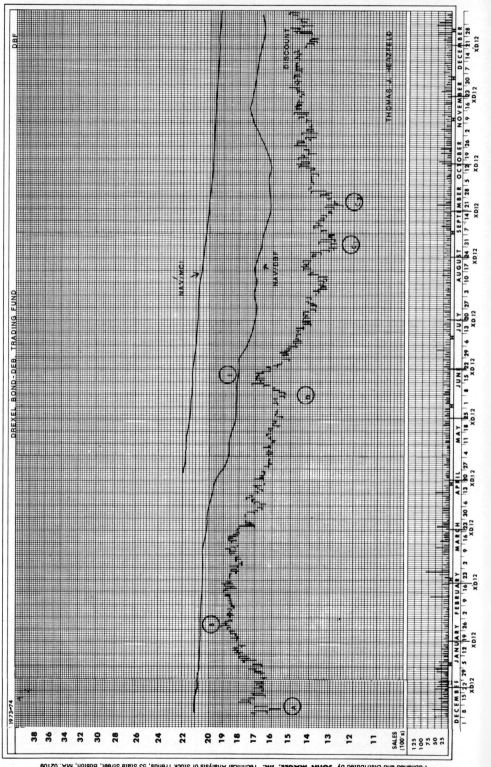

54

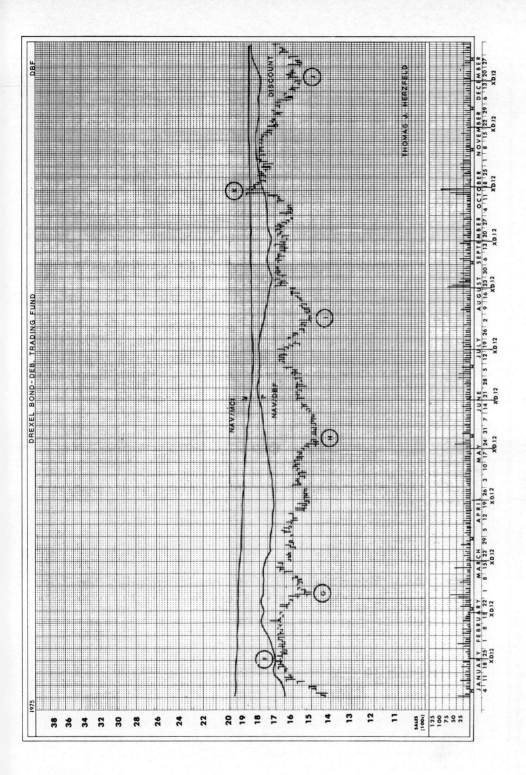

DREXEL BOND - DEB. TRADING FUND

THOMAS J. HERZFELD

55

**FIGURE 5.1**
**Drexel Bond-Debenture Trading Fund** (Cont.)

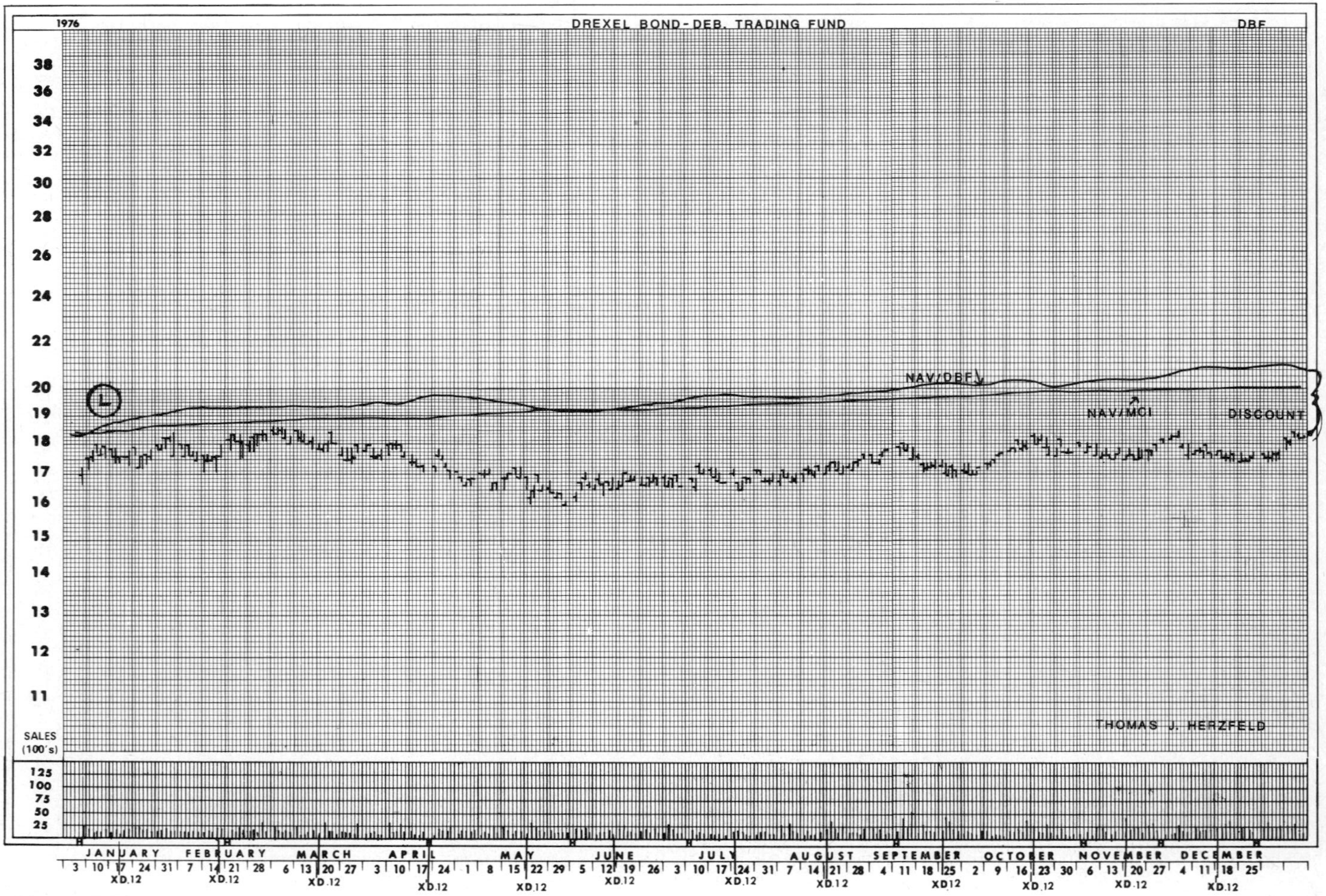

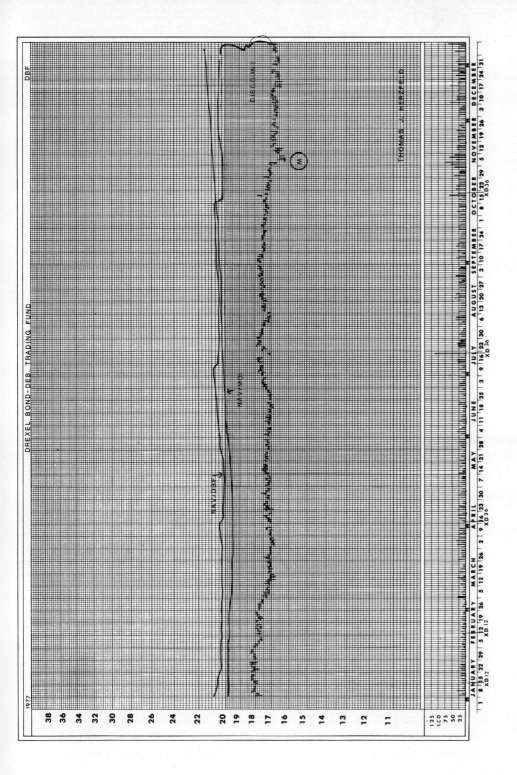

DREXEL BOND-DEB. TRADING FUND

DBF

1977

THOMAS J. HERZFELD

57

10. Who is managing the fund? It is important to know whether this function is a responsibility of a bank, a mutual fund advisory management company, or a regular brokerage house. Some funds managed by or affiliated with brokerage houses tend to have higher portfolio turnover than those which are managed by banks or insurance company subsidiaries. High turnover in itself might be considered an advantage if the trading is profitable. However, too many of the funds which are active traders seem to have disappointing track records.

Although it is not a variable requiring continual evaluation, a bond fund trader should be aware of the effects of an additional distribution below the fund's net asset value. Recently, one fund did succeed in making such a distribution, which automatically dilutes the fund's NAV. In my opinion, this dilution is unfair to existing stockholders and is in fact discouraged in the Investment Act of 1940. For example, if a fund has 5 million shares outstanding with a net asset value of $20 a share, its total net assets will be $100 million. But if that fund's market value is $16 a share, it has a 20 percent discount, and if an additional distribution is made at $16 a share, the net asset value of each share shrinks to $19.33. This would be based on the original 5 million shares being valued at $100 million and the additional 1 million shares at $16 million for a total value of $116 million. And that $116 million of assets divided by the new 6-million share capitalization results in a diluted net asset value per share of $19.33. A fund *issuing* shares below NAV for its dividend reinvestment plan is similarly diluting its net asset value.

## CHARTING BOND FUNDS

Once all the variables have been considered and assessed—once a firm evaluation of them has been made—the bond funds must be carefully charted. After 12 years, I am convinced that to be successful in bond fund trading, to make a good profit, there is nothing more essential than charting them, conscientiously, on a daily basis.

Of course, all the basics discussed in Chapter 3 on charting should be kept in mind. To recap the fundamentals of that chapter and expand on them as they apply to bond funds, let's examine Figure 5.2 on Pacific American Income Shares (PAI).[1]

As you can see in Figure 5.2, there is a daily calendar along the bottom of the chart. In the body of the chart, plotted on the standard method, is the price showing high, low, and closed on a daily basis.

**FIGURE 5.2**
**Pacific American Income Shares**
*(See note on page 88.)*

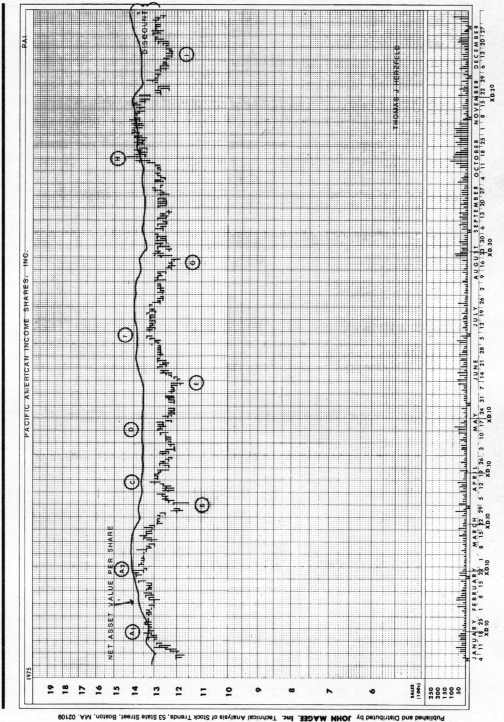

**FIGURE 5.2**
**Pacific American Income Shares** *(Cont.)*

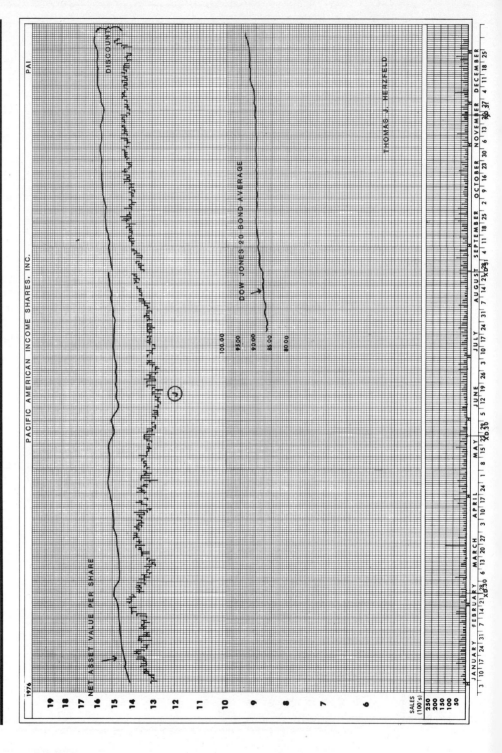

60

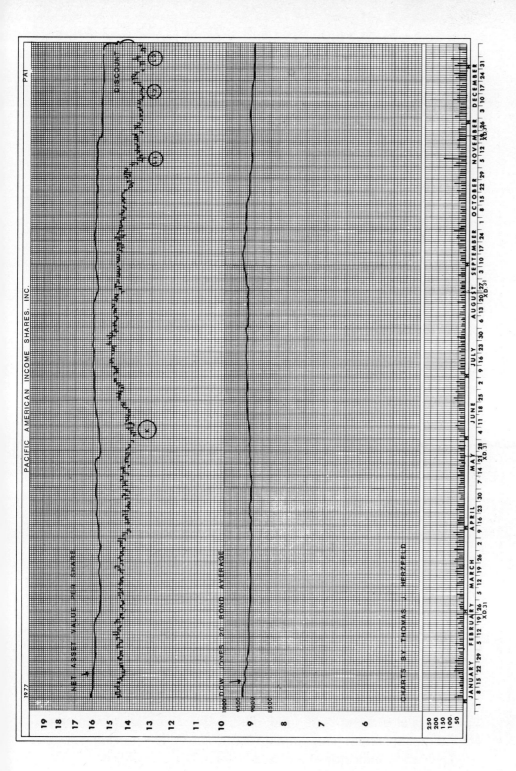

PACIFIC AMERICAN INCOME SHARES, INC.

1977

NET ASSET VALUE PER SHARE

DISCOUNT

DOW JONES 20 BOND AVERAGE

CHARTS BY THOMAS J. HERZFELD

JANUARY FEBRUARY MARCH APRIL MAY JUNE JULY AUGUST SEPTEMBER OCTOBER NOVEMBER DECEMBER

1 8 15 22 29 5 12 19 26 5 12 19 26 2 9 16 23 30 7 14 21 28 4 11 18 25 2 9 16 23 30 6 13 20 27 3 10 17 24 1 8 15 22 29 5 12 19 26 3 10 17 24 31
XD 31 XD 31 XD 31 XD 31 XD 31

19 18 17 16 15 14 13 12 11 10 9 8 7 6

1000 DOW
9000
9900
8500

250 200 150 100 50

61

The paper, as in all my charts, must be semilogarithmic so that the percentage moves of an average or a stock of one price will show in the space on the chart proportionate to the movement of other indices or averages on a percentage basis.

I have added two ingredients to the standard chart. The first is the line which runs more or less directly through the center; it shows the Dow Jones 20-Bond Average. The other is the straight line at the top which shows the NAV of the bond fund being tracked. As in earlier chapters where we compared the relationship of the Dow Jones Industrial Average to the net asset value of stock funds, it should be readily apparent that there is an almost perfect correlation between movements of the Dow bond average and the movements of the net asset value of the bond funds. There is usually only one deviation from this rule. This occurs when a fund goes ex dividend. Then the NAV is adjusted downward by the amount of the dividend, while the Dow bond fund average on that particular day, of course, has no similar adjustment.

Some of my charts have other elements which can be helpful in evaluation. In Figure 5.3 on John Hancock *Income Securities*—a closed-end fund—I also chart the net asset value of John Hancock *Bond Fund*, which is an open-end mutual fund. (It should be kept in mind that there are three Hancock funds—the open-end mutual fund; John Hancock Income Securities, a closed-end fund traded on the NYSE; and John Hancock Investors, which is also traded on the Big Board and which has a very high degree of privately placed bonds.)

The question might arise, "Why in the John Hancock Income Securities chart do I use two different net asset values—one for the closed-end fund and one for the open-end fund?" The reason is that the latter is my leading indicator. Those three "bibles" of regular financial information—*The Wall Street Journal*, *The New York Times*, and *Barron's*—publish the net asset values of closed-end funds only once a week. Stock funds and specialty funds appear in the *Times* on Saturday and in the *Journal* and *Barron's* on Monday. Bond funds, on the other hand, are published by the *Times* and *Journal* on Wednesday. This schedule means that between the end of the week—when net asset values are computed—and the time of publication, there is a lag of 5 days before the investor can see the NAV for the previous Friday of a closed-end bond fund. This is the reason for plotting the NAV of the open-end bond fund on a daily basis, thus providing up to a 5-day leading indicator of a closed-end fund's next published NAV.

**FIGURE 5.3**
**John Hancock Income Securities**

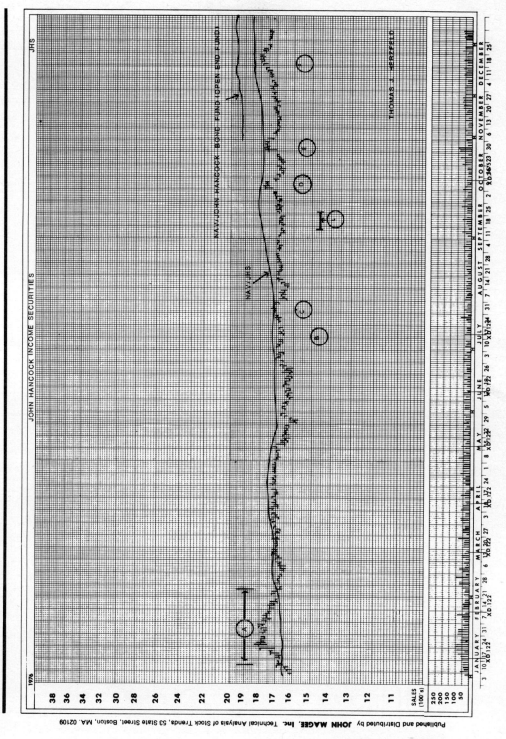

**TEKNIPLAT Chart Paper**

**64**

FIGURE 5.3
John Hancock Income Securities *(Cont.)*

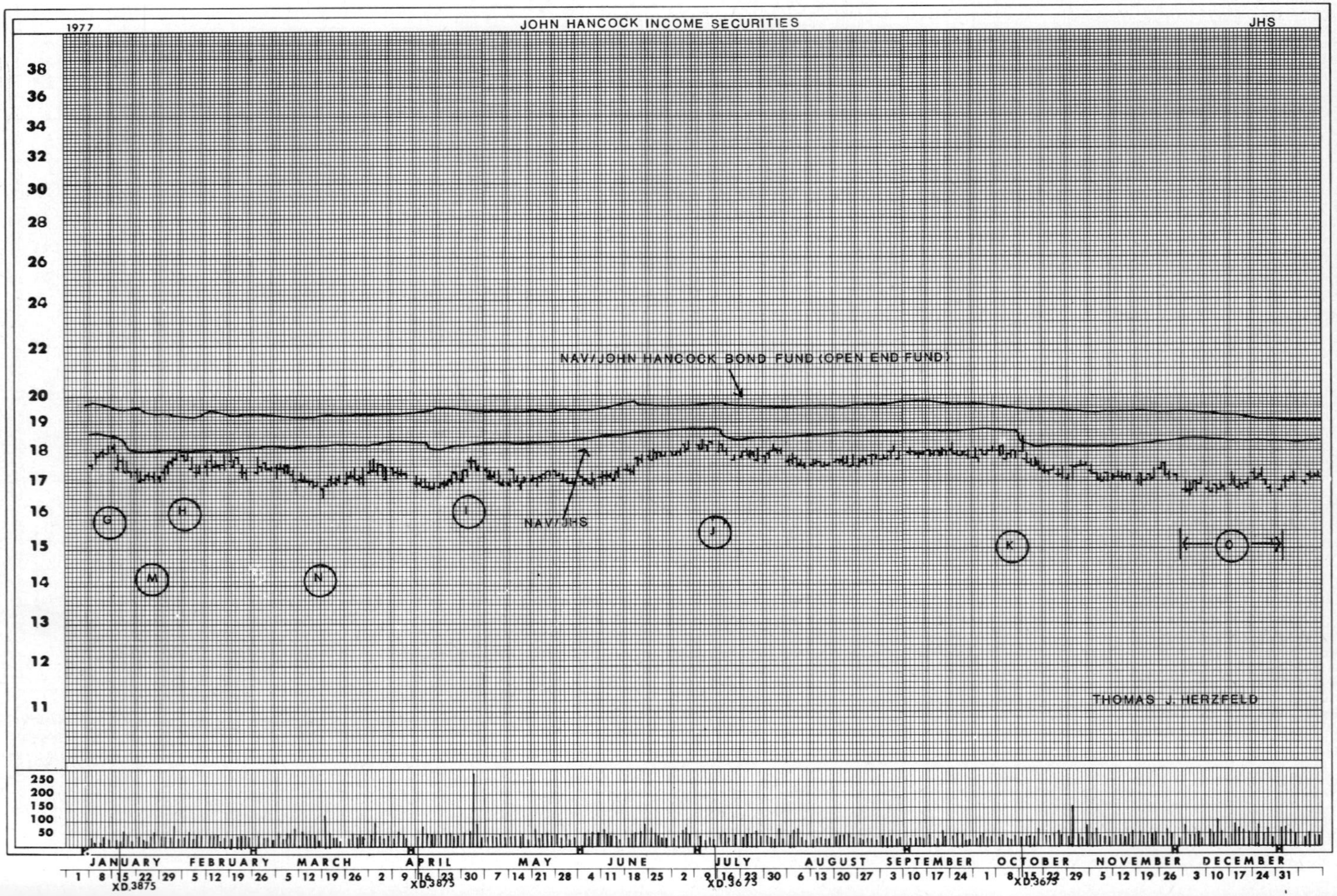

Most open-end mutual funds publish their net asset values daily. To almost a 1.0 coefficient of correlation, the relationship between the net asset value of an open-end bond fund and a closed-end fund are going to be the same. This can be demonstrated by examining Figure 5.3, where we have the Hancock Bond Fund (the open-end fund) above the line on which we have the Hancock Income Securities Fund (the closed-end issue).

The lines show that the movements of the two net asset values are virtually identical. But a look at the week of December 10–17, 1977, serves to dramatize the necessity of the leading indicator. If we had not used the open-end fund as a leading indicator, we would not have known until a week later—through the press's weekly publication of NAV—that the net asset value of the closed-end fund would be lower for the following week.

The only times there are deviations between the two movements are, again, on dividend dates, with the first fund paying monthly and the second, quarterly. With respect to open-end funds, on the payable date, some mathematical adjustment for the dividend is necessary to determine if the portfolio moved higher or lower. For example, if the net asset value of an open-end fund is recorded as being $8.80, down 8 cents on the ex dividend date, assuming a 10-cent dividend, the NAV was actually 2 cents higher that day.

Prices of the various funds are listed vertically on the left-hand side of my charts. In Figure 5.2 showing Pacific American Income Shares (PAI), for example, the prices on the left run from 6 to 19, plotted on a semilogarithmic scale. The plotting of the Dow Jones bond average shows the essential value of the semilogarithmic paper. On December 19, 1977, that average stood at 91.26; therefore, it was plotted at approximately 9¼ on the PAI price scale. If the Dow bond average had been 95.00 on that date, that average would have been plotted on the PAI chart exactly at a point corresponding with 9½ on the PAI price scale.

## TRADING BOND FUNDS

There are two basic approaches in determining when to buy and sell a bond fund. The first is to work solely from information provided by the chart (see Figure 5.2 on PAI). The other is to calculate deviations from the fund's normal discount. For instance, constructed on a moving average basis, the discount for Pacific American Income Shares in October 1977 was 7.2 percent; a year earlier, it was 7.5 percent. One could assume that the sole decision as to when to buy the fund could be at a 5 percent deviation greater than the 7.2 percent moving average figure—or in this case at a 12.2 percent discount. The initial temptation to buy at a fixed deviation should be moderated, for there are other considerations to keep in mind.

It is essential to look at what the discounts of all the bond funds are doing. If all bond fund discounts are narrowing, we might well buy the one with the greatest deviation beyond its normal discount from NAV, even if that deviation were only 3 or 4 percent. In other words, we must always seek the most attractive fund in the group, relative to the others.

The ideal way to trade bond funds is to start by buying a fund which not only has the highest discount relative to its normal one, but the highest discount relative to what the rest of the group is doing.

Now let's discuss the actual trading of bond funds. In theory, we will buy Fund A at a 10 percent discount, if its normal discount is 5 percent. We will also try to catch the fund's monthly or quarterly dividend, but as soon as the discount narrows 5 percent or perhaps even swings to the narrow side of 2 or 3 percent, we will sell Fund A. When we do, we will immediately switch into another fund selling at a discount 5 percent larger than the moving average of its discount. By leap-frogging, a trader may be able to increase his profitability dramatically—buying one fund, catching its dividend, selling that fund and buying another, catching its dividend, selling it when its discount narrows, etc. There can be no guarantees in this procedure, it must be emphasized. However, a reasonable profit objective in following this method of trading bond funds could be a total return of 20 percent per year, as opposed to the 9 to 11 percent yield to be realized by purchasing a single bond fund and holding on to it.

The potential profit aside, the most intriguing consideration behind this method of trading bond funds is that at no time during the trading cycle does the investor take any more risk than he would take if he bought a portfolio or investment grade bonds at a substantial discount from their actual value.

To the uninitiated, the fact that we're actively trading may make it seem as if we're taking heavy risks. Actually, I believe the opposite is true. Through active trading, we're actually minimizing our risks. Why do I say minimizing? The fact is that by "scalping" (taking) a point here and a fraction of a point there, we are always putting away profits not for their own sake alone but to act as a potential cushion for the day when the bond market goes unexpectedly into a decline and a position goes against us. The importance of this trading concept with closed-end bond funds cannot be overemphasized.

Compare it, if you will, to the individual investor or the institution seeking income through bonds in general. That investor will not, first of all, be getting his portfolio of bonds at a discount from their market value, as he would by buying closed-end bond funds at a discount. He will be paying market value for each individual bond. And if he does, when interest rates rise, he's going to watch the value of his portfolio decline.

One might argue that the same unfortunate sequence could occur with a closed-end bond fund—rising interest rates serving to erode the portfolio value of the fund. However, there is a safety valve built into our system of buying closed-end bond funds—the fact that we only buy the funds when they are trading at prices which are larger than their average discounts. In this case, in a period of rising interest rates where bond prices generally are eroding, producing a decline in the fund's net asset value, the discount may tend to narrow, negating the downward pressure being exerted on the fund's net asset value by the declining bond market.

There are other ways to make our approach to closed-end bond funds still more stable. One method I recommend occasionally is to go long a closed-end bond fund at a discount larger than its average and to go short Treasury bond futures as a hedge. Here, if interest rates decline and the bond market rallies, the investor will probably realize a larger profit on his closed-end fund position, primarily because the discount will tend to narrow, and he will be receiving 9 to 11 percent interest on his investment. On the Treasury bond short position, he will have an actual loss but that loss may be smaller than his profit on the long position in the bond fund. On the other hand, if interest rates rise and the bond market declines, the investor may realize a profit on his short position in Treasury bond futures while sustaining a loss on the long position in the fund. Some or all of that loss, it should be kept in mind, might well be absorbed by the fund's discount narrowing again. In addition, the possible loss is minimized by the fact that dividends continue to be received on the long bond fund position.

Some financial analysts assert that short sales are not conservative by their very nature. I disagree when it comes to short sales as a hedging strategy. Look at it this way. At certain times, some closed-end funds may be selling at premiums or extremely narrow discounts, and at the same time, others may be trading at extremely wide discounts. In periods in which it appears that rising interest rates and a declining bond market may be on the horizon, it can be considered conservative to establish long positions in deeply discounted bond funds and short positions in funds trading at premiums or narrow discounts.

One further piece of advice, based on personal experience, should be kept in mind whenever trading closed-end bond funds. That is, average down when buying funds and do not average up, contrary to what most books about the financial market advise.

Traders who concentrate in growth stocks always seem to be saying, "Average up and cut your losses." As we advised with closed-end stock funds (see Chapter 4), this is precisely what not to do with closed-end bond funds. Rather, the trader should average down and, when doing this, increase the size of his orders. The result is that the investor's average price should be close to the reversal price at the bottom.

With common stocks, the ultimate danger in averaging down is that a company can indeed go out of business, thus causing a severe loss for an investor who has increased the size of his orders while following a stock downward. To the best of my knowledge, no closed-end bond fund has ever been wiped out. Therefore, excessive discounts should not be regarded as signs of internal weakness but rather as indications of unusually fine buying opportunities. In periods of high inflation and sharply rising interest rates, however, it is essential to hedge long bond fund positions with either short positions in overpriced bond funds or short positions in Treasury bond futures.

Another important factor in closed-end bond fund trading is margin, especially if an investor trades at a brokerage house which offers him the most favored interest rate; the best rate available to customers is usually ½ percent above the broker's call rate. During the fall of 1977, customers buying on margin at the most favored rate were paying 7⅝ percent on their borrowings, and yet the yield on closed-end bond funds was 9 and in some cases over 9 percent.

Here's the classic example of how buying bond funds on margin works. If a person bought $100,000 aggregate value of bond funds with an average yield of 9 percent, his income would come to $9000. But, if he bought $200,000 in funds on a margin of 50 percent, putting up $100,000 of his own money, his gross income from the $200,000 would be $18,000. His interest expense on the $100,000 margin account at 7⅝ percent would be $7625. Therefore, his net income would be $18,000, minus the $7625 in interest charges, or $10,375. That figure represents a yield of 10⅜ percent versus a yield of 9 percent without the $100,000 in margin.

At this point, it should be apparent why a 20 percent return trading in closed-end bond funds is not an unreasonable objective through the combination of rotating profitable positions into new positions, utilizing margin, and catching dividends. For example, with an average fund which sells at $20 per share, if an investor can make a trading profit of 1 point net twice a year for a total of 2 points and if he catches the dividends, which would be about $1.80, he would garner 3.8 points in a year—which is virtually a 20 percent total return. Although in the above example an investor has to make only two trades per year for a 1-point profit, a more viable strategy is to seek ¾ of a point profits four or five times a year.

Before getting into specifics on why and how one should trade certain closed-end bond funds, I would like to return to the subject of timing for a moment. November and December have traditionally been attractive periods in which to purchase bond funds, and January is generally regarded as a profit-taking month. The buying opportunities in the last 2 months of the year are presented by investors selling to establish tax losses, usually to their misfortune, without considering what the future price performance of the fund may be. If tax loss seekers would, instead, wait until January to liquidate their funds, they would very often find that the fund is a point or two higher than its November–December level. To put it bluntly, selling a fund in January will more often than not be a lot more profitable than the value of any tax loss established at the depressed prices of year-end.

And now to the reasons why I traded—or should have traded—certain closed-end bond funds when I did, to the guidelines I employed, and to the significant role my charts played in my buy and sell decisions.

Let's again look at Figure 5.3 on John Hancock Income Securities, which is traded on the New York Stock Exchange under the ticker symbol JHS. Here is an example of what happens when dividends are switched from a monthly to a quarterly basis. For the first 2 months of 1976, at Point A, JHS sold at a premium over its net asset value. But July of 1976, Point B, was the last time the fund paid a monthly dividend, having switched over to a quarterly payout. After that switchover—with the exception of one single day when the fund went momentarily ⅛ above its net asset value at Point C—it never again traded at a premium in 1976 to 1977. However, from July 1976 to December 1977, the fund traded at varying levels, either at net asset value or to a discount of about 1½ or 1¼ points. On eight separate occasions during that period, it went from a 1½-point discount to almost touch its net asset value (see Points *D, E, F, G, H, I, J,* and *K*). From the time it shifted to quarterly dividend payments in July 1976 through December 1977, there were five good and as many as ten relatively good trading opportunities in JHS. The first good buying opportunity came in the week of September 18, 1976, at Point *L*, when the net asset value was $18 and the stock was selling at 16½, an 8.3 percent discount from NAV. The stock rallied at the end of September and in the beginning of October almost reached its net asset value, going as high as 17⅞. It went ex dividend in the week of October 9, 1976, thereby confronting the trader with a decision—whether to wait and collect the October dividend or sell beforehand.

My experience has taught me that in nine out of ten cases, the wise investor should sell before the ex dividend date. For example, in the week JHS went ex dividend by 36¾ cents, the stock itself dropped by considerably more than that amount. It fell from 17⅞ to 16½; that is, the drop was 1⅜, and the dividend was a mere ⅜. This kind of movement gave traders an opportunity to take a profit before the dividend, miss the dividend itself, and buy the fund back again at 16½. This, therefore, was an opportunity to take advantage of a 1⅜ drop while simply forfeiting the dividend.

Here's another way of looking at this potential for gain. The alert trader could have made two trades—one for 1½ points, the other for 1⅜ points and still have sacrificed the dividend, happily.

In January 1977, JHS again went ex dividend and declined by 1¼ points to $17 at Point *M* before rallying to $18 at Point *H*, thereby reattaining its net asset value within a 1-week period. By March, however, JHS had dropped to a wide discount again with the stock selling at 16⅝ (Point *N*), a 7.6 percent discount from NAV which was approximately 18. It could, in fact, have been bought again and sold at the end of April, with the astute trader even catching the dividend before selling out again at 17¾ for another profit (Point *I*).

John Hancock Securities again became a buy in the November-December period of 1977, when its net asset value was about $18.25, while the fund itself was selling in the 16⅝–17 range (Point 0).

(I must make it clear once again that this kind of trading is pursuing profits of 1 or 1½ to 1¾ points—after commissions. Such profits may seem small, but when such profitable trading is done four times a year—in 10 to 20 different funds—they do indeed add up to a rather satisfactory return. Those who hold out for 2- or 3-point gains in closed-end bond funds will very rarely find them.)

As for CNA Income Shares, plotted in Figure 5.4, outstanding buying opportunities presented themselves in the April-June 1977 period of Point A, when the fund's NAV was approximately $13.50, and the price of the fund was in the 12⅛–12⅜ range, an average discount of 9.2 percent. Then you will see that in the August-September period, Point B, the discount narrowed to 13⅜ where it virtually reached the net asset value.

From November 1976 through January 1978, there were four buying opportunities in USLIFE Income Fund (UIF), as shown in Figure 5.5. The buying opportunities were in November 1976 (Point A), March 1977 (Point B), April 1977 (Point C), and June 1977 (Point D). UIF traded at premiums during two periods and was a short sale on both occasions—January 1977 (Point E) and August-September 1977 (Point F). A short position established in UIF during August 1977 and held through December 1977 would not have been profitable, however. The trader would have been short over four ex dividend dates of 8 cents each. Short selling works better in funds that pay quarterly dividends for the above reason. Try not to be short on the ex dividend date.

Examination of State Mutual Securities (SMS) from late 1976 through the beginning of 1978 in Figure 5.6 will demonstrate the price fluctuation difference between funds paying monthly dividends and funds paying quarterly dividends: funds with monthly dividend payments have flatter and relatively stable price movements with gradual or long-term fluctuations. This means fewer trading opportunities during each year. However, the total return should prove just as satisfactory. The reason for this is the trader will be invested for longer periods and receive monthly dividends during those periods. For instance, during the November-December 1976 period, a buy signal was given at Point A, when the fund declined to 11¾–11⅞. The NAV at that time was over $13, a healthy 10 percent discount for SMS caused by year-end tax selling. In January, as with most closed-end funds, the discount narrowed, to about 1 percent. This is the normal December–January closed-end fund behavior—a wide discount in December and a narrow discount in January. A sell signal was given the week of February 5, at Point B, at 12¾–13.

**FIGURE 5.4**
**CNA Income Shares**

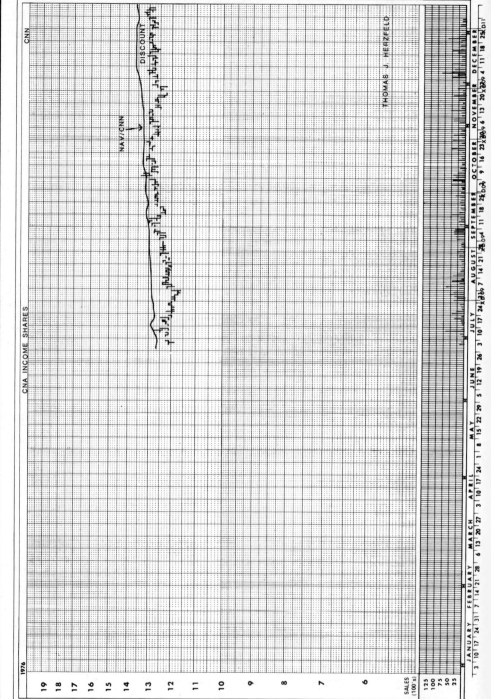

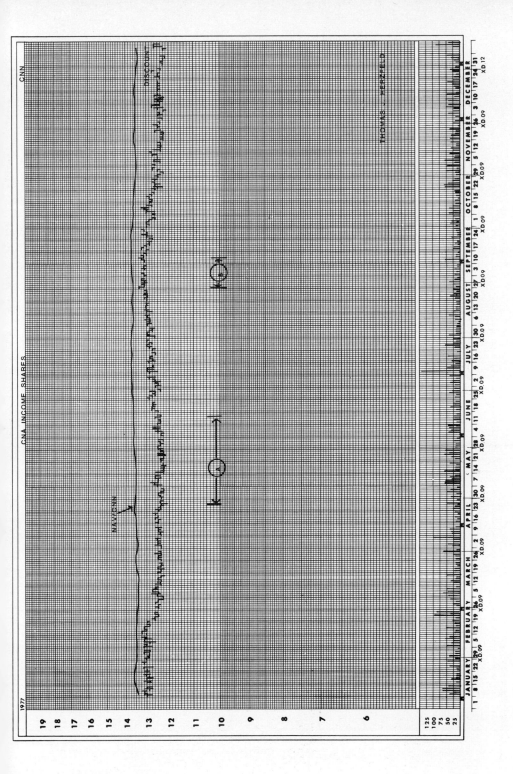

73

# FIGURE 5.5
## USLIFE Income Shares

74

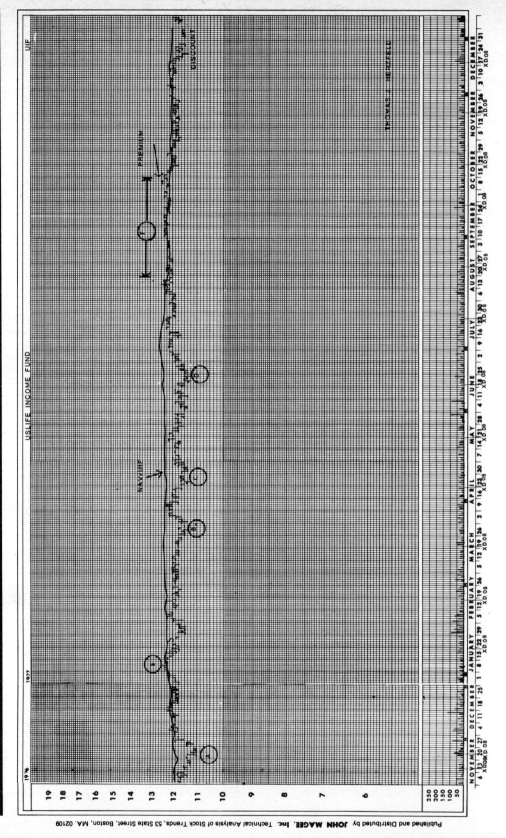

FIGURE 5.6
State Mutual Securities

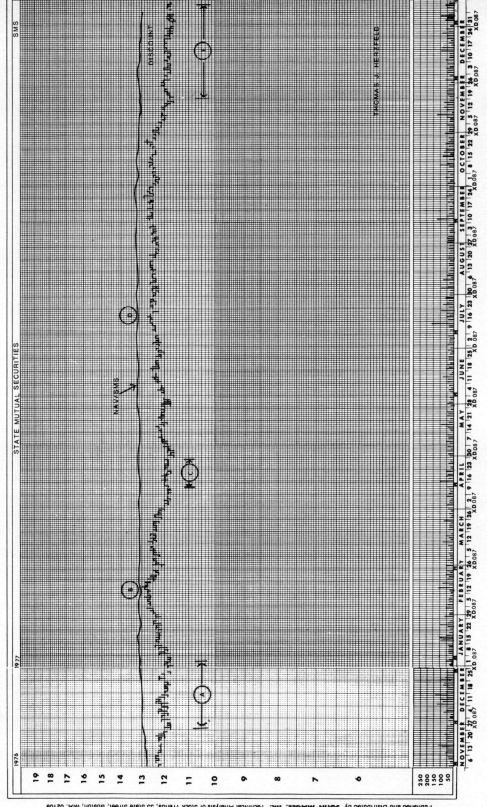

Two 8¼ cent dividends were paid in the December 1976–January 1977 trade. Point *B* was a short-selling opportunity for aggressive traders. Or at least it was an opportunity to create a hedge against long positions in funds then selling at excessive discounts, such as Mass Mutual Income Investors (MIV) whose NAV in February 1977 was $13.50, whose price was 11⅝, and whose discount was an unusual 13.9 percent. How remarkable it is that two bond funds with the same NAV (about $13) should simultaneously sell at such divergent prices—SMS at 13 and MIV at 11⅝.

Mid-April 1977 (Point *C*) was the time to buy (cover short positions) in SMS again. The price was 11⅝–11¾, the NAV was over 13, and the discount was 10.7 percent. It was a hold until the week of July 16, when it rose to 12¾ (Point *D*). Tax selling again created a buying opportunity in the November-December period of 1977 (Point E). The discount again widened, and the price fell to 11⅝.

As Figure 5.7 indicates, outstanding buy opportunities in Fort Dearborn Income Securities (FTD) came at the following times: May-June 1976 (Point A), August 1976 (Point B), the end of February 1977 (Point D), the end of May 1977 (Point E), and during the November-December period of 1977 (Point F). Conversely, clear sell signals came in FTD several times during the period as it approached its NAV or even went through it—in January (Point G) and February (Point H) of 1976 and again in January 1977 (Point I).

Drexel Bond-Debenture Trading Fund (DBF) has been an especially good fund to trade (see Figure 5.1). The management expenses are relatively high compared to other funds, causing its large discount. Also DBF had over 20 percent of its 1977 portfolio invested in equity-oriented investments, accounting for some of its relative volatility.

The late-1973 period had a buy signal the week of December 1 at 15½–16 (Point *A*). The NAV was 21, and the discount was 25 percent. Within 7 weeks, it rallied over 3 points to 19⅛. A sell signal was given the week of January 19, 1974 (Point *B*). The NAV was 20.62, and the discount was 7.3 percent. Again note the exceptionally large discount during the year-end tax selling in December.

Multiple buy signals were given in August and September of 1974 (points $C_1$ and $C_2$) at 12¾.

The week of June 15 (Point *E*) gave a short sale signal at $17. The NAV was 19.03, and the discount was only 5.7 percent. It is again interesting to note how investors tend to be aggressive before an ex dividend date. The then monthly dividend in DBF was 12 cents a

## FIGURE 5.7
## Fort Dearborn Income Shares

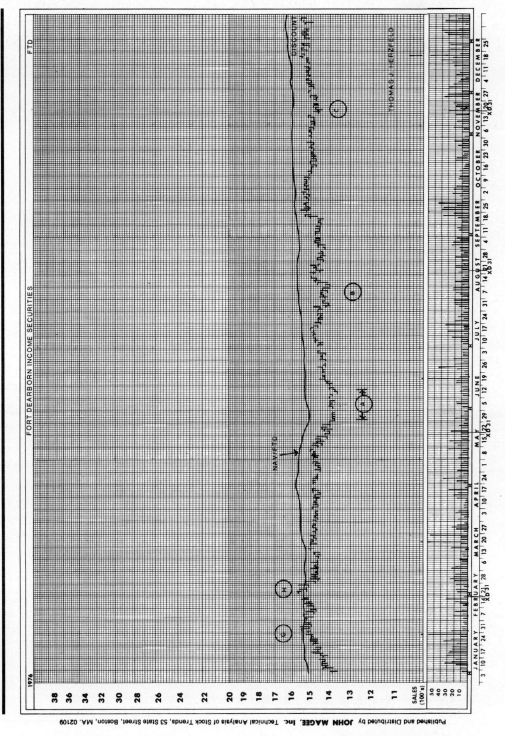

77

**FIGURE 5.7**
**Fort Dearborn Income Shares** *(Cont.)*

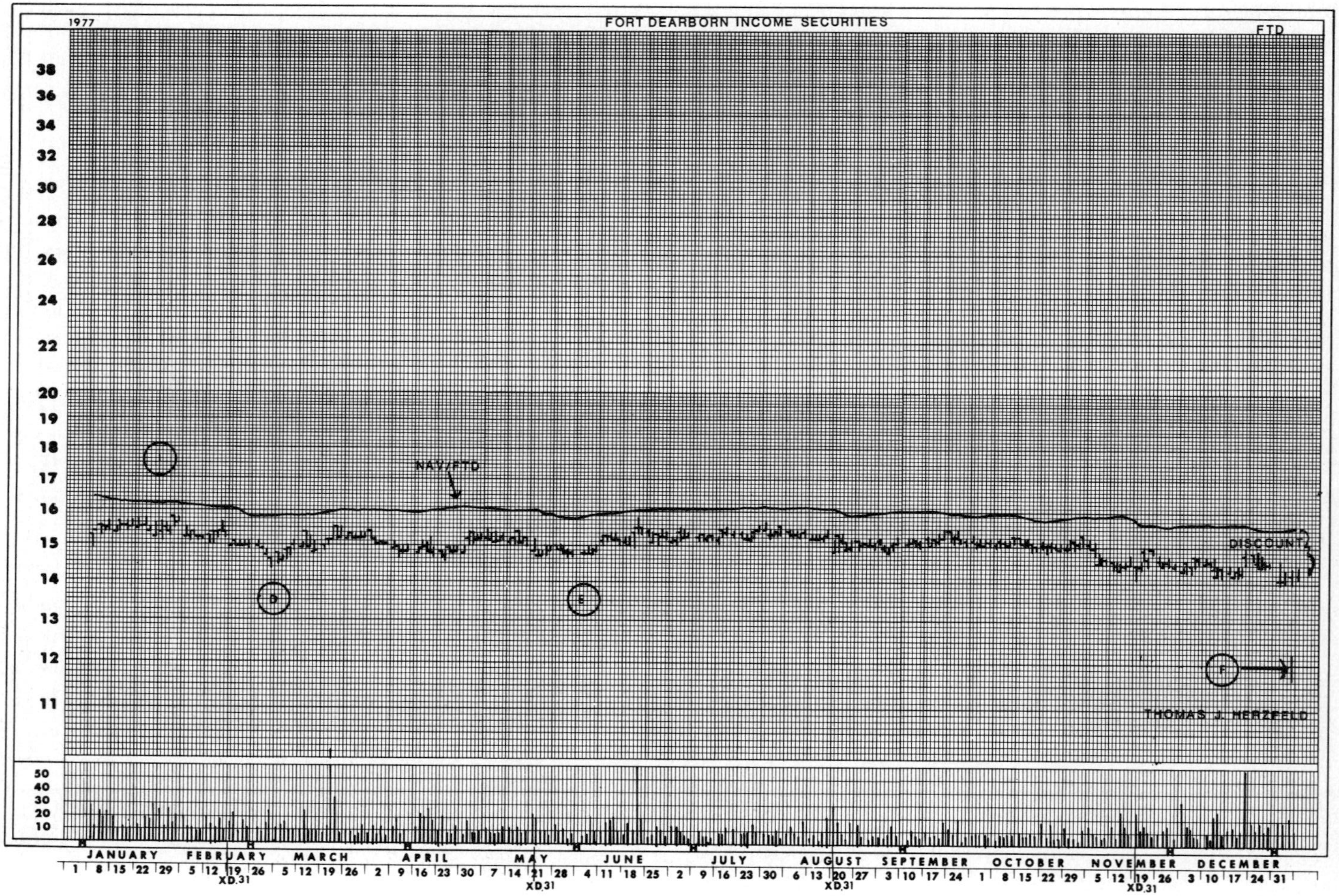

FORT DEARBORN INCOME SECURITIES

FTD

DISCOUNT

NAV/FTD

THOMAS J. HERTZFELD

share. To get the 12-cent dividend, the price of the stock was bid up from 15⅜ on June 1 (Point D) to 17¼ on June 11, 1974 (Point E). Of course, the stock dropped 2 points immediately after the dividend.

The sell signal after the August-September 1974 buy signal came in January 1975 (Point F), when DBF touched its NAV at 17. Always try to keep in mind that January is usually a strong month for closed-end funds. From Points $C_1$ and $C_2$ in August-September 1974, DBF rallied from 12½ to 17 (Point F) in January 1975—a 4½ point move plus 36 cents in dividends, for a total move of $4.86. During that time, the net asset value rose only $1. This kind of profit is the true excitement of trading closed-end funds.

As 1974 ended and 1975 began, the buy and sell levels with respect to deviations from normal discount had to be raised (bought and sold at narrower discounts) for two reasons: first, on a moving average basis the "normal" discount of DBF was narrowing, and second, the market had shifted from bear to bull.

There were four good buying opportunities in 1975 for DBF— Points G, H, I, and J, plus one of the best short-selling opportunities of that year (Point K). On October 10, 1975, DBF traded at 18⅞, its NAV was $17.63, a premium of 1¼ points or 7.1 percent. This short sale above 18½ (Point K) could have been covered 2 months later between 15½–16, (Point J), during the 1975 year-end tax selling period. The beginning of 1976 saw the usual January rally. DBF rose from 15½–16 (Point J) to 18 (Point L) in a 1-month period.

The remaining part of 1976 and 1977 was uneventful for DBF, except for Point M at the beginning of November 1977. The NAV was $20, the price was $16, and the discount was 20 percent, an unusually good buying opportunity in spite of the declining bond market.

Mass Mutual Income Investors (MIV), as shown in Figure 5.8, has sold at premiums and substantial discounts in the same year (1975). It has also been volatile one year (1975) and flat the next year (1976). In December 1974 it was selling at 10 (Point A), almost a 2-point discount. Within 2 months, it was at a half-point premium (Point B). The price was then 12⅞. By April (Point C), it was back to 10⅛. By the end of June 1975 (Point D), it rallied to 12 again. This volatility reoccurred in the period from December 1975 (Point E) to January 1976 (Point F), when it rallied from 10⅛ to 11¾. These were very unusual movements for a bond fund. But as more traders noticed these moves and began to increase their trading in MIV, the swings flattened out. This occurred in 1976 for MIV.

**FIGURE 5.8**
**Mass Mutual Income Investors**

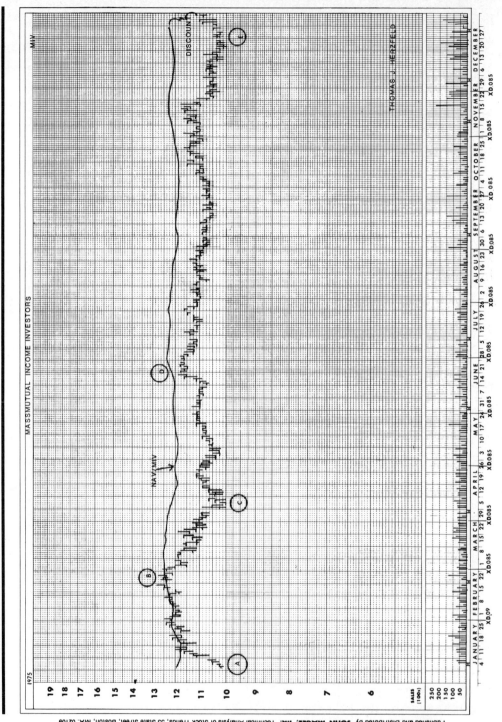

Published and Distributed by **JOHN MAGEE, Inc.** Technical Analysis of Stock Trends, 53 State Street, Boston, MA. 02109

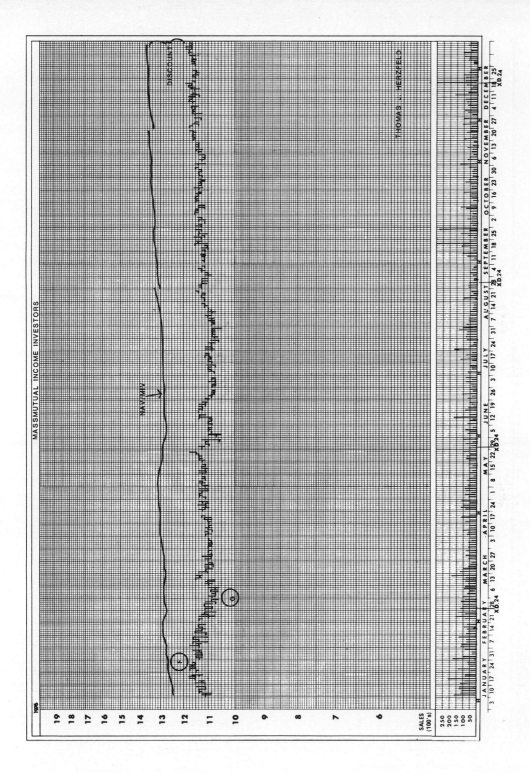

MASSMUTUAL INCOME INVESTORS

THOMAS J. HERZFELD

81

## FIGURE 5.8
**Mass Mutual Income Investors** *(Cont.)*

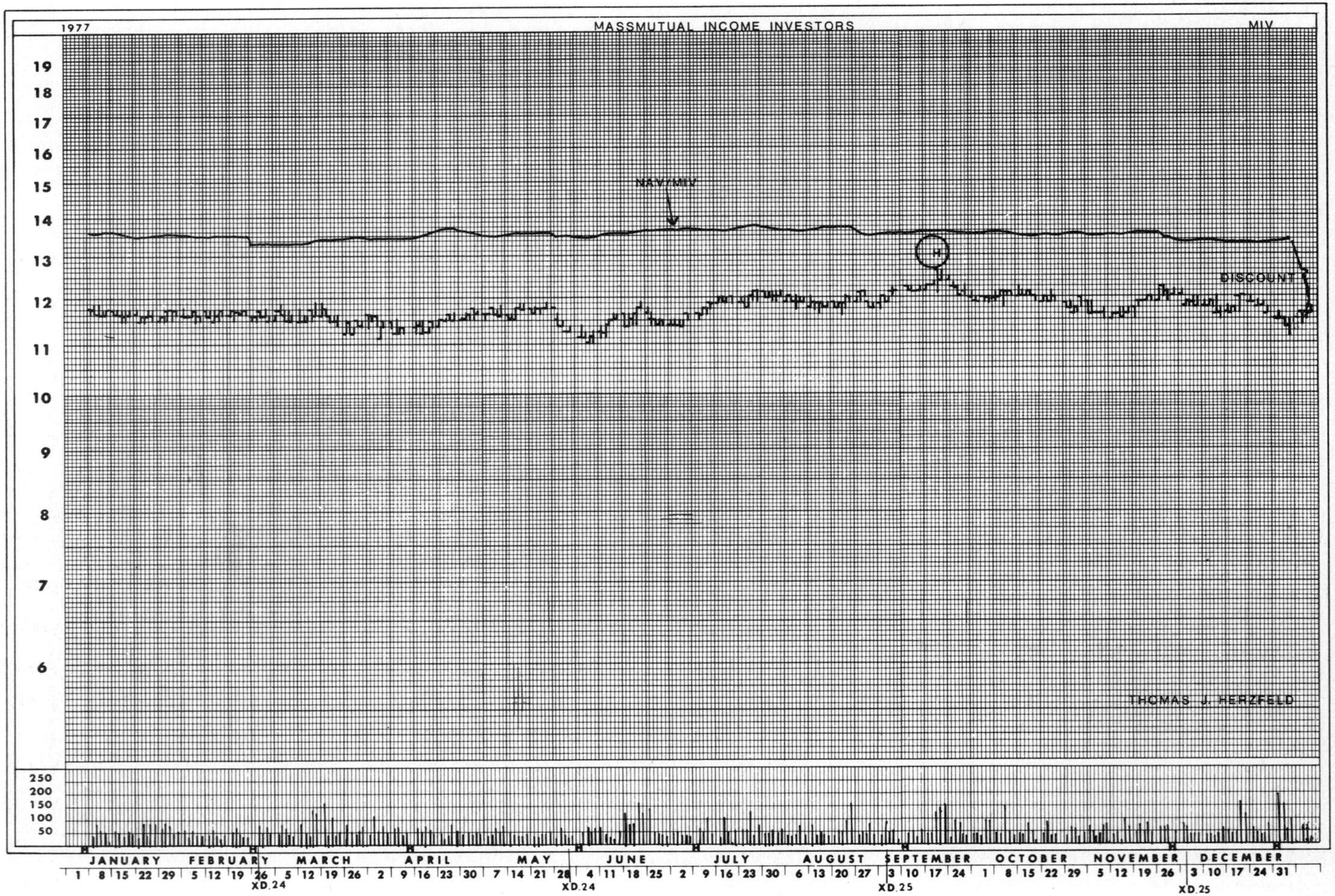

INA Investment Securities (IIS) had a relatively normal trading pattern through 1977 (see Figure 5.9), except for the excessive sell-off during December 1977 (Point B) and a zero discount in February 1977 (Point A). Scalpers could have made profitable trades if they bought at Points C, D, E, F, G, and H or made short sales at A, I, J, K, L, M, N, and O.

Excelsior Income Shares (EIS) tends to have wider trading swings, as do most of the other funds which have quarterly dividend payment schedules, than the funds which pay monthly.

As illustrated in Figure 5.10, there were four trading opportunities in the 1976–1977 period in EIS. The first buy signal for EIS in 1976 was the week of May 22 (Point A), when the fund declined to the 18–18½ range. The net asset value at that time was $21.53, and the discount (at 18¼) was 15 percent. Shares purchased the week of May 22 would have been entitled to the 42-cent June dividend. A sell signal came on June 19 (Point B), when the stock broke through 20. The discount had then narrowed to 6.4 percent. If purchased at Point A and sold at Point B, the gross profit (before commissions) would have been 1¾ points, plus a 42-cent dividend, for a $2.17 profit. The transaction costs for an individual would have been approximately ⅝ of a point (depending on the commission discount and whether the trader was a resident of New York). The net profit on the trade would have been $1.54. The *nonannualized* percentage profit would have been 8.3 percent in 4 weeks (assuming no margin).

A buy signal (for aggressive accounts) was given the week of July 17 at 18¾–18⅞ (Point C) at a discount of 12.2 percent. The subsequent sell signal came in the week of September 25 (Point D) at 20¾, or a 6.7 percent discount. The gross profit from that trade would have been 2 points, plus the September dividend of 42 cents. In 1977 a buy signal occurred the week of April 23 (Point E) at 19¾. A sell signal was given 10 weeks later at 21⅜ (Point F), after the 42-cent June dividend was paid. The next buy area was the week of October 29, (Point G) at 19. This buy was still well before the 42-cent December dividend.

During the 2-year period of 1976 and 1977 a trader would have been long for a period of 35 out of 104 weeks. What should he have been doing during the remaining 69 weeks? Presumably, he should have been trading in other bond funds or at least he should have invested in a money market fund.

A question may be puzzling the reader as to why EIS was a buy at a 15 percent discount on one occasion and a 12 percent discount on a

## FIGURE 5.9
## INA Investment Securities

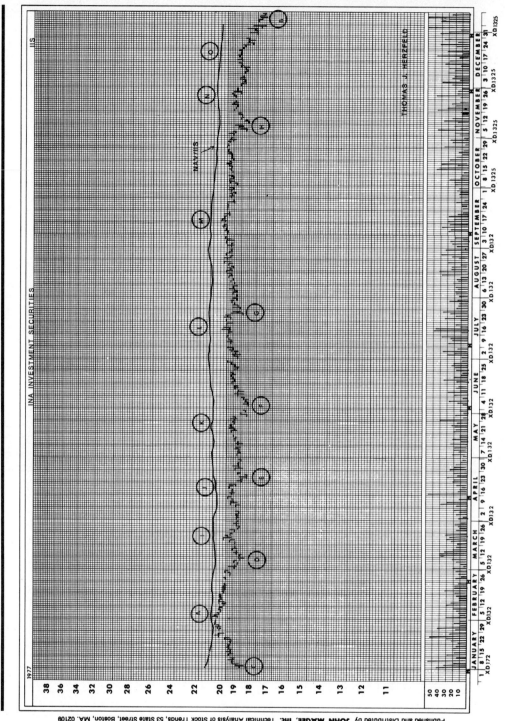

84

# FIGURE 5.10
## Excelsior Income Shares

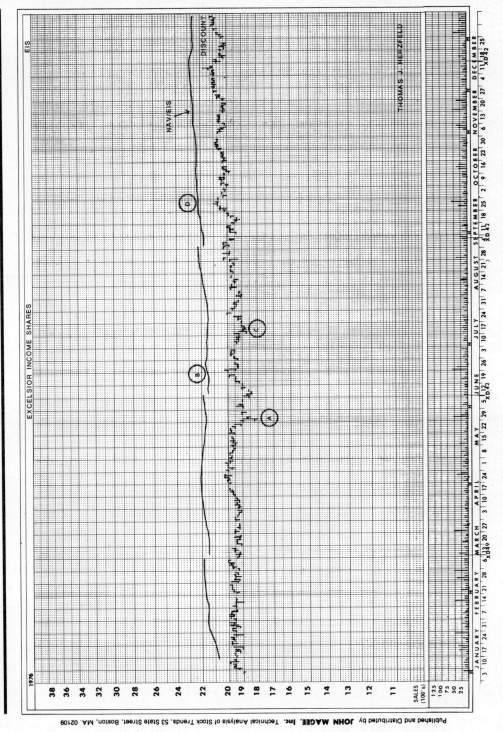

**TEKNIPLAT Chart Paper**

**FIGURE 5.10**
**Excelsior Income Shares** *(Cont.)*

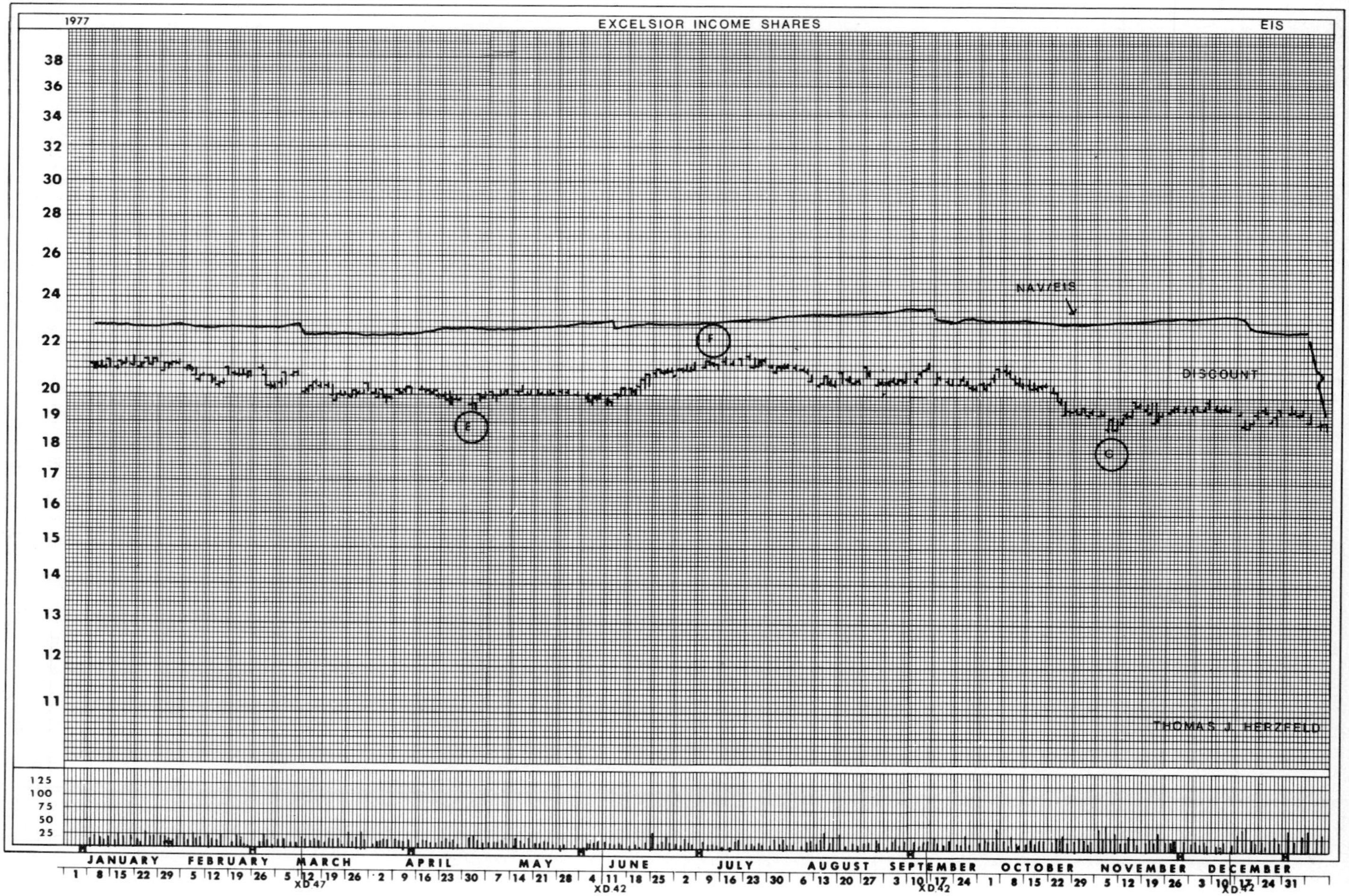

## FIGURE 5.11
## Mutual of Omaha Interest Shares

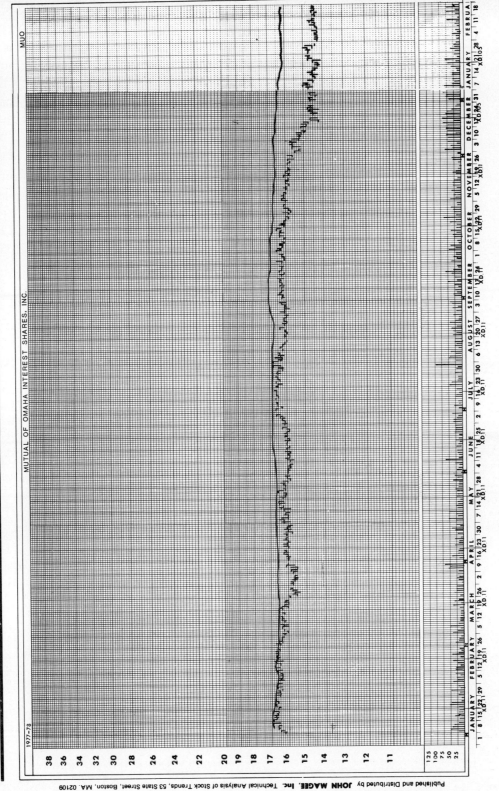

87

second occasion and a larger discount on the third buy signal. First, let me emphasize that no trading formula should be entirely mechanical; adjustments both subjective and objective must be made. If a bond fund has a normal discount of 5 percent assuming no adjustments, we should buy when the discount reaches 10 percent. But the important adjustments and considerations used to adjust the buy (or sell) points are, as previously discussed, the moving average of the discount, the direction of interest rates, and the relationship of the fund's deviation from normal discount to other funds' deviations at that moment. To summarize, the 5 percent deviation rule should be considered more of a guideline than a mechanical system.

Figure 5.11 is Mutual of Omaha Interest Shares (MUO). I have intentionally omitted what I considered the buy and sell signals in order to give the reader an opportunity to apply on his own the trading techniques we have suggested.

### NOTE

[1]Figure 5.2 shows Pacific American Income Shares (PAI), an example of a good trading vehicle. In 1975 the fund was trading at its NAV (Points $A_1$ and $A_2$) in January at $13\frac{1}{2}$–14. This was a short selling opportunity. By April 1975 the fund declined to a 15 percent discount. The price was $11\frac{1}{2}$. The NAV had declined only slightly from 14.03 in February 1975 to 13.62 in April (Point $B$). From April 1 (Point $B$) to April 11, 1975 (Point $C$), a trade could have been made from $11\frac{1}{2}$ to $13\frac{1}{4}$. The next buy signal was given the week of June 7, 1975. The NAV was 13.62, and the price was $11\frac{3}{4}$. The discount was 14 percent (Point $E$). A profit could have been realized on the rally to $13\frac{3}{8}$ (Point $F$) 4 weeks later. The discount narrowed to 4 percent. Point $G$, the week of August 9, 1975, was a buy signal at $11\frac{7}{8}$–12. The rally from that reversal carried to $14\frac{3}{8}$, a premium above its NAV, the week of October 11, 1975, at Point $H$, and it was of course a spot to sell short. Nine weeks later the premium disappeared, and the fund was selling at a 16 percent discount (Point $I$) in December 1975. The major buying opportunity for PAI in 1976 was in June (Point $J$), when the price was $12\frac{1}{2}$–13, the NAV was 14.75, and the discount was 14 percent. The major buying opportunity for PAI in 1977 was again in June after the May dividend (Point $K$). The end of 1977 saw wide discounts in all bond funds, including PAI. The stock market was falling, and interest rates were rising. Tax selling pressures were in force. PAI gave multiple buy signals in November and December 1977 at Points $L_1$, $L_2$, and $L_3$.

# Trading Closed-End Convertible Bond Funds

**6**

Convertible bond funds form a neat, easily comprehensible package. There are only four of them, all similar in size, objective, the general quality of their portfolios, and, most significantly, performance.

Before getting into details, however, it should be pointed out that the term "convertible bond fund" is a bit of a misnomer. A better description would be "convertible funds." This is because these funds have a large percentage of convertible preferred stocks in their portfolios. An excellent example is the Bancroft Convertible Fund, which has a portfolio mix of about 60 percent convertible bonds and 30 percent convertible preferreds. As for the often-used term "convertible bond," it usually means a convertible debenture. A debenture is not backed by any specific asset of a company; rather, it is an unsecured debt obligation. In this book, the terms debenture and bond are used interchangeably.

Following are general profiles of the four funds which make up the group.

• *American General Convertible Securities*   This fund is traded on the New York Stock Exchange under the symbol AGS. During the second half of 1977, it paid a monthly dividend of 11 cents per share and yielded approximately 7.3 percent based on a net asset value of $22 to $23, a price of $18, and a discount of 19 percent (as of August 1977). AGS is managed by American General Capital Management, a wholly owned subsidiary of American General Insurance Company. Some of its larger positions are Richmond Tank Car, which was acquired through conversion; Pennzoil 5¼s of 1996, which are rated BB by Standard & Poor's, convertible into 26.14 shares at $38.25 per share; Avco Corporation 9⅝s of 2001, rated B by S&P and convertible at $17 a share into 58.82 shares per bond; Connecticut General Mortgage and Realty 6s of 1996, not rated and convertible into 30.77 shares

**89**

per bond at 32.50 per share. AGS is capitalized at approximately 3.1 million shares. For investment purposes, it may borrow funds which do not exceed 25 percent of its assets.

• *Bancroft Convertible Fund* Traded on the American Stock Exchange with the symbol BCV, this fund had a net asset value of $23.06 at mid-1977, with a discount of almost 24 percent when it was selling at $17⅝. Its yield was 6.3 percent, with a quarterly dividend of 25 cents. Managed by Davis-Dinsmore Management Company, Bancroft is capitalized with slightly over 2 million shares. According to its semiannual report of 1977, some of the fund's larger positions are United Technologies $8 convertible preferreds; Fisher Scientific 5½s of 1996, rated B and convertible into 55.56 shares per bond at $18 per share; White Consolidated Industries 5½s of 1992, rated BB and convertible into 38.87 shares per bond at a price of $25.73; Allegheny Ludlum Industries $3 convertible preferreds; RLC Corporation 6¼s of 1997, rated CCC and convertible to 101.83 shares per bond at a price of $9.82. Bancroft also has positions in Harris International Financial NV, which is convertible into Harris Corporation common, and Beatrice Foods Overseas Financial NV.

• *Chase Convertible Fund* This fund which is traded on the New York Stock Exchange under the symbol CFB, as of August 1977 had a net asset value of $11.54, a price of $9⅛, and was selling at a discount of 21 percent. With a quarterly dividend at that time of 15 cents, it was yielding 6.6 percent. The fund is managed by Phoenix Investment Counsel of Boston, which was formerly called John P. Chase, Inc. Some of its larger positions are U.S. Steel 5¾s of 2001, rated A and convertible into 15.94 shares per bond at $62.95 per share; RCA 4½s of 1992, rated BBB, convertible into 16.95 shares per $1,000 bond at $59 per share; General Instrument 10¼s of 1996, rated BB, convertible into 34.67 shares per bond at $28.84 per share; and a large position in IC Industries $3.50 convertible preferreds. Thirteen percent of Chase's portfolio is in preferred stock, and the fund is capitalized at about 5½ million shares.

• *Castle Convertible Fund* Listed on the American Stock Exchange under the symbol CVF, as of August 1977, this fund had a net asset value of $24.22 and was selling at $21½ for a discount of 16.4 percent. With a quarterly dividend of 24 cents, it had a yield of 7 percent on an annualized basis. The fund, when it was managed by CI Management Fund, owned by City Investing, was known as the CI Convertible Fund. When Fred Alger Management, Inc., assumed direction of the fund in 1974, it was given its present name. Among its preferred stocks are Singer Corporation $3.50 cumulative convertibles and Lear Siegler $2.25 cumulative convertibles. Its larger positions in convertible bonds include TRE Corporation 9¾s of 2002, not rated, which are convertible into 62.50 shares per bond at a price of $16 per share; Host International 5¼ convertible subordinated debentures due 1994, rated BB, convertible into 23.67 shares per bond at $42.25 per share; General Instrument 10¼ convertible subordinated debentures due 1996, rated BB, convertible to 34.67 shares per bond at a price of $28.84 per share; and Chase Manhattan 6½ convertible subordinated debentures due 1996, not rated, convertible into 17.39 shares per bond at $57.40.

These capsulized descriptions should establish the overall similarity of the funds. As far as the performance of each is concerned, it can best be seen by examining Figure 6.1, which shows the net asset values from July 1975 through February 1978 (dollar prices have been omitted since we're simply showing comparative performances). Clearly, all four funds performed in very much the same manner, although Castle did run slightly better than the other three.

## ADVANTAGES OF CONVERTIBLE BONDS AND CONVERTIBLE BOND FUNDS

At this point, let us examine the general advantages of convertible bonds and convertible bond funds. Convertible bonds mature at a fixed date, assuring an investor that unless a company goes into bankruptcy, at maturity he will receive $1000 for each $1000 face value. Because a bond is a debt of the issuing company, bondholders have the right to force a company into insolvency if the interest and principal payments of the debt are not made.

Another plus lies in the fact that convertible bonds offer relatively high yields in comparison to other investments. In addition, these bonds have a potential capital gains factor. Since the bond is convertible into the common stock of a company, if the company's common rises, the bond's value will rise too.

All of the advantages of convertible bonds apply to the portfolios of convertible bond funds. In addition, the investor in a fund acquires a diversified portfolio at a discount from the value of the aggregate port-

FIGURE 6.1
Comparison of NAVs for Castle Convertible Fund, American General Convertible
Securities, Chase Convertible Fund, and Bancroft Convertible Fund

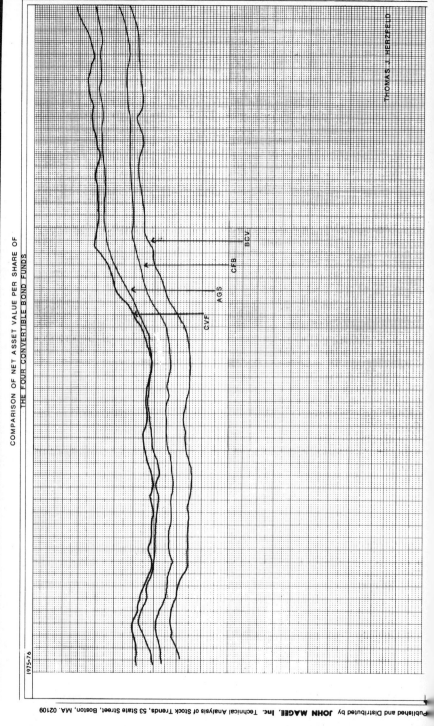

COMPARISON OF NET ASSET VALUE PER SHARE OF
THE FOUR CONVERTIBLE BOND FUNDS

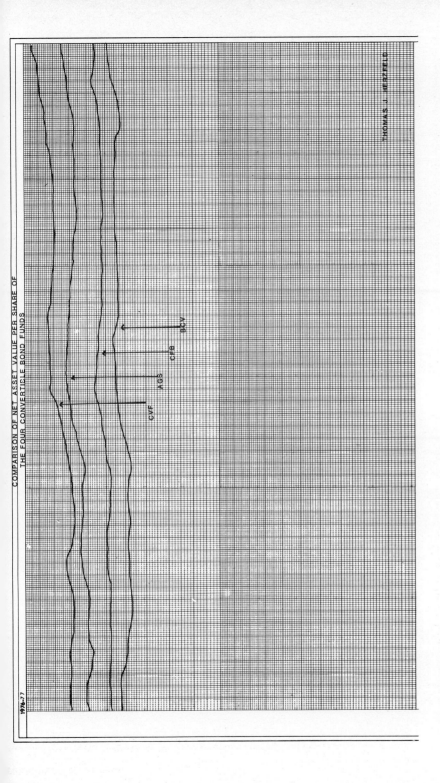

COMPARISON OF NET ASSET VALUE PER SHARE OF
THE FOUR CONVERTIBLE BOND FUNDS

1976-77

THOMAS J. HERZFELD

CVF    AGS    CFB    BCV

93

**94**

## FIGURE 6.1
## Comparison of NAVs for Castle Convertible Fund, American General Convertible Securities, Chase Convertible Fund, and Bancroft Convertible Fund   (*Cont.*)

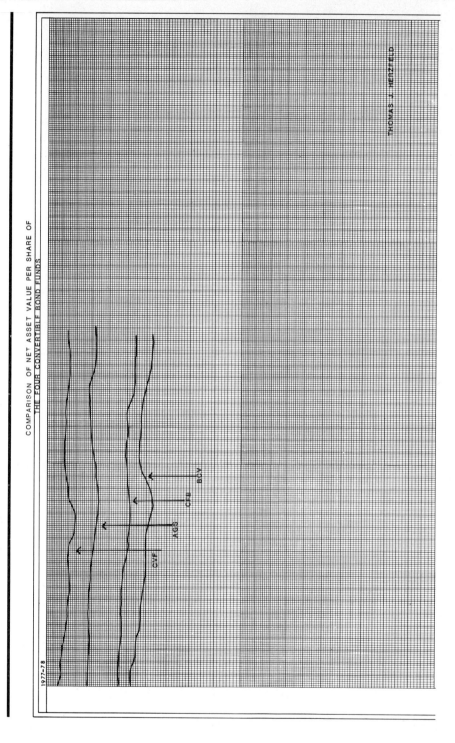

COMPARISON OF NET ASSET VALUE PER SHARE OF
THE FOUR CONVERTIBLE BOND FUNDS

folio and at a yield, because of this discount, which is higher than if he had purchased the bonds separately.

## A REVIEW OF CONVERTIBLE BOND ANALYSIS

In evaluating a convertible bond, priority should be given to a number of variables. These are the bond's maturity, its rating, its conversion ratio and investment value, and whether it is selling at a premium or discount or at parity with its conversion value. A bond's maturity and rating virtually speak for themselves: a shorter maturity will have a stabilizing influence on interest rate fluctuations. As for ratings, it is obvious that high-rated bonds are preferable to low-rated ones.

A bond's conversion ratio should also be considered. This term refers to the number of shares of common stock which will be received by the investor through conversion of a bond. For instance, if a bond is convertible at $25 a share, for each $1,000 bond, the holder would be entitled to convert into 40 shares.

In analyzing convertible bond funds, one must, of course, determine the more important variables which affect them. Since convertible bonds are affected by stock market as well as bond market swings, one might jump to the conclusion that all of the variables discussed in Chapter 2 should be taken into consideration. The fact is, however, that only seven variables are of truly significant weight.

Of these seven, four are comparatively simple—the quality of the fund, as indicated by ratings; the maturity of the portfolio, with shorter maturities providing a stabilizing influence against interest rate fluctuations; yield and dividend changes; and whether the fund stresses conversion value or investment value when buying bonds.

The key variables, besides the discount which necessarily ranks at the top of any such list, are the relationship of the funds to one another and whether the fund is a takeover or open-end possibility. As for their relationship, if three funds are selling at sharp discounts and one at a premium, the fund at a premium is a short-sell candidate. On the other hand, if three funds are selling without discounts or with very narrow ones and the fourth is at a sharp discount, that fund is a purchase candidate.

To qualify as a takeover candidate (which is discussed in depth in Chapter 10), a fund should have a poor record, a relatively high management fee, and a liquid portfolio and should sell at a substantial discount. At least one of the convertible bond funds has these "qualifications." As we shall see, this factor weighed quite heavily in a trading decision.

## CHARTS OF CONVERTIBLE BOND FUNDS

Now let's study the charts of the four funds over the past few years, examining their trading records and learning what could or should have been accomplished.

There are several methods which can be used in trading convertible bond funds. We can employ the basic approach, taking the average of the three widest discounts from the previous year and using it as our buy line. We can use the advanced method, taking a deviation from a moving average of the discount. Or, by combining the basic and the advanced approaches and adjusting for the relative discount of one fund to the group, we can employ a third concept.

Figure 6.2 shows American General Convertible Securities (AGS) from June 1975 through February 1978. In the second half of 1975, this fund fluctuated from a position of no discount to discounts as low as 2 or 3 percent and as high as 10 percent. Because of that discount history, the fund should not have been considered a buy, no matter what its deviation was from its net asset value or how closely it approached its widest discount of the previous year. The reason for this is found in the fact that the closed-end convertible bond funds as a group were selling at a 21 percent discount during the same period. Thus, the approach which has to be used in trading AGS is the third basic one in trading all closed-end funds: if a fund for no apparent reason is selling at a much narrower discount than the other funds in its group, that fund is a sale regardless of how excessive its deviation may be from its normal trading discount. This "rule" especially applies to the four convertible funds, whose objectives, quality, and size are so identifiably similar.

With AGS, then, the proper strategy was to plot the average discount for the group, instead of constructing deviations from moving averages of the discount or building a buy line based on its previous year's widest discount. As of July 1975, the average discount of the closed-end convertible bond group was 21 percent, which then became the buy line. The first and only time AGS hit that buy line was in the very end of June and the beginning of July 1976 at Point A. For a full year after that, there were no buy signals for AGS. This is because the buy line was adjusted in July 1976 to 27 percent, the then

FIGURE 6.2
American General Convertible Securities

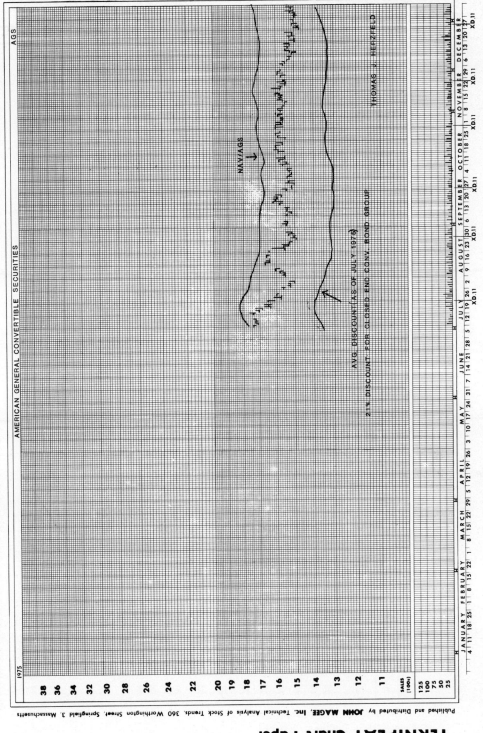

## FIGURE 6.2
**American General Convertible Securities**  *(Cont.)*

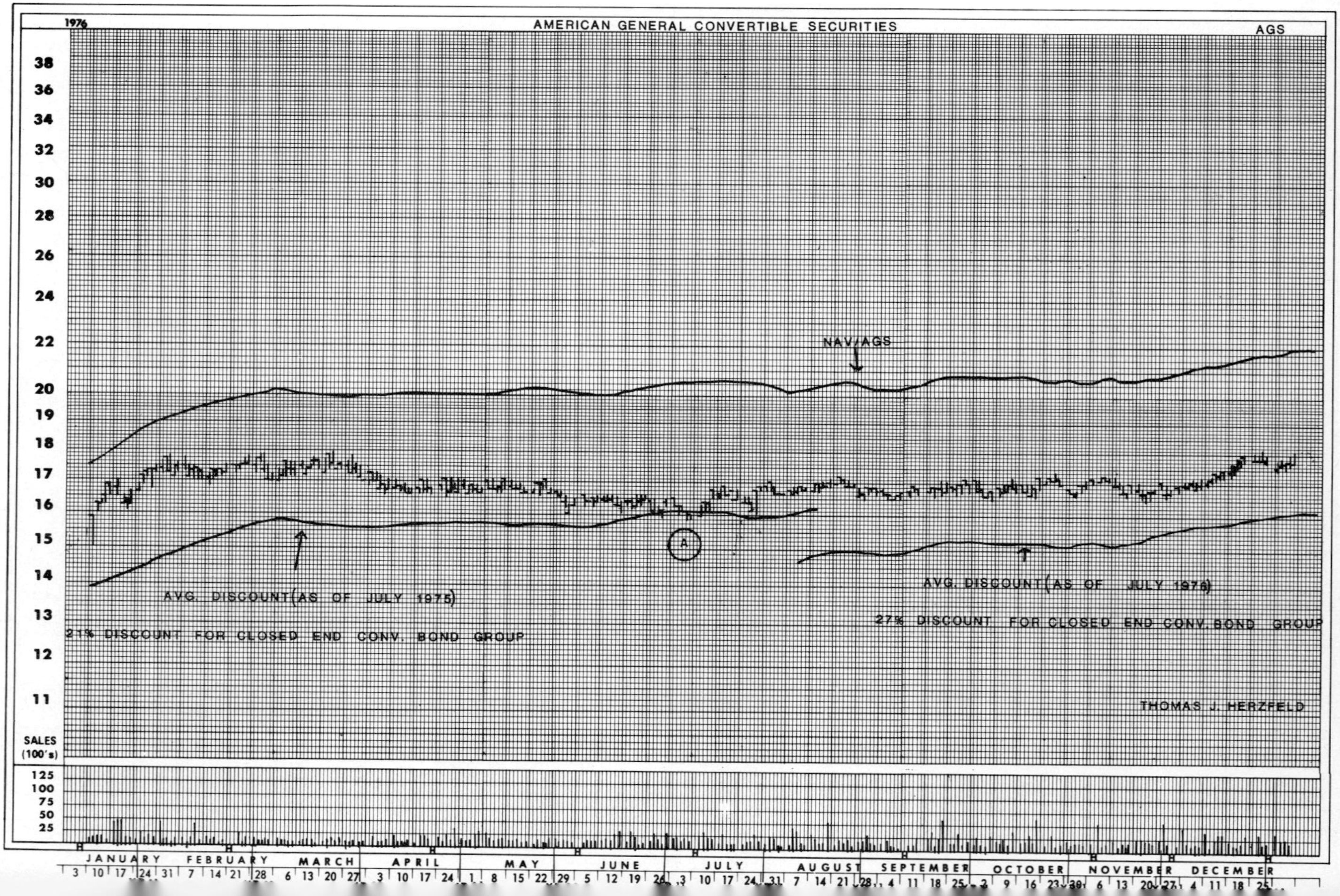

AMERICAN GENERAL CONVERTIBLE SECURITIES

AGS

NAV/AGS

AVG. DISCOUNT (AS OF JULY 1976)

27% DISCOUNT FOR CLOSED END CONV. BOND GROUP

AVG. DISCOUNT (AS OF JULY 1975)

21% DISCOUNT FOR CLOSED END CONV. BOND GROUP

THOMAS J. HERZFELD

98

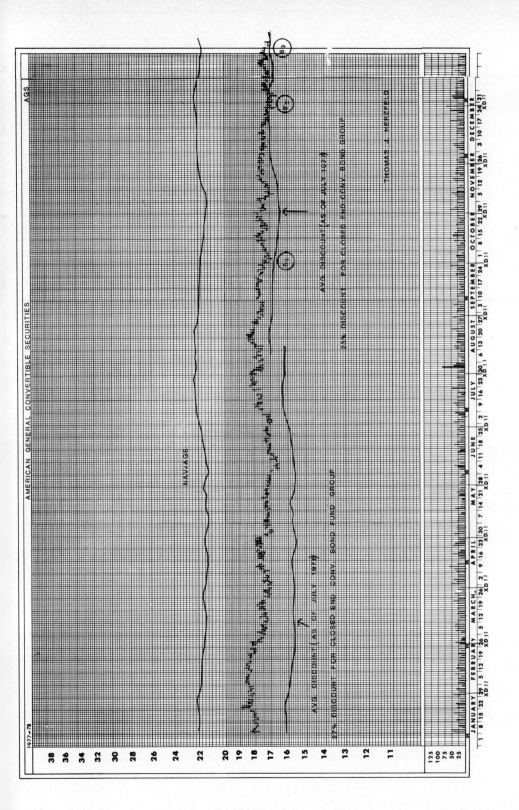

AMERICAN GENERAL CONVERTIBLE SECURITIES

AGS

1977-78

NAV/AGS

AVG. DISCOUNT (AS OF JULY 1976)

27% DISCOUNT FOR CLOSED END CONV. BOND FUND GROUP

AVG. DISCOUNT (AS OF JULY 1977)

25% DISCOUNT FOR CLOSED END CONV. BOND GROUP

THOMAS J. HERZFELD

| JANUARY | FEBRUARY | MARCH | APRIL | MAY | JUNE | JULY | AUGUST | SEPTEMBER | OCTOBER | NOVEMBER | DECEMBER |

99

current average discount of the group. As a result—and this applied to the other funds in the group as well—I certainly would not buy AGS if it was selling at a discount significantly narrower than 27 percent. As the chart shows, AGS did not trade at a 27 percent discount during the period through September 1977, its largest discount being 20 percent.

In August of 1977, AGS's buy line was adjusted to 23 percent, based on the group's moving average in the previous month. Multiple buy signals for AGS then appeared at Points *B-1*, *B-2*, and *B-3*, which were in September and December 1977 and January 1978. The interesting point here is that while the average discount of AGS widened over the 1975–1978 period from virtually no discount to a substantial one, the other funds in its group for the most part were experiencing narrowing discounts. As we explore the charts of the other funds, we will see that we were not buying AGS in 1975 for the same reason that we were buying in 1978. That reason also explains why we were buying the other funds in the group in 1975 and selling them in 1978.

It is reasonable to ask why AGS was not selling at a discount during certain times in 1975 and why, by 1978, it had gone to a large discount. Unfortunately, there is no logically apparent explanation for this movement. However, it is possible to explain why AGS went to a discount in 1977–1978. That explanation lies with a "sister" fund of AGS, Amercian General Bond Fund (AGB), which has a portfolio of high-grade corporate bonds and which usually does not sell at a discount. Perhaps in the past, in sympathy with AGB, AGS also did not sell at a discount. Or perhaps investors believed the lack of a discount in one fund was sufficient reason for the other not to sell at a discount. Obviously, if they persisted in this kind of analysis, they were making a fundamental mistake in trading.

A final note on AGS and the illustration of a fund whose discount is at a large disparity with the rest of the funds in its group. In May 1978, AGS was at a 24 percent discount, while Bancroft Convertible Fund and Castle Convertible Fund were at unusually narrow discounts, thus creating the exact opposite of the situation which occurred in 1975.

In Figure 6.3, showing Castle Convertible Fund (CVF) from 1975 through 1978, a different trading method is demonstrated. The buy line for CVF was established at 26 percent and the sell line at 13 percent, again based on the averages of the three widest and the three narrowest discounts.

**FIGURE 6.3**
**Castle Convertible Fund**

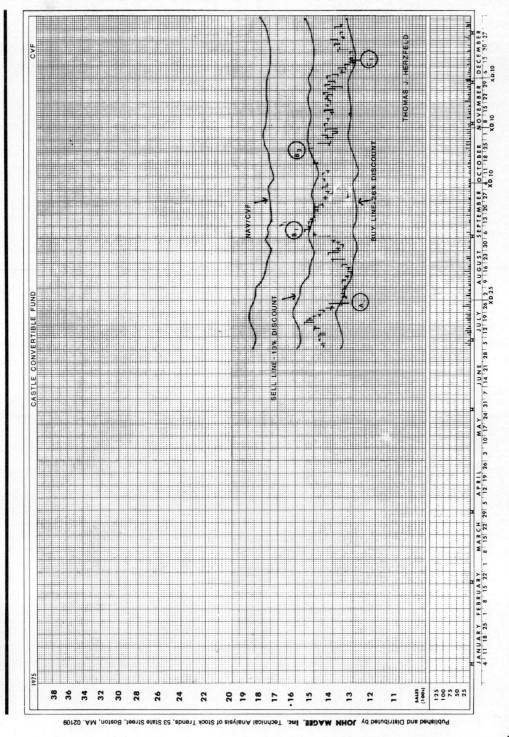

Published and Distributed by **JOHN MAGEE, Inc.** Technical Analysis of Stock Trends, 53 State Street, Boston, MA. 02109

**TEKNIPLAT Chart Paper**

**FIGURE 6.3**
**Castle Convertible Fund** *(Cont.)*

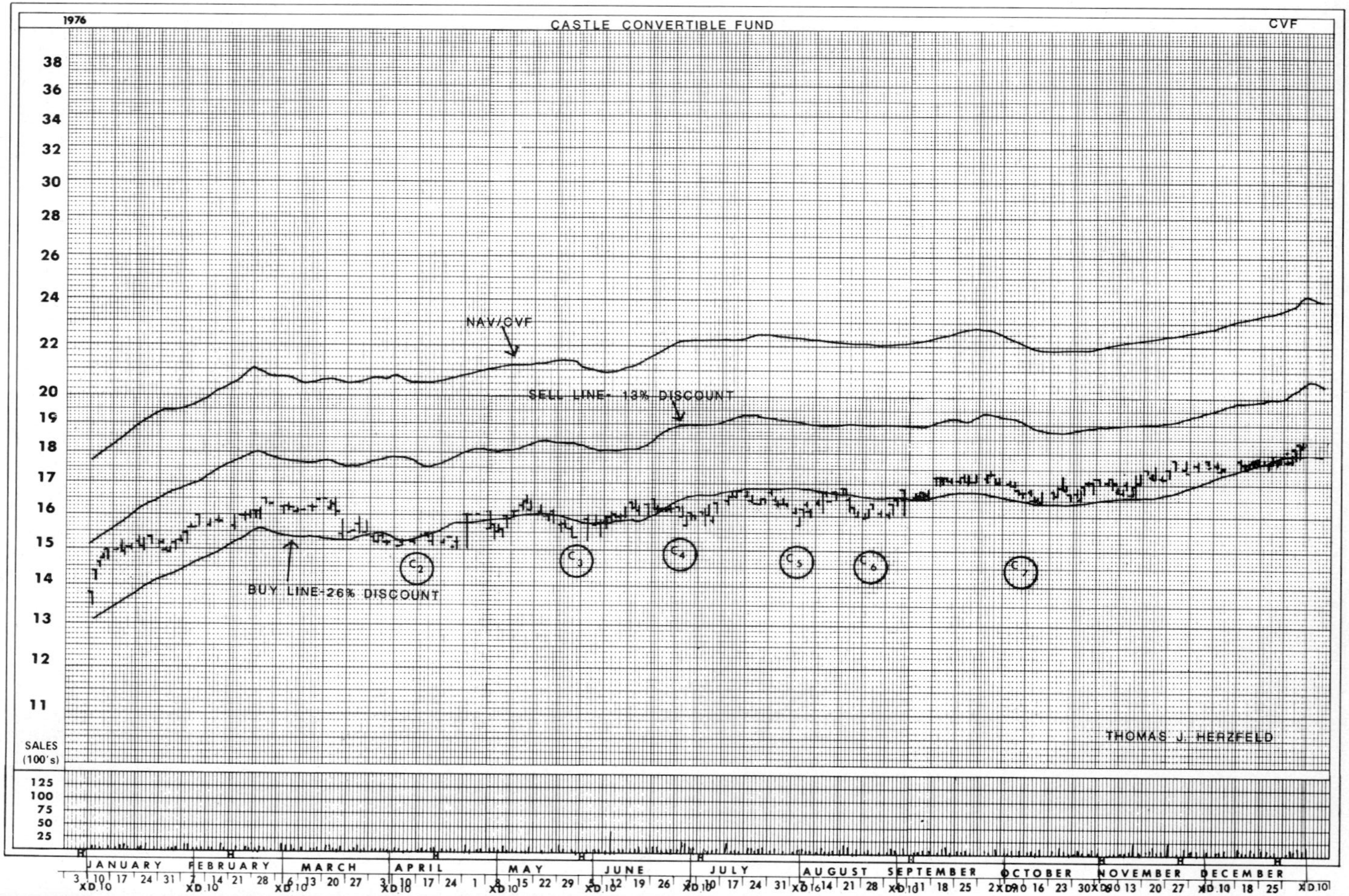

CASTLE CONVERTIBLE FUND

CVF

1976

NAV/CVF

SELL LINE -13% DISCOUNT

BUY LINE -26% DISCOUNT

THOMAS J. HERZFELD

SALES (100's)

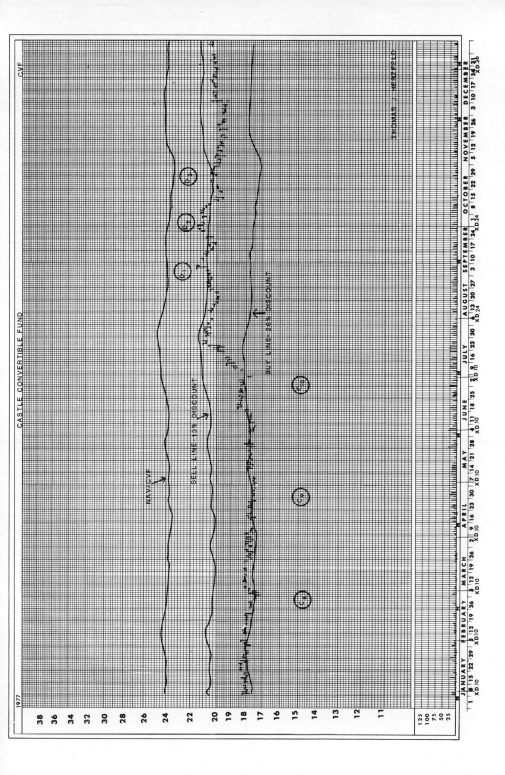

CASTLE CONVERTIBLE FUND

CVF

1977

THOMAS J. HERZFELD

NAV/CVF

SELL LINE -13% DISCOUNT

BUY LINE -26% DISCOUNT

38 36 34 32 30 28 26 24 22 20 19 18 17 16 15 14 13 12 11

125 100 75 50 25

JANUARY FEBRUARY MARCH APRIL MAY JUNE JULY AUGUST SEPTEMBER OCTOBER NOVEMBER DECEMBER

**103**

In July 1975 at Point A, we received the first buy signal when the fund declined to 13½. It then momentarily broke through the 26 percent line when it declined to 13¼, for a discount of about 28 percent. CVF rallied in August, and by the beginning of September it was 16½ at Point B-1; there it went through its sell line at a 13 percent discount and eventually narrowed to a discount of about 12 percent. A multiple sell signal appeared at Point B-2 in October 1975, and another buy signal came at Point C-1 in December 1975 at a price of 12⅞, again at a discount of 26 percent from net asset value which was then about 17⅝. Additional buy signals were given beginning at Points C-2, and continuing through C-3, C-4, C-5, C-6, C-7, C-8, C-9, and C-10.

It bears emphasizing that CVF was a buy at any of the points from C-1 to C-10 from December 1975 through all of 1976 and until the final buy signal at C-10 appeared at the beginning of July 1977. An investor at C-1 who held the fund through that entire period would have collected dividends which at that time were paid monthly. The rate was 10 cents per share with an extra dividend of 26 cents paid in August 1976.

After a sharp rally commencing at Point C-10 in July 1977, a sell signal was received at the end of August 1977, Point D-1, when the price of the fund was $21. This price was significantly higher, it must be noted, from the price of $13 when we received our first buy signal in 1975. For a closed-end fund, it indeed was a very profitable trading opportunity.

Multiple sell signals were given in CVF at D-1, D-2, and D-3 in August through October 1977, when the fund was selling at approximately a 13 percent discount. The fund then shifted into a neutral position, selling at approximately an 18 percent discount in the $20 per share range.

In 1977, a relatively important change was made by CVF's managers. The fund began to pay dividends on a quarterly basis at the rate of 36 cents per share, an increase over the previous rate of 10 cents per month. This caused CVF's yield to be higher than that of the other funds in the group while, at the same time, it was slightly outperforming them. The combination of higher yield and performance apparently is the reason why CVF's discount narrowed over the 3-year period. This should serve as an excellent example of yield coming into play as a heavily weighted variable in the trading of a closed-end convertible bond fund.

The experience of Castle Convertible Fund is further illustrated by what happened to the Chase Convertible Fund of Boston (CFB) after it lowered its dividend: the fund began to sell at a larger discount, as is shown in Figure 6.4, which runs from the end of 1974 to the beginning of 1978. In February 1975, CFB was trading at a slight premium at Point A. In the following month, the dividend was lowered from 6 cents to 5 cents a month, and the premium disappeared almost immediately. And by September of that year, in a truly dramatic shift, the fund was selling at a discount of 28 percent. (In the CFB chart, buy and sell lines were left out intentionally to give the reader an unassisted opportunity to pick the points at which he might have been a buyer or seller.)

Point C shows the Chase Fund selling in June 1976 at its largest discount during the period covered by the chart—approximately 34 percent from its net asset value. Point D, at the end of July 1977, shows that the fund was selling at $10 a share, which was a 15 percent discount from net asset value.

The reader should be aware of one other factor in making his theoretical buy and sell decisions on CFB. In 1976, the fund revised its dividend policy, changing the reduced 5 cents per month payout to 15 cents a quarter. In doing this, it joined an increasing number of funds shifting from monthly to quarterly dividend payments, primarily because of the savings derived from not sending monthly checks to shareholders.

Figures 6.5 and 6.6 deal with the Bancroft Convertible Fund (BCV); Figure 6.5 is without buy and sell lines, and Figure 6.6 has those lines. In these charts, to provide comparison of the fund's net asset value to the stock market in general, I also plotted the Dow Jones Industrial Average along the top.

Figure 6.6 shows that the buy line in Bancroft was at 33 percent and the sell line at 21 percent from the end of 1975 through 1976, dropping to 19 percent in 1977. The adjustment was made because at the end of 1976, it became apparent that reversals were beginning to be missed in buying Bancroft. The adjustment enabled trading in the fund at slightly narrower discounts.

The exact reversal points of the discounts have also been plotted on these charts, so that they have more information than my normal charts. Examples of these reversals are Point A at 16 percent, Point B at 25 percent, Points C and D at 18 percent, etc.

**FIGURE 6.4**
**Chase Convertible Fund of Boston**

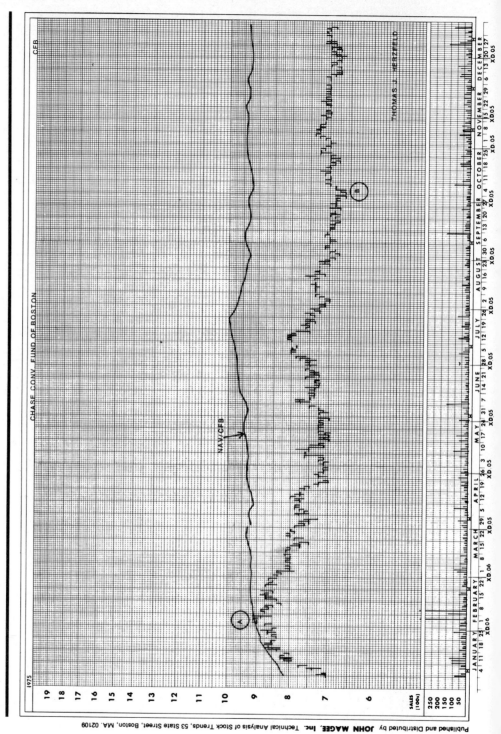

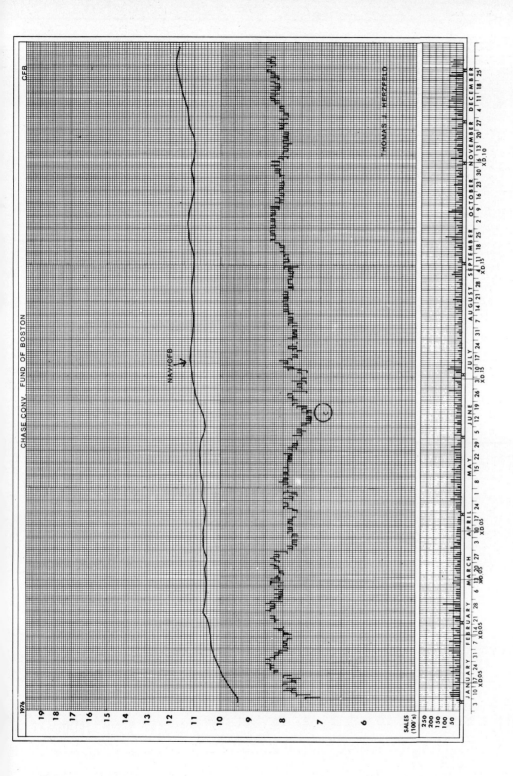

CHASE CONV. FUND OF BOSTON

CFB

1976

THOMAS J. HERZFELD

NAV CFB

SALES
(100's)

250
200
150
100
50

19
18
17
16
15
14
13
12
11
10
9
8
7
6

JANUARY FEBRUARY MARCH APRIL MAY JUNE JULY AUGUST SEPTEMBER OCTOBER NOVEMBER DECEMBER
3 10 17 24 31 7 14 21 28 6 13 20 27 3 10 17 24 1 8 15 22 29 5 12 19 26 3 10 17 24 31 7 14 21 28 4 11 18 25 2 9 16 23 30 6 13 20 27 4 11 18 25
XD.05 XD.05 XD.05 XD.05 XD.05 XD.15 XD.15 XD.10

**107**

FIGURE 6.4
Chase Convertible Fund of Boston  (Cont.)

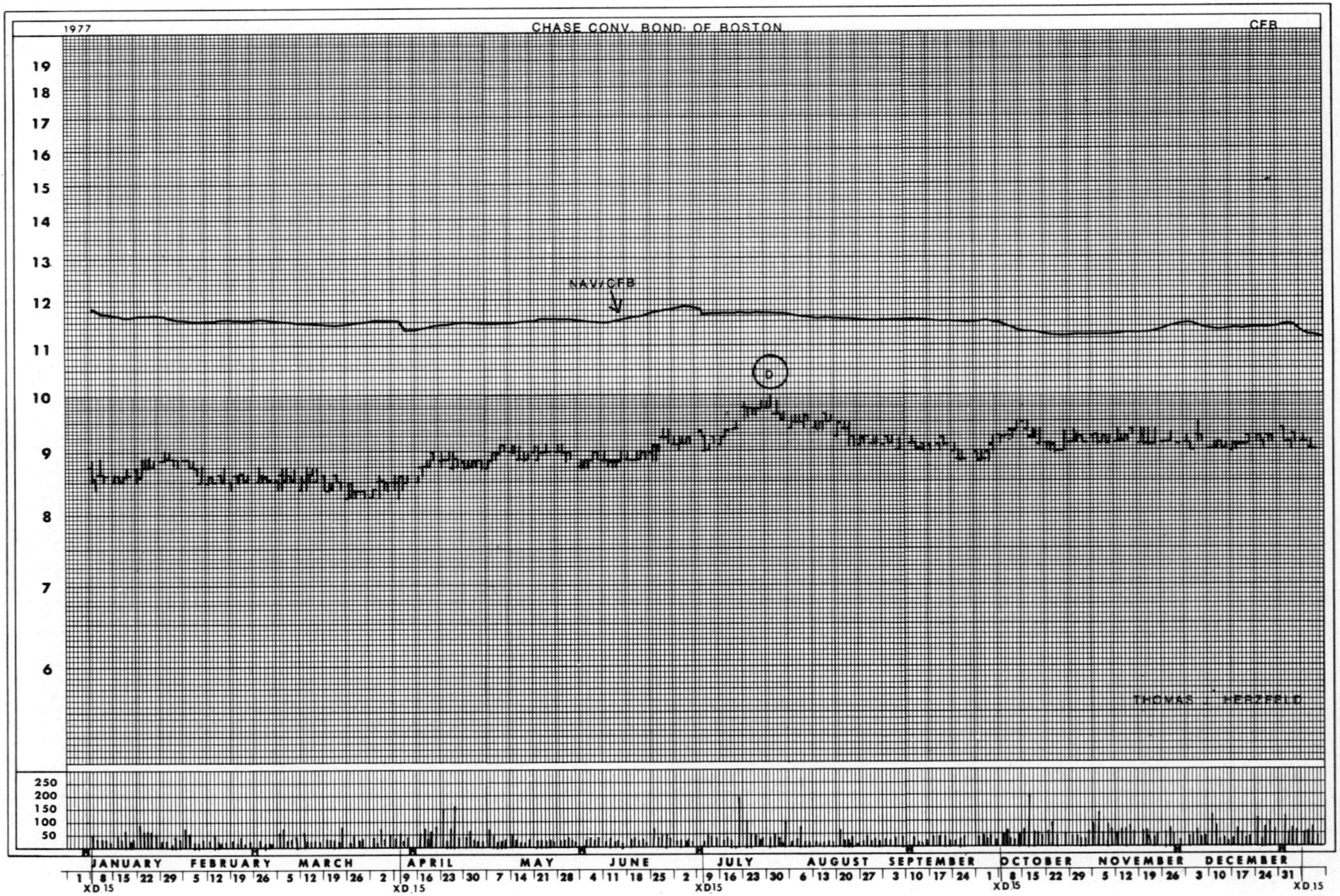

# FIGURE 6.5
## Bancroft Convertible Fund

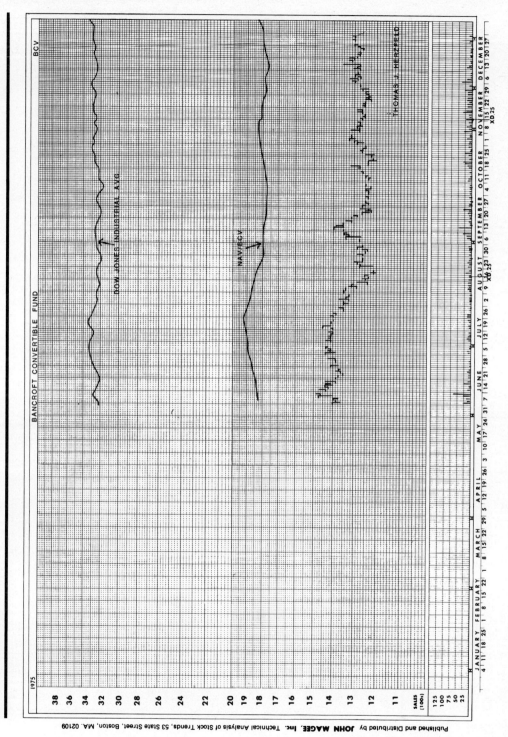

Published and Distributed by **JOHN MAGEE, Inc.** Technical Analysis of Stock Trends, 53 State Street, Boston, MA. 02109

**TEKNIPLAT Chart Paper**

**FIGURE 6.5**
**Bancroft Convertible Fund** (*Cont.*)

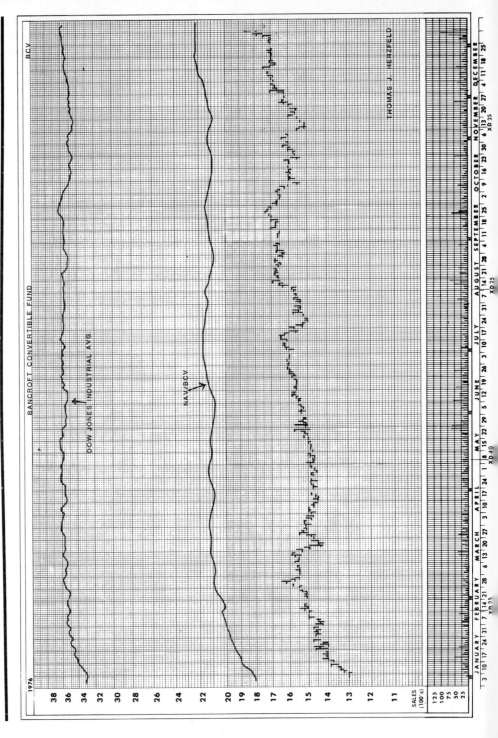

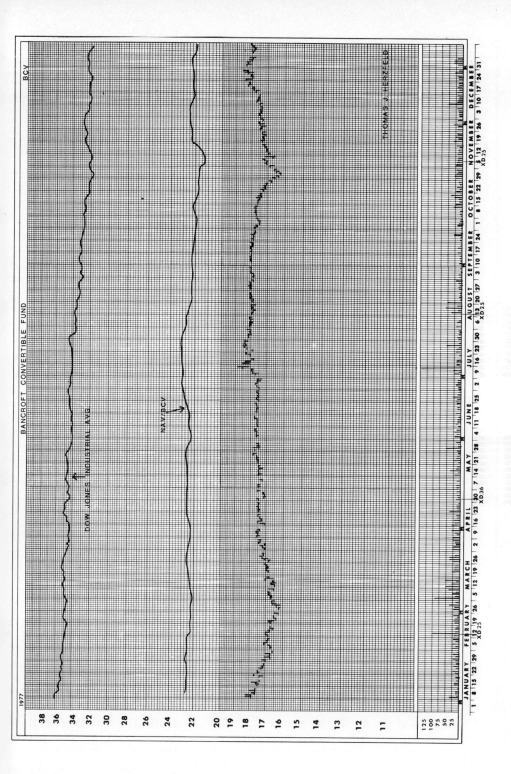

BANCROFT CONVERTIBLE FUND

BCV

1977

DOW JONES INDUSTRIAL AVG

NAV/BCV

THOMAS J. HERZFELD

JANUARY FEBRUARY MARCH APRIL MAY JUNE JULY AUGUST SEPTEMBER OCTOBER NOVEMBER DECEMBER

111

## FIGURE 6.6
## Bancroft Convertible Fund with Buy and Sell Lines

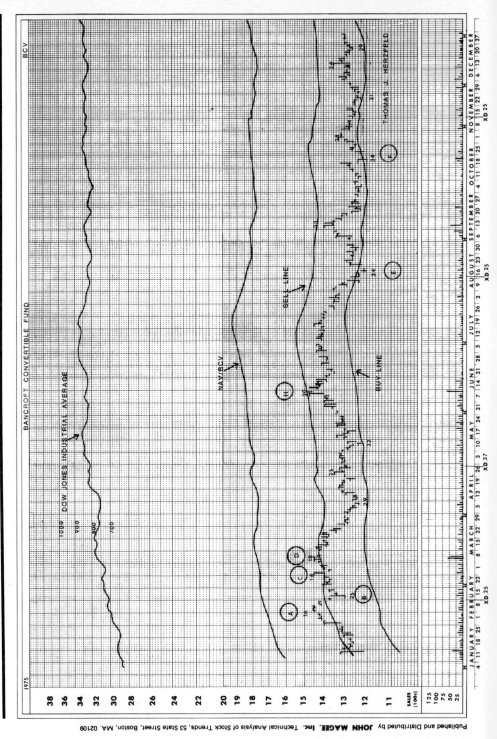

**TEKNIPLAT Chart Paper**

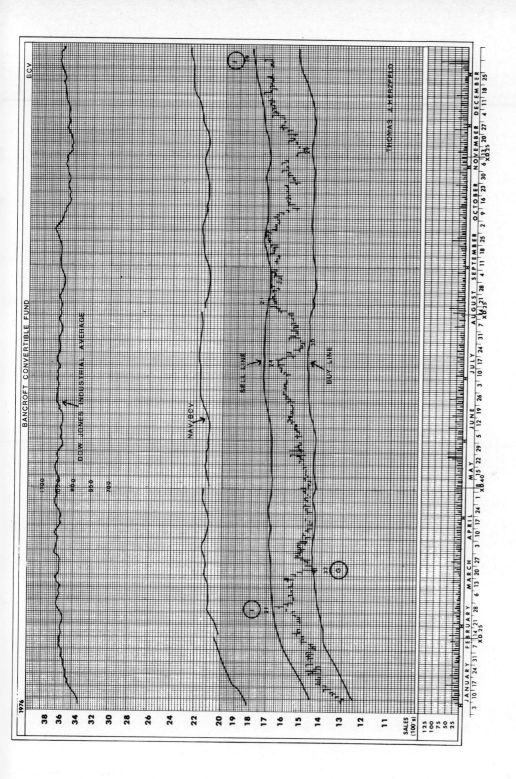

BANCROFT CONVERTIBLE FUND

BCV

1976

DOW JONES INDUSTRIAL AVERAGE

NAV/BCV

SELL LINE

BUY LINE

THOMAS J. HERZFELD

38
36
34
32
30
28
26
24
22
20
19
18
17
16
15
14
13
12
11

SALES
(100's)
125
100
75
50
25

JANUARY FEBRUARY MARCH APRIL MAY JUNE JULY AUGUST SEPTEMBER OCTOBER NOVEMBER DECEMBER

3 10 17 24 31 7 14 21 28 6 13 20 27 3 10 17 24 1 8 15 22 29 5 12 19 26 3 10 17 24 31 7 14 21 28 4 11 18 25 2 9 16 23 30 6 13 20 27 4 11 18 25

113

**114**

FIGURE 6.6
**Bancroft Convertible Fund with Buy and Sell Lines** *(Cont.)*

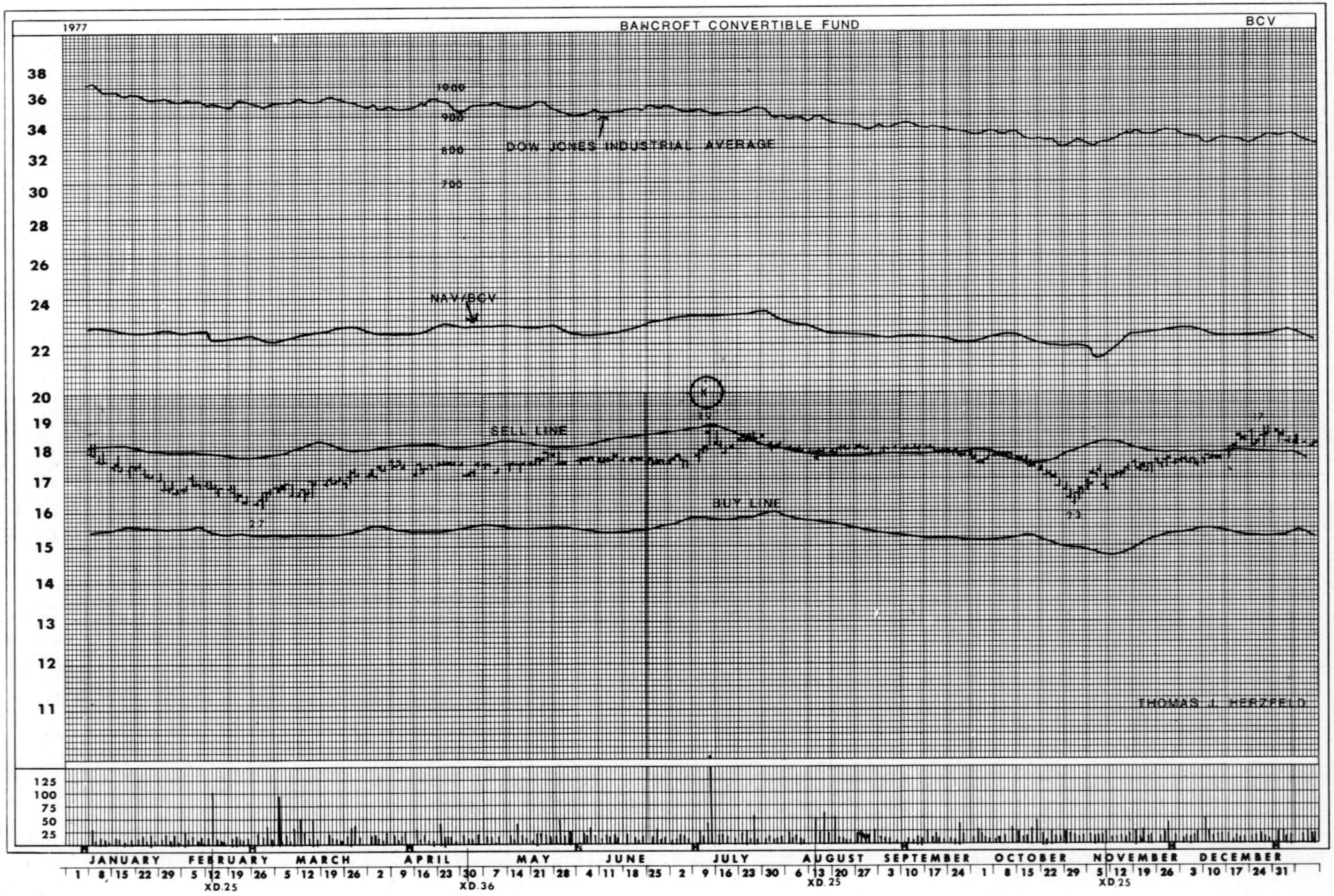

Until 1977, trading Bancroft Fund was a relatively routine matter. Buy signals appeared at Points *E*, *F*, and G; sell signals came at Points *A*, *C*, *D*, *H*, *I*, *J*, and *K*. In 1977 and 1978, the major trading problem with Bancroft was the fact that the discount narrowed considerably.

During that period, a trader had to decide whether or not to adjust to much more aggressive buy and sell lines or to avoid the fund entirely. My decision was to be a more aggressive buyer, even at much narrower discounts. I did this because Bancroft had several of the elements which I considered made it an ideal candidate for an open-end attempt. After assessing the possibilities, I felt that the downside risk would be about 5 percent but that if the fund were to go open-end, the profit potential would be in the neighborhood of 20 percent. An open-end attempt materialized in 1978.

From all of the above, it should be apparent that trading closed-end convertible bond funds—for profit—is not an unreasonably complex enterprise. There are only four of them, and they are quite similar in their basic aspects. As for my own guidelines and charts, they should prove quite simple to understand and master. But it must be stressed that even with a mere four closed-end convertible bond funds to consider, there are no guarantees.

# Trading Closed-End Specialty Funds

## 7

There are very few hard and fast rules which can be applied to trading closed-end specialty funds as a group. Purely and simply, these funds confront the trader with decisions unlike those involved in other closed-end funds. As a result of this situation, a great deal of highly individual analysis is required to trade successfully in closed-end specialty funds.

There are many closed-end funds which can be placed in the specialty category. I have made this placement on a somewhat arbitrary basis because a very fine line divides some of the specialty funds from stock or bond funds; the latter are treated as a separate group in Chapter 5. My own basic list of specialty funds is divided into seven categories. They are:

1. Gold and precious metals funds

2. Venture capital funds

3. Utility funds

4. Funds with concentrated positions in a few companies

5. Funds which invest in the stocks of companies in a single country

6. Funds investing in a single industry

7. Small funds

Some 21 different funds are mentioned in this chapter. I will devote greater attention to the funds I actively trade, beginning with their profiles by category.

## GOLD AND PRECIOUS METAL FUNDS

This group consists of three companies:

• *Precious Metals Holdings Inc.* This fund trades in the over-the-counter market under the symbol PMHD. It is managed by Phoenix Investment Counsel of Boston, the same firm which manages the Chase Convertible Fund of Boston. A proposal to open-end this fund was rejected in 1977. The fund invests in companies which are in the mining or processing of gold and other precious metals and minerals. It is capitalized with approximately 4.5 million shares. The fund occasionally sells at a premium above its net asset value—a premium that would be eliminated if the fund were converted to an open-end company.

• *Anglo-American Gold Investment Company Ltd.* Usually referred to on Wall Street as Am-Gold, this fund trades over the counter with the symbol AAGIY. It is a relatively large closed-end fund, being capitalized with almost 22 million shares. Am-Gold's sizable investments are in South American gold and uranium shares. Because of the unpredictable political situation in South Africa, trading in Am-Gold, as well as in some of the other closed-end gold funds, is comparatively difficult. This variable is compounded by the problem in predicting the conversion value of the South African rand. That rate influences Am-Gold's dividend which is distributed to shareholders in dollars.

• *ASA Limited* Formerly called American South African Investment Company Ltd., this fund is traded on the New York Stock Exchange under the symbol ASA. It also has listed options which are traded on the American Stock Exchange. ASA, which is capitalized with approximately 9.6 million shares, usually sells at a premium above its NAV. This automatically makes ASA relatively unattractive as an investment because an investor can purchase the stocks ASA holds directly and at a cost which would be lower than buying them through the fund.

The three funds in this group hold many of the same stocks in their portfolios and, therefore, their net asset values behave quite similarly. In trading them, some of the basic rules can be applied, particularly when it comes to deviations in a specific fund's average discount or, in ASA's case, deviations from the fund's average premium.

One of the essential variables to be evaluated in the group is the prices of the stocks held in the funds' portfolios. The gold shares of many companies owned by these funds are traded over the counter and can be quoted instantly on the NASDAQ, or else they can usually be found in the financial sections of daily newspapers. These three funds definitely offer many hedging possibilities which will be discussed in Chapter 9.

## VENTURE CAPITAL FUNDS

Among the principal funds followed in this group are the following.

• *Midland Capital Corporation* This over-the-counter fund whose NASDAQ symbol is MCAP is licensed under the Small Business Investment Act to invest in small businesses. It is capitalized at approximately 1.4 million shares.

• *Capital Southwest Corporation* Traded over the counter with the symbol CSWC, this fund makes venture capital investments. It also owns a small Business Investment Company. The fund is capitalized with 1.2 million shares.

• *Claremont Capital Corporation* This Amex fund with the ticker symbol CCM makes venture capital investments mostly in technology-oriented issues. It was known as Diebold Venture Capital until 1976, when control changed hands. This fund, which is capitalized with approximately 1.5 million shares, will also be discussed in Chapter 10 on takeovers and open ending. The Steadman Investment Fund tried to take over Claremont in 1977.

• *Southeastern Capital Corporation* With the symbol SOE, this Amex-listed fund is another which makes venture capital investments in small companies. It is capitalized with less than 1 million shares.

• *Value Line Development Capital Corporation* Traded on the Amex with the symbol VLD, it concentrates most of its investments in small technology-oriented companies. It is capitalized with 2.5 million shares.

The successful trading of funds in the venture capital group depends essentially on traditional analysis of the stocks in each portfolio, in addition to analysis of the funds' average discounts.

To be as candid as possible, study and experience have convinced me that truly productive short-term trading opportunities are not to be found in the venture capital closed-end fund group. The reader—meaning the potential investor—can be personally more productive by concentrating his studies and energies in other sectors of the closed-end fund industry, including other specialty groups.

## UTILITY FUNDS

Here is a specialty fund group which definitely presents some very sound trading opportunities. Among the interesting individual funds are:

• *American Utility Shares*   This Amex-listed fund with the symbol AU was capitalized at approximately 1.2 million shares. It was known as Bayrock Utility Securities Inc., when it was managed by Bayrock Advisors Inc. It was given its present name when Lord, Abbett assumed its management in 1975. (At the end of 1977, AU was merged into an open-end fund. This is discussed in Chapter 10.)

Despite the fact that AU was open ended, a look at its trading history proves interesting. The inherent advantage in buying AU clearly lay in the fact that the investor received a portfolio of high-grade utility securities at a discount from their net asset value.

Of course, buying any closed-end fund on a new issue means that the investor is paying a premium for his shares. Shortly after AU came out in the summer of 1972, it went from a premium to a rather substantial discount and by the end of 1975, the fund was selling at a discount of about 25 percent of its net asset value.

Particular attention should be paid to AU because it was a prime example of how a closed-end fund could be traded for small profits but with a large turnover. The basic trading approach which we applied to AU was to buy whenever the discount reached 25 percent and to sell when the discount slipped to 18 percent.

As shown in Figure 7.1, in which the history of the fund is plotted from 1975 to 1978, AU gave a sell signal at Points A-1 and A-2, where it rallied to less than an 18 percent discount. That took place during the weeks of October 18 and November 8, 1975, when the fund was selling at 9¼ and 9¾.

A buy signal was later given at Point B in December 1975 with the stock selling at 8¾. Within eight trading days, at Point C-1, AU shares rallied to 10, where a sell signal was given. Multiple sell signals were given through January, February, and the beginning of March 1976 at Points C-1, C-2, C-3, and C-4. At each of these points, the fund was selling at a discount of 18 percent.

## FIGURE 7.1
## American Utility Shares

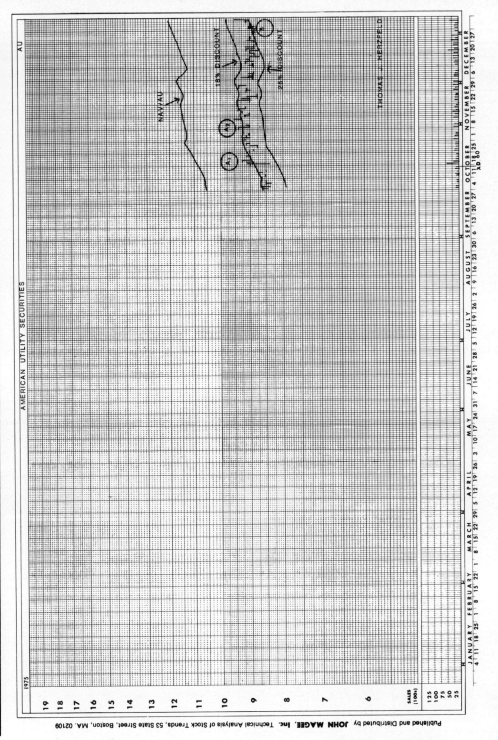

Published and Distributed by **JOHN MAGEE, Inc.** Technical Analysis of Stock Trends, 53 State Street, Boston, MA. 02109

**FIGURE 7.1**
**American Utility Shares** (Cont.)

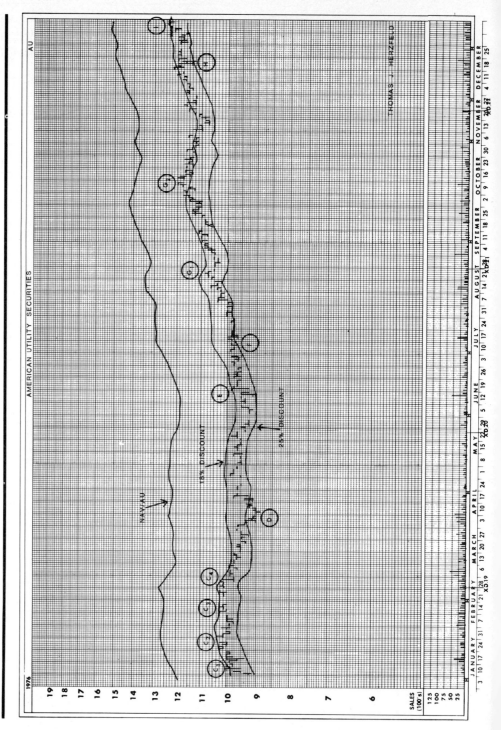

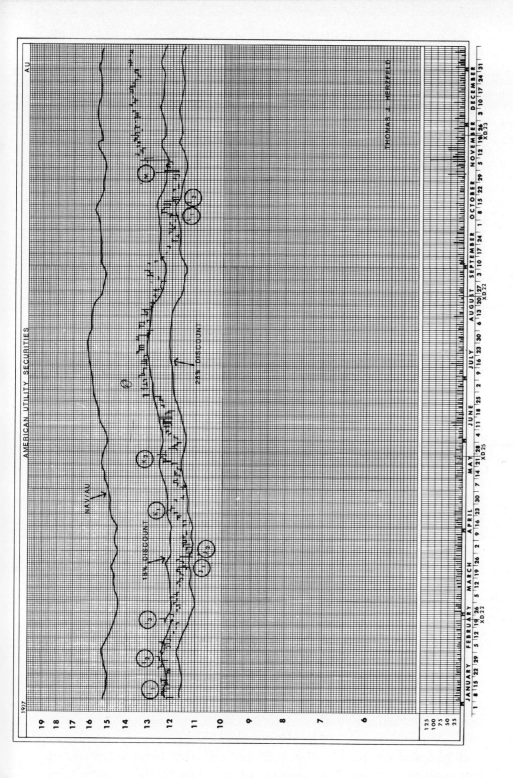

AMERICAN UTILITY SECURITIES

THOMAS J. HERZFELD

123

A buy signal then cropped up at the beginning of April 1976 at Point *D-1*, when the fund traded through its buy line and went to a wider than 25 percent discount. The price of a share at that time was $9.

For the next several weeks, AU was in a holding pattern but in the middle of June it rallied to 9⅞ at Point *E*, where a sell signal was given. A buy signal was given in July at Point *F*, a sell signal in August at Point *G-1*, and a second sell signal in October at Point *G-2*. By that time, the stock had rallied to $12 per share.

American Utility Shares then went into another of its periodic "stalls," emerging as a buy in December of 1976 at Point *H*. Sell signals quickly followed in January and February of 1977 at Points *I-1*, *I-2*, and *I-3*. The consistent buying opportunities presented by AU and many other funds in December as well as the traditional rally carrying into January should be carefully noted by the potential trader.

From January to October 1977, trading in AU was rather routine, as the chart illustrates. Buy signals appeared at Points *J-1* and *J-2* and sell signals at Points *K-1* and *K-2*. New buy signals appeared at Points *L-1* and *L-2* in October 1977, and then a sell signal surfaced in November 1977. This sell signal was entirely consistent with our basic trading methods. Unfortunately, and it must be put on the record, it represents the single example of when our closed-end fund trading system does not necessarily work—specifically, a vote to open-end a fund.

The trader who was carefully following AU would have been aware that a vote was to be taken by shareholders in November 1977 on a proposal to convert the fund to an open-end vehicle. As a result, because of that "knowledge," he may have ignored the sell signal which was given at Point *M*. The proposal to make the fund open-ended passed by a wide majority. After that decision, until it was open-ended, AU sold at a relatively narrow discount—approximately 10 to 14 percent.

In our discussion of variables, open ending was cited as one of those factors which merited consideration in the trading of closed-end funds. With American Utility Shares, open ending was a variable which should have weighed very heavily in a trader's decisions.

• ***Drexel Utility Shares*** This fund is traded on the American Stock Exchange with the symbol DUS and is capitalized with about 600,000 shares. The fund is managed by Drexel Burnham Management Company, which also manages the Drexel Bond Fund.

A typical discount for DUS is 20 percent from net asset value. At this point, it is sufficient to say that our standard method can be used in trading DUS with close attention being given to when it is moving at deviations from its net asset value.

Experience demonstrated that with DUS a variable of considerable importance was the relationship of its discount, on a comparative basis, to the discount of American Utility Shares. (In my opinion, DUS is a strong candidate to become an open-end fund.)

## FUNDS WITH CONCENTRATED POSITIONS IN A FEW COMPANIES

This is a relatively limited group, including:

• *Baldwin Securities*  Listed on the Amex and traded under the symbol BAL, this fund is capitalized with about 3.8 million shares. In addition to investments in special situations, BAL has positions in corporate and government securities. It also owns Beco Stores.

• *Highland Capital*  This is another fund traded on the Amex. Its ticker symbol is HLD, and it is capitalized at about 1 million shares. Highland is noted for its large position in Athlone Industries.

• *Standard Shares*  This fund is capitalized at 3 million shares and is traded on the Amex with the symbol SWD. It effectively controls Pittway Corporation.

It should be sufficient to say that this group of funds, as trading vehicles, offers relatively fewer opportunities than most of the other groups.

## FUNDS WHICH INVEST IN THE STOCKS OF INDUSTRIES IN A SINGLE COUNTRY

This group essentially is composed of two funds. One has a small capitalization and is relatively inactive. The other has a large capitalization and is comparatively active.

• *Israel Development Corporation*  This fund, listed on the Amex and traded under the symbol IDC, obviously invests in Israeli companies. It is capitalized at approximately 1.4 million shares.

• *Japan Fund*  This fund is traded on the New York Stock Exchange under the symbol JPN, and there is no room for doubt about its focus.

Capitalized with 13 million shares, JPN actively invests in Japanese companies whose shares present, in a closed-end fund, genuine trading opportunities. JPN usually sells at a quite wide discount. And when its discounts become excessive, as measured by our previously discussed methods, it is most definitely a good fund to trade.

But it must be stated that the trading of JPN does carry with it a very definite handicap. The Japan Fund, for all intents and purposes, exists in a world of its own, compared with funds whose portfolios are concentrated in domestic securities. As a result, it is extremely difficult to form an accurate and reliable frame of reference for trading the fund.

At the end of 1977, there was considerable discussion and debate in financial circles about the problems of the Japanese economy and the direction it would ultimately take. Quite naturally, the resulting uncertainty virtually forced JPN to go to an excessive discount. Ironically, the net asset value of the fund throughout December 1977 and into January 1978 rose steadily. It was quite obvious that knowledgeable investors were looking to other sources of information and were wisely ignoring what the newspaper headlines were shouting about the gloomy outlook for the Japanese economy.

In a confirmation of the idea that the market is often subject to mystical forces beyond rational explanations, a very large block of JPN was dumped on the market December 7, 1977 (Pearl Harbor day). That date proved to be the lowest point for a short-term move in JPN. After that, within a 1-month period, the stock rallied more than 10 percent.

## FUNDS INVESTING IN ONE INDUSTRY

Here is a group which offers at least four highly interesting funds to trade:

• *National Aviation and Technology* This fund was traded on the New York Stock Exchange with the symbol NTA and was capitalized with about 4.4 million shares. Until 1976, the fund was known as National Aviation, changing its name to reflect the fact that it had started trading in technology-oriented stocks, as well as in airline and aerospace issues. In 1977, Hobart Associates was successful with its shareholder proposal to open-end the fund. National Aviation's management was vigorously opposed, but Hobart's proposal passed by a narrow margin. (For further information, see Chapter 10 on open ending.)

Even before the proposal, National Aviation was, among those who followed closed-end funds, a logical candidate for open ending. As a result, that variable was given what could be considered overriding weight in trading decisions. From 1975 through 1978, the average discount of the fund continually narrowed, and traders in the fund had to initiate positions at more aggressive (narrower) discounts. This was essentially because they were convinced that the open-ending "kicker" made the pursuit worthwhile.

For several years, National Aviation was regarded as an excellent trading vehicle, trading until 1977 at highly predictable levels. However, after that period at Point J in Figure 7.2, when it was subject to either a takeover or open ending, its use as a trading vehicle faded. From the week of August 6, 1977, it moved to substantially narrower discounts and, therefore, had to be approached differently.

To understand this changeover, let's take a look at National Aviation from 1975 to 1977—before the open-ending proposal—to see how the fund could have been traded.

Buy lines were established at a 36 percent discount from net asset value and sell lines at 24 percent. Multiple buy signals were given at Points A-1 and A-2 in January and in the beginning of February 1975, when the per share price was about $9. Another buy signal was given at the beginning of March 1975 at Point A-3, when the per share price was about $10. The stock rallied sharply over the next few days to $12 a share, where a sell signal was given at Point B. Multiple buy signals followed at Points C-1 and C-2 in April and May of 1975, first at $10 a share and later at 11½. Then sell signals came at Point D-1 in June, with the stock at $13 a share, and again at D-2 in July.

The stock and its net asset value dropped in the July–August 1975 period. On a percentage basis, it should be noted, the decline in the price of the stock was much sharper than the decline in the fund's net asset value. As a result, the discount increased between July and August from Point D-2 to Point E-1, an increase in discount from approximately 20 percent to 36 percent. Then from Point E-2 in September 1975, when NTA was selling at a 35 percent discount and at $11 per share, it rallied to Point F in October 1975. Here it penetrated its 24 percent discount line by ¼ of a point and rallied to a price of $13 a share.

The next sell-off came a month later, when National Aviation

# 128

**FIGURE 7.2**
National Aviation

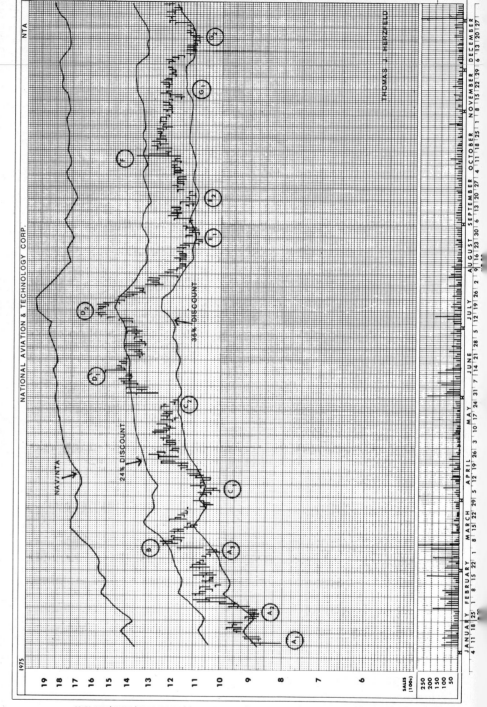

Published and Distributed by **JOHN MAGEE, Inc.,** Technical Analysis of Stock Trends, 53 State Street, Boston, MA. 02109

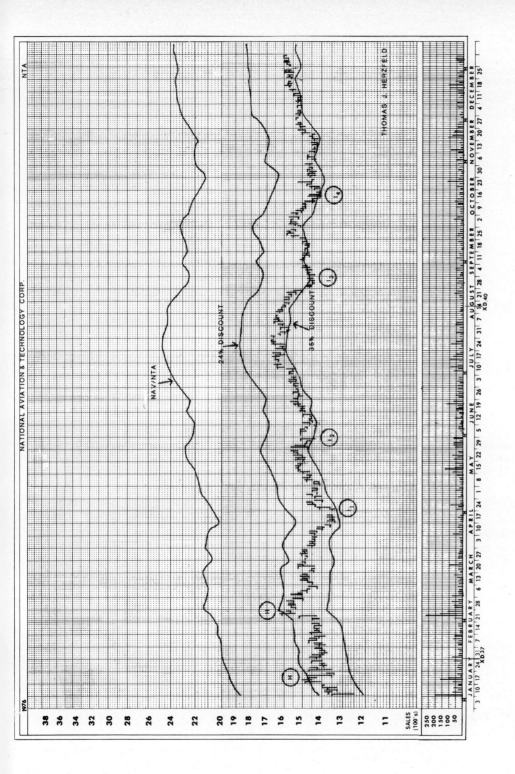

NATIONAL AVIATION & TECHNOLOGY CORP.

NTA

NAV/NTA

24% DISCOUNT

35% DISCOUNT

THOMAS J. HERZFELD

1976

JANUARY 3 10 17 24 31 FEBRUARY 7 14 21 28 MARCH 6 13 20 27 APRIL 3 10 17 24 MAY 1 8 15 22 29 JUNE 5 12 19 26 JULY 3 10 17 24 31 AUGUST 7 14 21 28 SEPTEMBER 4 11 18 25 OCTOBER 2 9 16 23 30 NOVEMBER 6 13 20 27 DECEMBER 4 11 18 25

XD.37

XD.40

38 36 34 32 30 28 26 24 22 20 19 18 17 16 15 14 13 12 11

SALES (100's) 250 200 150 100 50

**129**

**FIGURE 7.2**
**National Aviation** *(Cont.)*

130

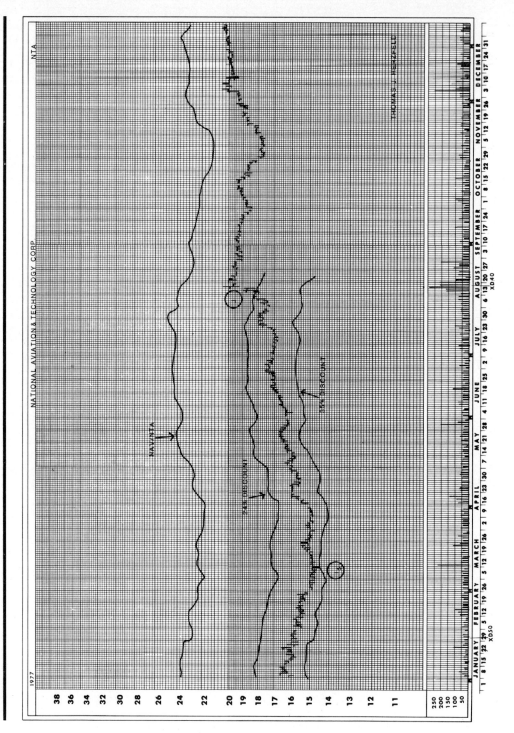

declined at Points *G-1* and *G-2* at around $11 per share. As most funds tend to do, it rallied sharply in January to Point *H-1*, carrying the fund through $14 a share. Eventually, when the second multiple sell signal was given at Point *H-2*, the fund was selling at $16 per share.

The net asset value again declined in the March-April 1976 period, but on a percentage basis the price of the fund declined more than its net asset value. This was another excellent example of a fund's discount narrowing in a rising market and widening in a declining market.

A fresh series of buy signals was initiated at Point *I-1* in April 1976, with the stock selling at $13 a share. The second buy was at Point *I-2* in May 1976 at $14 per share, followed by multiple buys at Points *I-3* and *I-4* in August and October 1976, when the stock was in the $14 range. The final buy in this sequence was in March 1977 at Point *I-5*, with the fund selling at approximately $15 per share.

A sell signal finally came after more than a year—during which accumulations should have been taking place—at Point *J* in August 1977, when the stock had risen to $18 per share.

Thus, it is quite clear that from 1975 all the way into the middle of 1977, National Aviation traded at highly predictable ranges and provided, as a result, an excellent example of how to trade closed-end funds.

However, when the open-ending proposal became a more-or-less regular item in the financial press, National Aviation's discount narrowed very sharply, and from August 1977 until the reorganization, the fund sold at a discount of approximately 14 percent.

As was the case with American Utilities in a similar situation, alert traders would not have been sellers at Point *J* because the open-ending variable would have negated the sell signal given by the chart.

• ***Petroleum & Resources Corporation***    This fund, traded on the New York Stock Exchange with the symbol PEO, is capitalized at about 4½ million common shares, plus about 1 million preferred. It was known as Petroleum Corporation of America until 1977, when its name was changed to reflect that it was buying natural resource issues for its portfolio in addition to those of petroleum companies. Approximately 17 percent of PEO is owned by another closed-end fund, Adams Express Company, which is discussed in Chapter 4 on stock funds.

Trading PEO, it must be said in all candor, is relatively simple.

There is a single overriding consideration in trading the fund—its premium. Experience has demonstrated that if PEO's premium is higher than 10 percent, the stock is most usually a sell. When the fund sells at its NAV or below, PEO is a buy.

Figure 7.3 shows the price movement and the net asset value of PEO from February 1977 through February 1978. This figure differs from our other ones in that the chart's bottom line represents the net asset value and is our buy line. The sell line is plotted at a 10 percent premium.

The last two funds in this group originally were formed to invest in the Real Estate Investment Trust (REIT) industry: SG Securities, Inc., and RET Income Fund. The rapid downfall of REITs on all fronts is illustrated by the fact that the net asset value of SG Securities in 1973 was $13.97 and by the following year it had plunged to below $1 per share. At that juncture, the company shifted its investment policy, investing a substantial portion of its remaining funds in investment grade bonds. This is also an example of the effect of a declining market on *leveraged* funds.

• *SG Securities, Inc.* SG Securities, traded on the American Stock Exchange with the symbol SGO, has two classes of stock, a common and a preferred. The latter is interesting from an income point of view and should be regarded as similar to a bond fund. Because of the income from SGO's portfolio, now primarily bonds, the preferred is able to cover its dividend of $1.70. This means that the preferred which was selling between $14 and $15 per share during 1978 and into 1979 was yielding more than 11 percent. An interesting "kicker" for the preferred is that it is callable at a higher price.

As for the common shares of SG Securities, their net asset value rose during 1976, 1977, and 1978. In my opinion, SG Securities represented a very interesting situation, both in its common and preferred issues. Not surprisingly, in July 1978 a tender offer was made at a premium above NAV for about one-third of the common shares.

• *RET Income Fund* This fund is traded on the Amex with the symbol RET. Like SGO, it has changed its investment strategy and no longer concentrates on REITs; recently, more than 75 percent of its assets were in nonREIT securities, with a substantial portion in investment grade bonds and commercial paper. The fund also has a preferred stock which is quite similar to SGO's in investment and yield.

## FIGURE 7.3
Petroleum & Resources Corporation

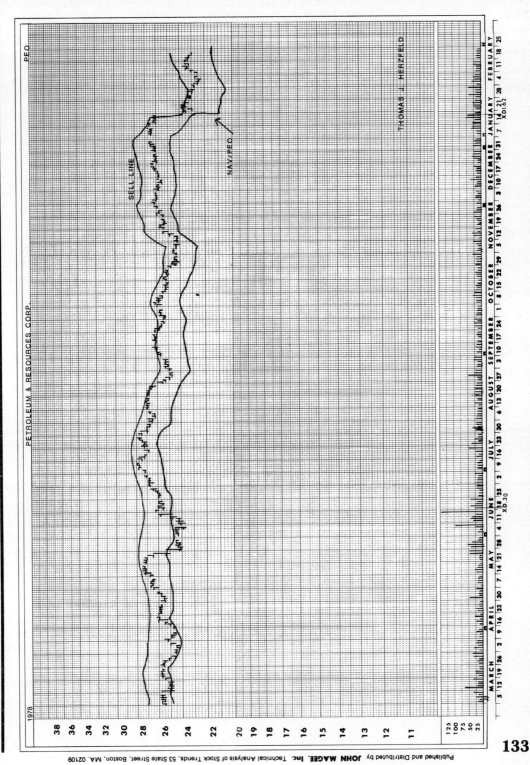

**133**

**SMALL FUNDS**

• *OTF Equities*  This fund, which is traded over the counter, is typical of this group. It is capitalized with about 200,000 shares.

• *Overseas Securities*  Overseas Securities, which trades on the Amex with the symbol OVU, is another in this group. It is capitalized with approximately 270,000 shares. It is not unusual for OVU to sell at a discount of 30 percent or more. In 1975, Gault Malleable Iron Ltd. acquired 48 percent of its shares. Trading in OVU is minimal. However, whenever it sells at substantial discounts beyond its 30 percent average, it can be accumulated and traded out when the discount narrows.

It should be apparent at this point that closed-end specialty funds do not necessarily have behavior patterns which correspond to the general stock or bond markets. Their performance, it should therefore be kept in mind at all times, is essentially dependent on the particular stocks in their portfolios which are, by broad definition, specialized into one or possibly two areas.

# Trading Dual-Purpose Funds

**8**

It is clearly time for a light note as we begin this chapter on dual-purpose funds. Dual-purpose funds and the author came to Wall Street at the same time—in 1967. We have no idea whatever how this coincidence—this convergence of stars or buy and sell lines—may be regarded by astrologers, but as they examine their charts and we study ours, it should be put on the record that dual-purpose funds and the author are quite different in at least one important aspect: dual-purpose funds will be leaving Wall Street at clearly known fixed dates; the author will remain, hopefully, long after they are gone.

To be perfectly frank, dual-purpose funds, despite the special label the investment community has given to them, are surprisingly similar to the other closed-end stock funds we have been discussing in earlier chapters. As a matter of fact, an examination of their portfolios reveals that they are virtually identical with most of the stock funds we have been looking at. Take the portfolio of the dual-purpose Gemini Fund as an example. It includes many of the names we found in ordinary stock funds—for instance, Celanese, General Tire, CIT Financial, McGraw-Hill, Colonial Penn, Tenneco, Pennzoil, etc.

Then if the portfolios of dual-purpose funds are so similar to those of regular closed-end funds, what makes the former different and, therefore, merit special attention? The difference essentially boils down to (1) the way dual-purpose funds are capitalized, and (2) the fact that they have fixed expiration dates.

Specifically, dual-purpose funds are closed-end funds with two classes of stock—capital shares and preferred shares. Each of these two classes is designed to serve the aspirations and interests of two distinctly different breeds of investors:

1. The preferred shares are for investors seeking income.
2. The capital shares, as their name connotes, are for those investors in search of capital gains.

**135**

Dual-purpose funds issue equal amounts of common and preferred shares. Preferred shareholders are entitled to the income from the entire portfolio which the fund holds, and capital shareholders are entitled to the capital gains which the entire portfolio generates.

The investor's leverage is, therefore, 2 to 1. Here's how that leverage evolves. If 1 million shares of preferred stock are issued by a dual-purpose fund at $10 per share and a million shares of common shares are issued at the same price, the fund would have $20 million in assets, less, of course, underwriting costs. With preferred shareholders receiving the dividends or income from the entire $20 million and the common shareholders receiving the capital gains, if any, from the $20 million portfolio, the result is a 2-to-1 leverage for each class of shareholder. A dual-purpose fund selling at a discount from net asset value would possess even greater leverage.

When a dual-purpose fund is formed, a specific date is established—usually 10 to 15 years in the future—when the fund's preferred shares will be redeemed at a specific price. After those preferred shares are redeemed, the capital shareholders are entitled to divide the fund's remaining assets on a basis proportionate to the shares they hold. This "divvying up" of the pot can be done in one of two ways:

1. The fund can be liquidated with each shareholder receiving his proper portion of the assets.

2. Or at the election of the common shareholders, the fund can be converted into an open-end operation, continuing as an investment company. Here, as in all open-end funds, the shareholders can redeem their individual shares at whatever their net asset value may be.

The year 1967 was the key one for dual-purpose funds in the United States. Before that date, such funds did not exist in this country, although several of them were formed in England in the early 1960s. Then in 1967, seven different dual-purpose funds were brought to market in the United States. They were:

• **American Dual Vest** Traded on the New York Stock Exchange under the symbol ADV, this fund has approximately 1.6 million preferred shares and a like amount of common stock, with the preferred redeemable at $15 a share on June 29, 1979. After being initially issued in December 1966 at a price of $15, the net asset value of the capital shares rose to $20 per share in 1968. However, by 1974 the net asset value had plunged to $4 a share. Then, it began recovering, reaching $9.80 by 1976, and by May 1978 it was $10.30. ADV is managed by Weiss, Peck and Greer. Some of its larger holdings include AT&T, Studebaker-Worthington, and United Telecommunications.

• **Hemisphere Fund** Traded on the New York Stock Exchange with the symbol HEM, this fund is capitalized with approximately 1.4 million cumulative income shares redeemable at $11.44 per share on June 30, 1985, and a similar amount of common shares. Some of HEM's larger positions are in IBM, Ford, Exxon, Mobil, and Phillips Petroleum. The fund, which is managed by CNA Management Corporation, has had wide fluctuations in its net asset value since it was first issued. For example, in 1967 it was over $13 per common share, but in 1974 the net asset value was down to a meager 4 cents per share.

• **Gemini Fund** Traded on the New York Stock Exchange under the ticker symbol GEM, this fund was brought to market in March 1967 with 1,650,000 income shares and the same number of common shares. Gemini, which was underwritten by Drexel, Harriman and Ripley and Bache and Company, has large positions in Philadelphia Suburban, General Motors, Martin-Marietta, Interco, Harsco Corporation, International Minerals and Metals Corporation, General Telephone & Electronics, and Philadelphia National Corporation. Under the direction of Wellington Management, over the 10-year period from 1967 to 1977, Gemini's net asset has been as low as $6.97 (in 1974) and more than $25 (in 1977). Its preferred shares are redeemable on December 31, 1984, at $11 per share.

• **Income and Capital Shares** With the symbol ICS, this fund is traded on the New York Stock Exchange. It has approximately 1.5 million common shares and the same number of preferreds, which are redeemable at $10 per share in 1982. ICS is managed by Phoenix Investment Counsel of Boston, which manages several open-end funds as well as another closed-end fund. From 1966 to 1977, its net asset value had some sharp swings, being as high as $17 in 1968 and as low as $3.78 in 1974.

• **Putnam Duofund** This issue, traded over-the-counter with the symbol PUTNC, was underwritten in 1967 by Francis I. duPont and

Company with 1.5 million common shares. PUTNC, managed by the Putnam Management Company, includes among its major holdings Occidental Petroleum, Colt Industries, Kaiser Aluminum, Hanes, American Standard, Mobil, and General Motors. The income shares are redeemable on January 3, 1983, at $19.75 a share.

• *Scudder-Duo Vest*    Traded on the NYSE with the symbol SDV, it is one of the larger dual-purpose funds. It was underwritten in 1967 by E. F. Hutton with 5.5 million shares each of capital and preferred stock. The proceeds of the offering were approximately $100 million. The fund's net asset value has fluctuated from its initial offering to a high in 1972 of about $11 and to a low of under $7 a share in 1974. Some of Scudder's major positions are in Exxon, Goodrich, IBM, and Dresser Industries. On April 1, 1982, the preferred shares will be redeemable at $9.15.

• *Leverage Fund of Boston*    Under the symbol LFB, this fund is traded on the New York Stock Exchange and has 1.9 million common shares and an equal number of preferred. The preferred shares are redeemable at $13.725 in January 1982. LFB, managed by Vance Sanders & Company, is another dual-purpose fund whose net asset value has shown comparatively wide fluctuations. For example, the NAV was above $18 in 1972, below $6 in 1974, and above $19 in 1978. Among LFB's important holdings are Exxon, Boeing, R. J. Reynolds, and Westinghouse.

Before getting into some of the harsher realities of dual-purpose funds, it would be well to point out that their essential strategies are similar to those of the closed-end stock funds we discussed in Chapter 4. But dual-purpose funds, because of the leverage involved, tend to be a little more on the dramatic side in rising and falling markets.

However, and let's be candid about this, dual-purpose funds are a fine but sad example of jacks-of-all-trades who are masters of none. This is because they attempt to meet two distinctly diverse objectives, namely, income on the one side and capital gains on the other. And, to be perfectly blunt about it, as their records affirm, dual-purpose funds do not meet either of their objectives very well. This double failure results in the complete negation of the advantage of leverage.

As a result, I am less than interested in dual-purpose funds as a group. In my judgment, for capital gains it is far better and more sensible to trade in closed-end stock funds whose prime objective is exactly what they are designed for—capital gains. Buying those kinds of funds on margin creates the same leverage in and of itself. And in the pursuit of capital gains, the investor is not—as with dual-purpose funds—burdened with a portfolio containing securities designed to protect the yield of the preferred shareholders.

As income candidates, dual-purpose funds offer little to generate excitement, comparing unfavorably with yields available in bond funds. Their only clear-cut advantage in this area is that their preferred shares are redeemed at a fixed date so that they should behave quite similarly to intermediate-term bonds, reflecting the yields of the intermediate bond market rather than those of the long-term bond market.

But again, since dual-purpose fund portfolios are at least half designed to serve the aspirations of investors seeking capital gains, their yields, even with 2-to-1 leverage, are lower than what can be obtained in the bond funds.

Trading rules for dual-purpose funds can be broken down into two categories:

1. Common shares should be traded like stock funds, as discussed in Chapter 4.

2. Preferred shares should be treated in the same manner as bond funds, as discussed in Chapter 5.

The only rule which can be revised has to do with timing. As each year passes and a dual-purpose fund gets closer to the point where its shares will be redeemed or the fund will be liquidated, its trading discount should, theoretically, be adjusted a notch narrower. But that's theoretical. In practice, I have found that this narrowing does not work over the long haul. Chances are it will work better in the last 2 or 3 years of the life of the fund, if ever.

The annual report of Income and Capital Shares for 1976 portrays one of the principal shortcomings of dual-purpose funds—the serving of two different objectives. Only 68.2 percent of the fund's portfolio was in common stocks, although there were some convertible bonds and convertible preferreds. Some 9 percent of the portfolio was in nonconvertible bonds, including U.S. government and agency issues, utility, foreign, and oil company bonds. These kinds of holdings held out practically no growth potential for the fund's investors. In addition, almost 9 percent of the fund was in short-term credit obligations. As a result, the fund had virtually segregated about 18 percent of its portfolio in order to protect the yield on its preferred stock—and at the expense of investors looking for capital gains. The remainder of the fund's portfolio also appeared to have been purchased with the purpose of safeguarding the yield of the preferred.

A similar situation is found in the annual report of the Hemisphere Fund for 1976. It shows that 57.1 percent of the portfolio was composed of common stocks; 33 percent was in bonds, a small portion of which were convertible; and the remainder, about 11 percent of the fund's holdings, was in short-term notes. Here, once again, is an obvious case of a dual-purpose fund attempting to satisfy both preferred and capital shareholders without much efficiency possible on behalf of either.

It is true that when dual-purpose funds get to excessive discounts, their common shares will show dramatic increases in rising markets. The reason for this sort of action may lie in the fact that investors bid them up aggressively in the belief that their potential in rising markets is better than the potential of regular funds. As a result, in such rising markets, the discounts of dual-purpose funds tend to narrow faster than those of stock funds and, conversely, in declining markets, they tend to widen faster.

In our discussion of the whys and wherefores of discounts in closed-end funds, we came up with a long list of reasons for them. In the case of dual-purpose funds, there is a highly valid reason why their common shares should sell at discounts. It is this: since there is no yield on the fund's common shares, the investor is losing anywhere from 3 to 8 percent a year income which he would have received by investing in closed-end stock or convertible bond funds. Therefore, a rule of thumb in establishing a discount for a dual-purpose fund is to determine the comparable yield on a regular closed-end fund with the same growth potential as the dual-purpose fund and then multiply that yield times the number of years the fund will remain in existence. For instance, if the average stock fund is yielding 6 percent, a dual-purpose fund with 4 years of life remaining should properly sell at a discount of at least 24 percent; with 3 years until expiration, at least 18 percent; and with 2 years, at least 12 percent. And of course, it would trade at a smaller discount in the fund's last year of operation.

Much of what we have been discussing is illustrated in Figure 8.1, showing the Leverage Fund of Boston from the end of 1975 through the beginning of 1978. Notice that in the rising market of 1976, the fund's discount was continually narrowing. However, in the declining market which began in 1977 the discount in general widened, and in the 1978 rally the discount narrowed again.

**FIGURE 8.1**
Leverage Fund of Boston

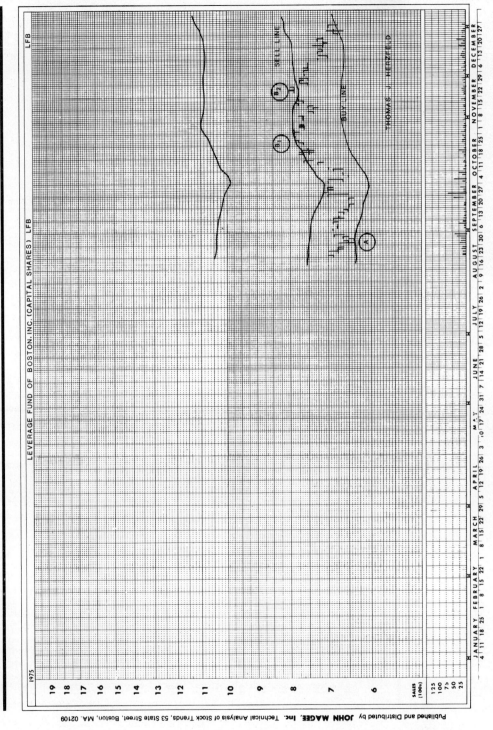

**FIGURE 8.1**
**Leverage Fund of Boston** *(Cont.)*

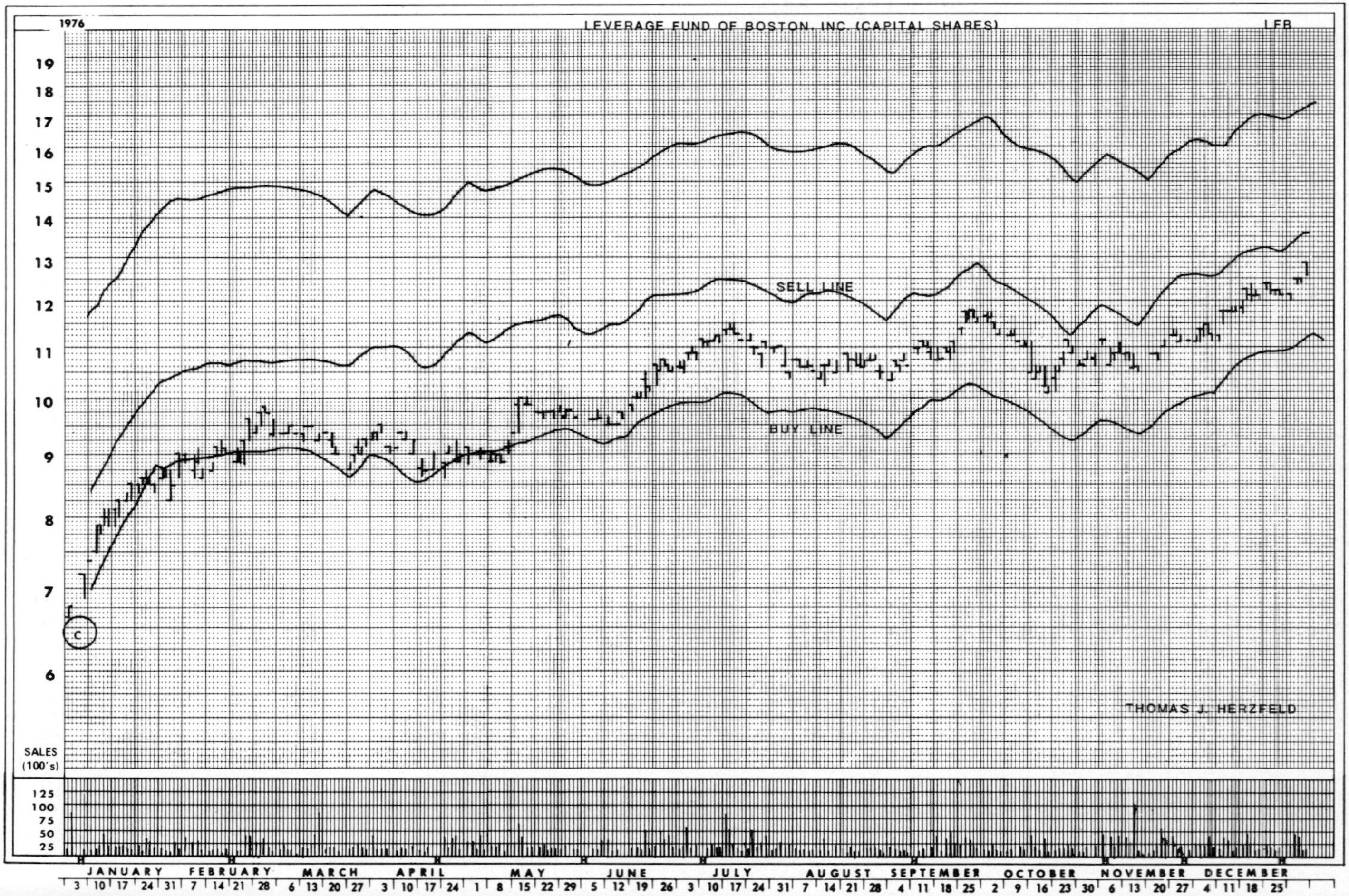

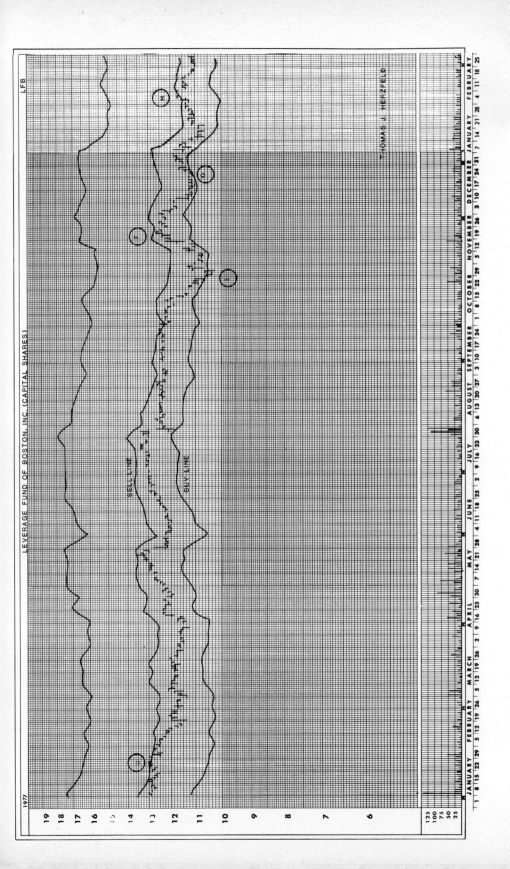

LEVERAGE FUND OF BOSTON, INC. (CAPITAL SHARES)

LFB

THOMAS J. HERZFELD

SELL LINE

BUY LINE

1977

JANUARY FEBRUARY MARCH APRIL MAY JUNE JULY AUGUST SEPTEMBER OCTOBER NOVEMBER DECEMBER JANUARY FEBRUARY

**143**

The virtual predictability of this sort of behavior does make dual-purpose funds interesting strictly from the point of view of analyzing their discounts. Had we applied the basic trading rules discussed in Chapter 4 to trading Leverage Fund of Boston, adjusting for the slight modifications mentioned in this chapter, our buy line in 1975 was slightly over 35 percent, narrowing to 33 percent in 1977 and to 28 percent in 1978. Our sell line in 1975 was at a 26 percent discount, narrowing to 23 percent in 1978.

The first buy signal was given at Point A in Figure 8.1 in August 1975 at 6⅜, and multiple sell signals were given in October and November 1975 at the 7¾–8 area at Points B-1 and B-2. Another buy signal came at the end of December 1975 at 6⅝ (Point C), when the fund went to an unusually large discount, probably because of year-end tax selling. From that time the fund was a hold until more than a year later in January 1977 at Point D, when the price rallied to $13 per share. As we can see, throughout the rising market of 1976, the discount was continually narrowing. This narrowing, plus the rise in the fund's net asset value, generated a highly generous trading move—almost a double.

In the declining market of 1977, no buy signals appeared until Point E, when the fund went through its buy line to the 10½ area. Then it made a sharp but very short-term rally in November to 12½ at Point F. In December a buy signal was given, again at $11 at Point G, followed by a sell signal at the beginning of 1978, at Point H, with the stock at about 11½ per share.

My final point about dual-purpose funds—a point to which I have more than alluded in this chapter—is that the closed-end fund industry offers other far more attractive and lucrative trading vehicles. The investor who wants growth will be much better off buying on margin closed-end funds concentrating on growth stocks. And the investor who wants yield will better serve himself by investing in bond funds selling at discounts. Dual-purpose funds, striving to meet both of these objectives at the same time, cannot compete with well-managed funds with a singleness of purpose. However, now that the funds are approaching maturity, I'm moderating my point of view, finding them more attractive than they have been over the last 5 years.

# Closed-End Fund Hedging and Arbitrage (Including the Herzfeld Hedge)

# 9

"Hedging" and "arbitrage" seem to carry a mystique in the minds of a large percentage of investors. One of the principal reasons for this phenomenon is that very little has been written on the subject. Another is that arbitrageurs tend to be highly secretive about their work.

I would like to try to put an end to the mystique and the secrecy by showing that arbitrage can be little more than an exercise in high school-level mathematics.

It must be admitted that the confusion about hedging and arbitrage, even on the part of top-level executives in Wall Street, may stem from the fact that there is a broad area of disagreement on just what the two terms mean. If you ask five reasonably sophisticated and skilled Wall Street traders or investors for their definitions, you will get, at the least, five different answers.

A general-reference dictionary might define arbitrage as the buying and selling of the same securities at the same time but in two separate markets so that a profit is made from the difference in price.

The New York Stock Exchange defines an arbitrage as "a technique involved to take advantage of differences in prices."[1]

One of the better definitions which I have seen appears in *The Stock Market Handbook*. It says that arbitrage "is the simultaneous buying of securities on one market and selling in another market at a price advantage."[2] This same book offers another definition which is probably the best I have seen as it applies to the general term of arbitrage: "The buying of a security convertible into another one at a price advantage because the first one is selling for less than its converted equivalent."[3]

This definition begins to approach my own meaning of the term arbitrage as it applies to closed-end funds. It must be emphasized that my definition of arbitrage, which follows, applies only to closed-end funds. That definition is this: "The simultaneous buying and selling of

**145**

closed-end funds and the securities in their portfolios or similar securities or options on those securities to take advantage of the temporary price difference between the market price of a fund and its net asset value per share."

A hedge as defined by the Chicago Board of Trade in a booklet discussing interest rate hedging is: "The initiation of a position in a futures market which is intended as a temporary substitute for the sale or purchase of the actual commodity."[4]

*The Stock Market Handbook* provides a definition of hedging which is more oriented to the stock market. It says hedging is "to offset or reduce a possible loss by buying and selling securities likely to rise and fall in opposite directions under the same conditions."[5]

This chapter deals with four basic forms of hedging and arbitrage in closed-end funds. They are:

1. Simple hedges and arbitrage
2. The Herzfeld Hedge involving closed-end funds and listed options
3. Bond fund hedges and cross hedges
4. Hedges and arbitrages which have been done or can be done in the specialty fund area

The examples of trades given in this chapter must be regarded as hypothetical. Even though I use the names of actual funds and specific prices and dates, I am not trying to convey the idea that actual trading was done in all instances. Of course, some trades were in fact made. Whenever we discuss hypothetical trades, three key points—volume, prices, and expenses—should be kept in mind.

With respect to *volume*, we will assume that a trade was made, even though in reality it might not have been possible. This situation would occur if I said we bought 3000 to 4000 shares of a fund on a specific date, even though a trade of that volume might not have been possible. This is because on that date the total trading volume of the issue might in fact have been only 5000 or 6000 shares, making the completion of our entire buy order virtually out of the question. In my illustrations, I attempt to use examples of larger trading positions for active funds and smaller positions for inactive funds. Therefore, it is my calculated guess that with respect to volume, the trades cited could have been made, although, to emphasize the point, there is no way of knowing that with any certainty.

With respect to *prices*, quite often I will use the closing price for the day in my examples. However, the stock could have had a range on that specific day, and I could have picked the high or the low. Usually I pick the close or a mean price between the high and low. It should again be noted, however, that the buying of large quantities of stocks or closed-end funds may affect their price movements. In my examples we will assume that prices were not thus affected.

With respect to *expenses*, brokerage commissions are especially important when it comes to arbitrage. However, for specific reasons, I do not take them into consideration in any of my examples. Most forms of arbitrage in today's stock market are being practiced by professional traders at firms which are members of the major exchanges. I personally feel that in closed-end fund arbitrage, there is room for the private investor to participate, and this chapter is written with the general investing public in mind. However, when it comes to expenses, the reader should be aware that they vary widely, being quite different for various types of investors and depending on several factors. In the case of a member firm trading for its own account, for example, expenses may be limited to stock transfer taxes. If the firm clears for itself and executes its own orders on an exchange floor, it may not have any floor brokerage or clearing expenses. A nonclearing firm, on the other hand, will have a clearing expense and in some cases, it may also have to pay for floor brokerage, as may the clearing firm itself. Over-the-counter transactions usually take place at net prices, with the market maker having the edge.

As for large institutional accounts, they will pay commissions but usually at sharply discounted rates, much like active individual traders who can find brokers happy to handle their business at reduced commissions.

It is practically impossible when dealing with arbitrage to fix a definite commission, clearing, or brokerage expense. The reader—that is, the potential individual investor—must determine beforehand what his own expenses will be in making trades. Then he will have to make the necessary adjustments to conform to the examples I will give in regards to specific situations. Let us now turn to those specifics.

## SIMPLE HEDGES AND ARBITRAGE

This strategy involves *establishing a long position in a closed-end fund trading at an excessive discount while going short in a closed-end fund selling at a premium*. To illustrate this case, I went (theoretically, it must be remembered) long in Madison Fund (MAD) and short in Niagara Shares (NGS) from January 1976 to December 1977. During that period, the Dow Jones Industrial Average declined from 910 to 830.

What transpired is shown in Figure 9.1. At Point A on the chart in January 1976, Madison was selling at $9.50, its net asset value was 13.37, and the discount from its net asset value was 28.9 percent. At the same time, Niagara was selling at $13.75, its net asset value was 13.46 and had a premium of 2.2 percent.

By December 1977 (Point B) Madison was selling at $13.25, its net asset value had risen to 16.42, and its discount had narrowed to 19.3 percent. As for Niagara, its price had declined to 10⅝, its NAV was down to 12.51 and from its premium of 2.2 percent at the beginning of the year, it had gone to a discount of 15.1 percent.

As Table 9.1 shows, if an arbitrageur had established a long position of 1000 shares of Madison Fund in January 1976 at $9.50 per share and simultaneously sold short 1000 shares of Niagara at 13.75, almost 2 years later, in December 1977, he could have achieved a substantial profit. He could have done this by selling his 1000 shares of Madison at $13.25, realizing a gain of $3,750, and covering his short position in Niagara at 10⅝, for a gain of $3.125. This would have given him a net gain of $6,875.

The term "net gain" is used instead of "total gain" because in most forms of arbitrage, there is usually a gain on one side of the transaction and a loss on the other. The hope is that the gain is larger than the loss, whether the gain comes from the long or the short position. In many of the closed-end arbitrages which we will examine, gains often resulted on both sides. Such two-sided gains are quite unusual in most other forms of arbitrage.

Admittedly, the example of Madison and Niagara was described here because it is one of the better ones of the 1976–1977 period. In this form of arbitrage, it is more than likely that in a declining market the net asset value of both funds would also decline. The investor must recognize that what took place with Madison and Niagara cannot be depended on to be repeated in all arbitrages involving the establishment of long and short positions in different funds.

In this case, Madison's net asset value rose through a declining market while Niagara's NAV declined. However, the following is the basic theory of this arbitrage which should be kept in mind: when the trader has a long position in a fund with an excessive discount and a short

FIGURE 9.1
Price vs. NAV for Madison Fund and Niagara Shares

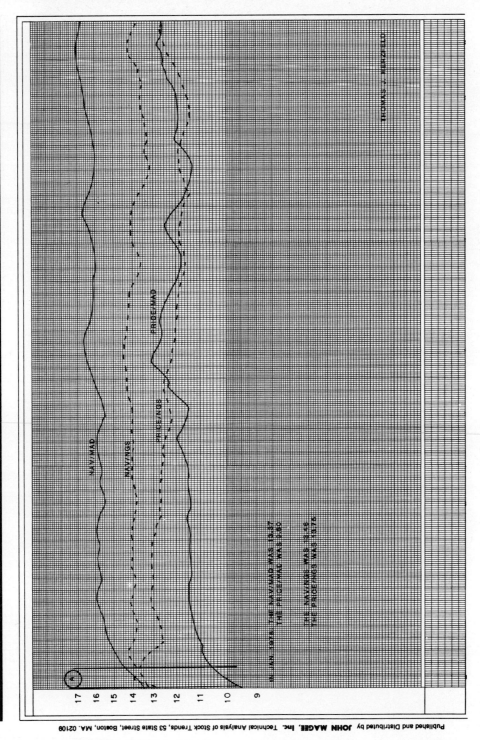

FIGURE 9.1
Price vs. NAV for Madison Fund and Niagara Shares   *(Cont.)*

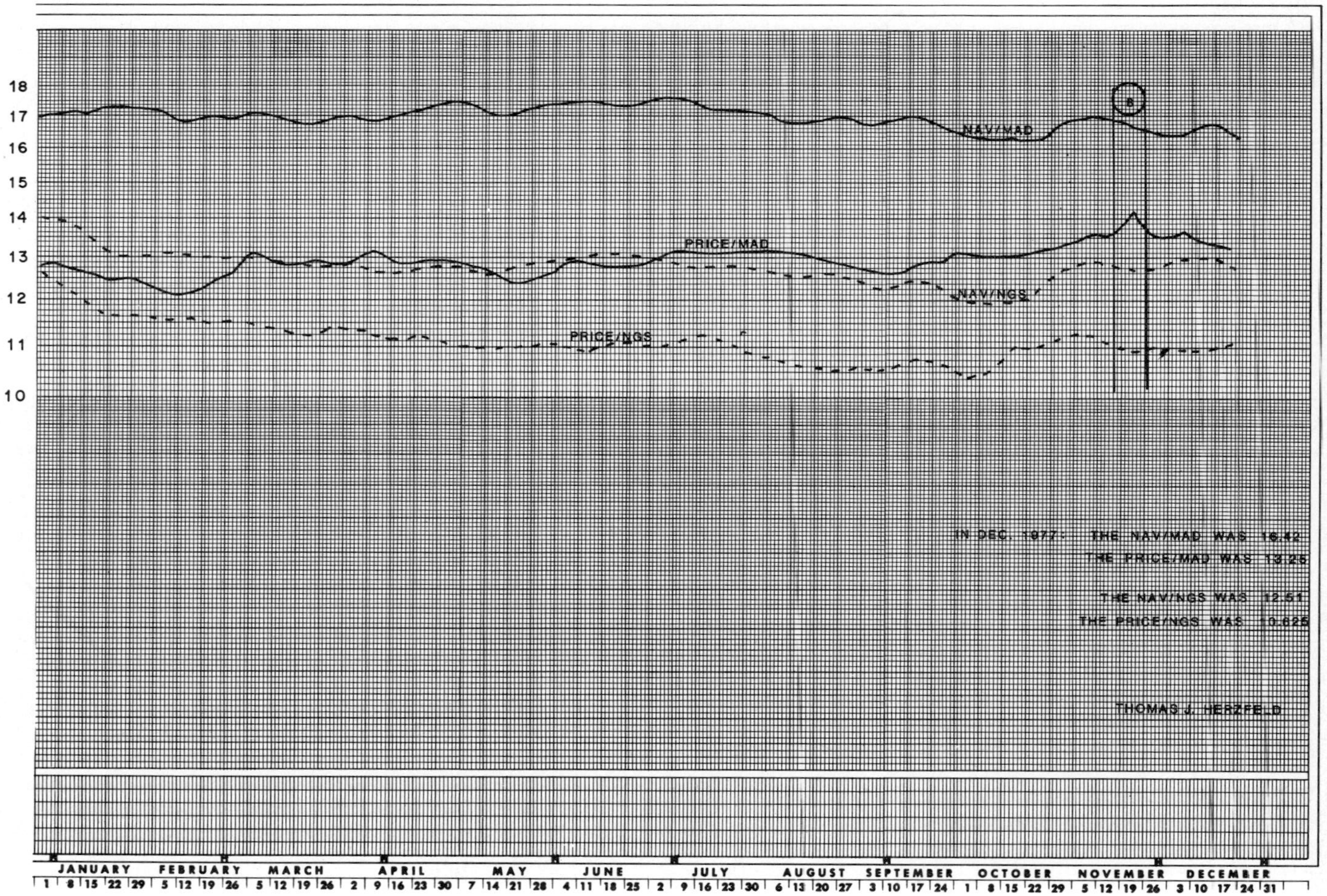

150

**TABLE 9.1**

**Example of Going Long a Closed-End Fund at an Excessive Discount
and Going Short a Closed-End Fund at a Premium (Falling Market)**

JANUARY 1976 (DJIA 910)

| Go long | | | Sell short | | |
|---|---|---|---|---|---|
| 1000 MAD | @ | 9.50 | 1000 NGS | @ | 13.75 |
| NAV/MAD | | 13.37 | NAV/NGS | | 13.46 |
| Discount/MAD | | 28.9% | Premium/NGS | | 2.2% |
| Cost | | $ 9,500 | Proceeds | | $13,750 |

DECEMBER 1977 (DJIA 830)

| Sell | | | Buy to cover | | |
|---|---|---|---|---|---|
| 1000 MAD | @ | 13.25 | 1000 NGS | @ | 10.62 |
| NAV/MAD | | 16.42 | NAV/NGS | | 12.51 |
| Discount/MAD | | 19.3% | Discount/NGS | | 15.1% |
| Proceeds | | $13,250 | Cost | | $10,625 |
| Long position gain | | $ 3,750 | Short position gain | | $ 3,125 |
| | | Net gain = $6,875* | | | |

*Not including taxes, commissions, and floor brokerage or clearing expenses.

position in a fund selling, for no apparent reason, at a premium, the excessive discount will narrow, and the premium will either narrow or disappear. Therefore, on the assumption that the net asset values should behave similarly, the converging or narrowing of the deviations of the two discounts will result in a profit on the trade.

Another fascinating arbitrage can take place when a fund is selling at an excessive discount. Here *the trader simultaneously buys the fund and sells short the stocks which the fund holds, particularly those stocks in which the fund has major positions*. Table 9.2 provides a guide to this technique. As an example, we will use Tri-Continental Corporation as the long position and that closed-end fund's major holdings as the short positions from the end of November 1976 through the end of December 1977, a period in which the Dow Jones Industrial Average dropped from 948 to 830.

At the beginning of November 1976, a long position of 5000 shares of Tri-Continental could have been established at 20⅛ for a total cost of $100,625. At that time, the fund's NAV was 26.47, and it was selling at a 24 percent discount. At the same time, the following short positions could have been established: 50 IBM at 274⅛; 300 Standard Oil

**TABLE 9.2**

**Example of Going Long a Closed-End Fund at an Excessive Discount and
Selling Short the Fund's Major Positions**

END OF NOVEMBER 1976 (DJIA 948)

| Go long | | | Sell short | | | |
|---------|-------|----------|-------|-------|-------|
| | | Quantity | Stock | Price | Proceeds |
| 5000 TY | @ 20.125 | 50 | IBM | 274.125 | $13,706.25 |
| | | 300 | SD | 36.375 | 10,912.50 |
| NAV/TY | 26.47 | 100 | GM | 70.75 | 7,075.00 |
| | | 100 | DD | 125.375 | 12,537.50 |
| Discount/TY | 24% | 200 | UCL | 53.50 | 10,700.00 |
| | | 200 | XON | 51.75 | 10,350.00 |
| Cost | $100,625.00 | 100 | MO | 61.875 | 6,187.50 |
| | | 200 | AVP | 48.875 | 9,775.00 |
| | | 100 | MTC | 82.25 | 8,225.00 |
| | | 200 | UK | 57.50 | 11,500.00 |
| | | Total proceeds | | | $100,968.75 |

END OF DECEMBER 1977 (DJIA 830)

| Sell | | | Buy to cover | | | |
|------|-------|----------|-------|-------|------|
| | | Quantity | Stock | Price | Cost |
| 5000 TY | @ 20.50 | 50 | IBM | 273.50 | 13,675.00 |
| | | 300 | SD | 38.875 | 11,662.50 |
| NAV/TY | 23.27 | 100 | GM | 62.875 | 6,287.50 |
| | | 100 | DD | 120.375 | 12,037.50 |
| Discount/TY | 11.9% | 200 | UCL | 52.875 | 10,575.00 |
| | | 200 | XON | 48.125 | 9,625.00 |
| Proceeds | $102,500.00 | 100 | MO | 61.875 | 6,187.50 |
| | | 200 | AVP | 48.125 | 9,625.00 |
| | | 100 | MTC | 57.625 | 5,762.50 |
| | | 200 | UK | 41.00 | 8,200.00 |
| | | Total cost | | | $93,637.50 |

Long position gain $1,875.00 Short position gain $7,331.25
Total gain = $9,206.25*
During this period: NAV −12.1%,
DJIA −12.4%

*Not including taxes, commissions, and floor brokerage or clearing expenses, if applicable.

of California at 36⅜; 100 General Motors at 70¾; 100 duPont at 125⅜; 200 Union Oil of California at 53½; 200 Exxon at 51¾; 100 Philip Morris at 61⅞; 200 Avon Products at 48⅞; 100 Monsanto at 82¼; 200 Union Carbide at 57½.

The decision on the number of shares to be sold short in each stock can be based on either or both of the following considerations:

1. The proportionate value of an individual stock in relation to the fund's entire portfolio
2. The attempt to make short sales of more or less equal dollar amounts

This example uses a combination. The proceeds from the short sale of the 10 stocks were $100,968.75—an amount virtually equal to the total cost of 5000 shares in the long position in Tri-Continental. At the time of this arbitrage, if we had thought that the market was going higher, we would have increased the size of the long position relative to the short. But if we had felt that the market was going lower, we might have been biased in favor of the short position. Most of the time, to minimize market risk, equal short and long positions are used.

By the end of 1977 when the Dow was at 830, Tri-Continental's net asset value had declined to 23.27. This was a drop of 12.1 percent from November 1976. In the same period, the Dow showed a decline of 12.4 percent. (There is a strong correlation between Tri-Continental's net asset value and the Dow. This is probably explained by the fact that many of the stocks in Tri-Continental's portfolio are also components of the Dow-Jones Industrial Average.) However, while the stock market in general was declining, Tri-Continental's discount was narrowing. By the end of 1977, it was only 11.9 percent. At that time, if the 5000-share long position in Tri-Continental had been sold at 20½, the proceeds would have been $102,500, resulting in a long position gain of $1875. Covering the short position in the original 10 stocks would have cost $93,637.50, representing a short position gain of $7331.25. (This was because of the rather sharp decline in some of those stocks: General Motors had dropped by about 9 points, duPont by about 5, Union Carbide by approximately 16, and Monsanto by more than 20 points.) Finally, the total gain on the arbitrage was $9206.25, consisting of $1,875 from the long position, plus $7331.25 from the short.

A variation on this strategy might have been the substitution, on the short side, of a stock, similar to one which was in the fund's portfolio, that the investor judged to be more overpriced at the time of the short sale. Texaco, as an example, could have been substituted for one of the portfolio's oil stocks, or Ford for General Motors. Such substitutions may well have represented opportunities to increase the total gain on the transaction.

While our previous example dealt with establishing a long position in a fund at a wide discount and a short position in the fund's portfolio, the very opposite arbitrage, with highly interesting possibilities, can be set up—that is, *selling short a fund which is at a premium and going long in individual stocks in the fund's portfolio.*

Figure 9.2 on Petroleum & Resources shows that at Point A in May 1977, the fund was selling at a substantial premium above its net asset value. The stock was selling at 27⅜, the NAV was 25.09, and the premium was 9.1 percent. As the first part of Table 9.3 shows, if 1700 shares of Petroleum & Resources had been sold short at 27⅜, the proceeds would have been $46,537.50. If on the same date, May 13, 1977, we had established long positions in some of the stocks in which the fund's holdings were rather large, we would have purchased 200 Royal Dutch, 200 Standard Oil of California, 200 Marathon Oil, 100 Cities Service, 100 Standard Oil of Indiana, 200 Gulf Oil, 100 Exxon, and 300 British Petroleum. The cost of these purchases would have been $45,025. As in the example with Tri-Continental, we sought to make the purchases of the eight securities as close as possible to each other in cost, and we also designed the arbitrage so that the long position's value was close to the value of the short position. Again, this may not always be possible, but the combination does serve to decrease the market risk.

On June 4, 1977, the entire portfolio could have been sold for a total of $43,750, or a loss on the long position of $1275. However, since there was an unusually weak market for oil stocks, the net asset value of Petroleum & Resources declined during that period from 25.09 to 24.80 and the 9.1 percent premium disappeared completely by June 4, becoming instead a discount of 4.2 percent at Point B. The cost to cover the 1700-share short position in the fund would have been $40,-375, resulting in a gain of $6162.50, or a net gain on the entire transaction of $4887.50.

At the same Point B, the entire strategy of the arbitrage was ready for a total reversal through the establishment of a long position in Petroleum & Resources and short positions in the stocks which had

**FIGURE 9.2**
Petroleum & Resources Chart Showing Successful Trading Points

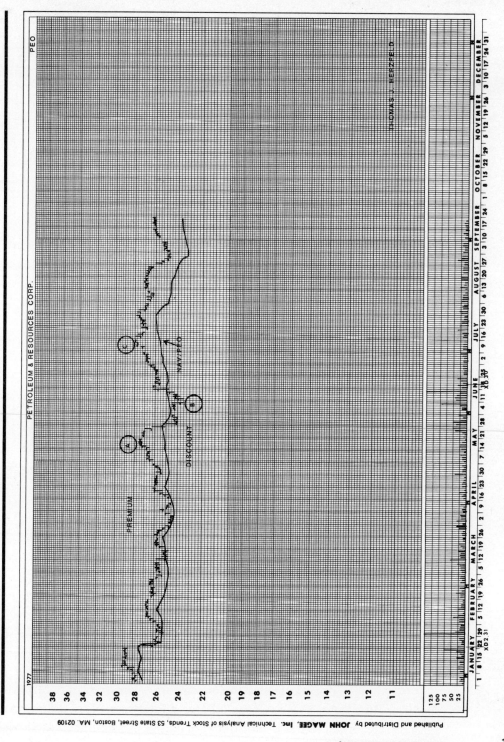

PETROLEUM & RESOURCES CORP.

PEO

1977

PREMIUM

DISCOUNT

NAV/PEO

THOMAS J. HERZFELD

38 36 34 32 30 28 26 24 22 20 19 18 17 16 15 14 13 12 11

125 100 75 50 25

JANUARY FEBRUARY MARCH APRIL MAY JUNE JULY AUGUST SEPTEMBER OCTOBER NOVEMBER DECEMBER

Published and Distributed by **JOHN MAGEE, Inc.** Technical Analysis of Stock Trends, 53 State Street, Boston, MA. 02109

**TEKNIPLAT Chart Paper**

**155**

**TABLE 9.3**
**Example of Going Short a Closed-End Fund at a Premium and Going Long Major Positions of the Fund's Portfolio**

MAY 13, 1977

| Quantity | Stock | Price | Cost | Sell short | |
|---|---|---|---|---|---|
| 200 | RD | 23.25 | $4,650.00 | 1700 PEO | @ 27.375 |
| 200 | SD | 30.50 | 6,100.00 | NAV/PEO | 25.09 |
| 200 | MRO | 37.25 | 7,450.00 | | |
| 100 | CS | 60.00 | 6,000.00 | Premium/PEO | 9.1% |
| 100 | SN | 52.50 | 5,250.00 | | |
| 200 | GO | 27.50 | 5,500.00 | Proceeds | $46,537.50 |
| 100 | XON | 51.25 | 5,125.00 | | |
| 300 | BP | 16.50 | 4,950.00 | | |
| | | | Total cost 45,025.00 | | |

JUNE 4, 1977

| Quantity | Stock | Price | Proceeds | Buy to cover | |
|---|---|---|---|---|---|
| 200 | RD | 20.75 | $4,150.00 | 1700 PEO | @ 23.75 |
| 200 | SD | 29.75 | 5,950.00 | NAV/PEO | 24.80 |
| 200 | MRO | 37.50 | 7,500.00 | | |
| 100 | CS | 56.875 | 5,687.50 | Discount/PEO | 4.2% |
| 100 | SN | 52.25 | 5,225.00 | | |
| 200 | GO | 27.00 | 5,400.00 | Cost | $40,375.00 |
| 100 | XON | 50.75 | 5,075.00 | | |
| 300 | BP | 15.875 | 4,762.50 | | |
| Total proceeds | | | $43,750.00 | | |

Long position loss  $ 1,275.00          Short position gain          $ 6,162.50

Net gain = $4,887.50*

*Not including taxes, commissions, and floor brokerage or clearing expenses.

just been sold. Then, at Point C at the beginning of July 1977, the program could have been reversed again, going short the fund and long the portfolio.

Emphasis must be placed on the following: arbitrage does not involve isolated trades, such as in one year setting up an arbitrage in Petroleum & Resources and in another, in Tri-Continental. There are, in all markets, continual arbitrage possibilities. Such trading can be set up on what amounts to a rotating basis—in one fund and out of the other; long in one fund and short in stocks; or long in the stocks and short in the fund, etc. The objective in an arbitrage program is to keep the total values of all long and short positions in balance.

Here is a variation of the form of arbitrage illustrated above. At the end of 1976, when gold was at $134 an ounce, ASA Limited was selling at a premium of almost 33 percent. Its net asset value was 15.91, and it was selling at 21⅛ per share. A short position was established through the sale of 2100 shares whose proceeds generated $44,362.50. Simul-

**TABLE 9.4**
**Another Example of Going Short a Closed-End Fund at a Premium and Going Long Major Positions of the Fund's Portfolio**

YEAR-END 1976 (Gold $134/oz.)

| Quantity | Go long Stock | Price | Cost | Sell short | |
|---|---|---|---|---|---|
| 400 | West Driefontein Gold Mining | 20.25 | $ 8,100.00 | 2100 ASA @ 21.125 | |
| 900 | Vaal Reefs Exploration & Mining | 10.375 | 9,337.50 | NAV/ASA | 15.91 |
| 4000 | DeBeers Consolidated Mines | 2.375 | $9,500.00 | Premium/ASA | 32.8% |
| 2100 | Kloof Gold Mining | 4.125 | 8,662.50 | Proceeds | $44,362.50 |
| 1200 | President Steyn Gold Mining | 7.0 | 8,400.00 | | |
| Total cost | | | $44,000.00 | | |

YEAR-END 1977 (Gold $167/oz.)

| Quantity | Sell Stock | Price | Proceeds | Buy to cover | |
|---|---|---|---|---|---|
| 400 | West Driefontein Gold Mining | 24.875 | $ 9,950.00 | 2100 ASA @ 20.50 | |
| 900 | Vaal Reefs Exploration & Mining | 15.75 | 14,175.00 | NAV/ASA | 19.90 |
| 4000 | DeBeers Consolidated Mines | 4.25 | 17,000.00 | Premium/ASA | 3% |
| 2100 | Kloof Gold Mining | 6.25 | 13,125.00 | Cost | $43,050.00 |
| 1200 | President Steyn Gold Mining | 8.375 | 10,050.00 | | |
| Total proceeds | | | $64,300.00 | | |
| Long position gain | | | $20,300.00 | Short position gain | $1,312.50 |
| | | Total gain = $21,612.50* | | | |

*Not counting trading expenses.

taneous with establishing that short position at a very wide premium, it was possible to establish long positions in the major portfolio holdings of ASA. The following purchases could have been made: 400 West Driefontein Gold Mining at 20¼ per share costing $8100; 900 Vaal Reefs Exploration & Mining at 10⅜, costing $9337.50; 4000 DeBeers Consolidated Mines at 2⅜, costing $9500; 2100 Kloof Gold Mining at 4⅛, costing $8662.50; 1200 President Steyn Gold Mining at $7, costing $8400. The total price of the long position was $44,000 (see Table 9.4).

If we had been bullish on South African gold stocks and gold in general, we could have established long positions whose total value would have been larger than the value of the short sale. However, by taking a neutral position on gold, our ratios were appropriate.

By the end of 1977 gold had risen to $167 per ounce, and the net asset value was up to 19.90, against 15.91 at the end of 1976. However, the premium on ASA had almost disappeared, from 33 percent to a mere 3 percent in little more than a year. Buying 2100 shares of ASA to cover the short position cost $43,050. In spite of the rising gold market and South African gold mining in particular, this represented a gain on the short position of $1312.50 over the original investment of $44,362.50.

More importantly, a remarkable profit was realized on the long positions in the gold shares. West Driefontein rose to 24⅞, Vaal to 15¾, DeBeers to 4¼, Kloof to 6¼, and President Steyn to 8⅜. The proceeds from the sale would have been $64,300 for a gain on the long position of $20,300 and a total gain on the long and short transactions of $21,612.50.

## THE HERZFELD HEDGE

It is probably safe to say that all students of the stock market, as well as all investment advisors and professional traders, have found one particular area of the market which they have adopted and, to one degree or another, made their own—at least in their own eyes.

I am no exception. Mine, quite obviously, centers on closed-end funds and on hedging and arbitrage. Applying a host of techniques, modifying some and discarding others, and always testing my theories and methods where they count—in the actual market place—I devised what has come to be known in some Wall Street circles as the Herzfeld Hedge.

Before getting into specific details of my strategy, however, I must post a firm warning. Since the Herzfeld Hedge involves dealing in options, I refuse to recommend that anyone attempt to employ any of the strategies of the hedge unless that individual has made himself thoroughly familiar with option trading. And by this, I must stress that the individual be as aware as possible of the inherent risks involved in trading options and especially in the selling of naked options. (A thorough reading of the Options Clearing Corporation's prospectus is essential.)

It should be pointed out that the established option exchanges offer the investor an opportunity to employ various trading strategies involving leverage, arbitrage, and hedging that are not available in common stock trading. However, before discussing option trading, I want to define certain key terms I will be using:

## Definitions of Key Terms

**Option**  A contract to buy (or sell) a specified number of shares of a specified common stock at a specified price within a specified time. In our discussion we'll distinguish between the following:

*Call option.*  Entitles the holder to buy a specified number of shares at a specified price within a specified time.

*Put option.*  Entitles the holder to sell a specified number of shares at a specified price within a specified time.

**Strike price**  The price at which the option contract may be exercised.

**Exercise**  An option contract's being fulfilled. For a call option this would refer to the holder of the option *purchasing* the stock from the option seller at the strike price. This transaction is sometimes referred to as "calling" the stock. For a put option this would refer to the holder of the option *selling* the stock to the option seller at the strike price. This is sometimes referred to as "putting" the stock.

**Expiration**  The last day on which the option can be exercised.

**Buyer**  The one who purchases the option contract. It is the decision of the buyer to exercise the option contract. He may exercise the option at any time up to the expiration date.

**Seller or writer**  The one who sells the option contract to the buyer. The seller can be of two basic types:

1. *Covered writer.* The option writer who has a stock position so that he can perform his function if the option is exercised. For example, let's say the writer owns 100 shares of XYZ Inc. and

sells a call option against his stock. If the buyer of the option decides to exercise his option and calls the stock, the writer then delivers his stock to the buyer.

2. *Uncovered writer*, also called *naked writer*. This is a key factor in the Herzfeld Hedge. In this case the option seller does not have the stock position to fulfill his obligations if the option contract is exercised. Using the same example as above, the uncovered writer either must go to market and purchase the stock and deliver it to the buyer, or must remain short. In any event, the naked option writer must have sufficient funds to cover his liabilities in case the option is exercised. The funds required are determined by margin requirements as dictated by the Federal Reserve. The requirements are sometimes altered by brokerage firms' "house requirements."

**In the money**   Term showing the relationship of the option strike price to market price of underlying stock. If a call option strike price is below the market price of the stock, the option is said to be *in the money*. For a put option the opposite would be the case, that is, an in-the-money put would occur when the option strike price is above the market price of the underlying stock.

**Out of the money**   The inverse of in the money. For call options, *out of the money* refers to a situation in which the call option strike price is above the market price of the stock. For put options, out of the money describes a situation in which the put option strike price is below the market price of the underlying stock.

**On the money**   A situation in which the option strike price is identical to the market price of the underlying stock.

**Intrinsic Value**   The market price of the option in a parity relationship to the market price of the underlying stock. Let's say the call option strike price is 20, and the market price of the underlying stock is 21. The intrinsic value of the option would, therefore, be 1. Thus, the option could be purchased at 1, the stock called at 20, and the stock then sold at the market price of 21. The net result would be even, that is, at parity. The buyer of the option would lose 1 on the purchase of the option and gain 1 by calling the stock at 20 and selling it at the market price of 21.

**Premium**   The option market price in excess of the intrinsic value. In the preceding example with the strike price of 20 and the market price of the underlying stock at 21, the market price of the option may be 2. This price is 1 above the intrinsic value. This excess over the intrinsic value is the premium.

**Discount**   The option market price below the intrinsic value. This is fairly common in those situations in which the option is deep "in the money" and near expiration. These situations develop because many option buyers do not have the financial ability to exercise their options and are forced to accept a discounted price by closing their option positions in the option markets rather than by exercising the option. The arbitrage possibilities are obvious.

**Open interest**   The number of contracts outstanding for a particular option. For every buyer there must be a seller, and effectively for every long position there is an offsetting short position. The number of contracts (open interest) is important in determining the liquidity (that is, ease of purchase and sale) of the option.

**Trading unit**   In option trading, each option contract represents the equivalent of 100 shares of the underlying stock. Therefore, the purchase of one option contract is actually the purchase of 100 options. If a stock dividend should occur, its effect is reflected by changing the strike price.

*Option Trading.* At this point, let's consider the constant dilemma of the option writer: should he buy the underlying stock in a market correction and then attempt to sell the corresponding option in a rally, or should he simultaneously buy the stock and sell the option? In the first case, he has increased his return but has assumed an additional market risk. In the second, he has less market risk, but less potential return. *The Herzfeld Hedge* may accomplish both objectives.

*Instead of buying the underlying stock, the investor buys a closed-end fund which sells at what he considers an excessive discount and has a portfolio of stocks with which he feels comfortable. He then simultaneously sells naked options on the fund's largest positions, whose corresponding options are selling at the largest premiums at that time.*

(In the example I am about to give, I did not make an analysis of which options were the richest at the time; I made a random selection of options. In using the Herzfeld Hedge in practice rather than in theory, when it comes to the selection of options, I find that one of several computer approaches is preferable to the random selection used here for the purpose of illustration only.)

The thrust of the strategy is that if the stock market declines, the diminishing time factor of the option plus the probable erosion of the price of the underlying stock exerts pressure on the excessive premium of the option. This probably would result in a greater gain on the short option position than the resulting loss in the long position on the excessively discounted fund. If the market rises, in the money options will tend to lose their rich premiums and will probably not rise as fast as their underlying stocks. In addition, the diminishing time factor is working against the option. At the same time as the underlying stocks rise, the net asset value of the fund should increase, combined with the probable narrowing of its discount, possibly causing it to become more profitable than the loss developing in the options. The hedge may also result in dividends' being received on the long positions in the fund.

And now to an example whose details are shown in Table 9.5. In June 1977, U.S. & Foreign Securities (UFO) was selling at an excessive discount of 26.7 percent. Its net asset value was 20.97, and the fund was selling at 15⅜. The Dow Jones Industrial Average was at 912. A purchase of 4100 shares of UFO at 15⅜ would have cost $63,375.

Had one of each of the following naked calls been sold on the major positions of UFO, the proceeds from the sale would have been $3718.75: IBM October 260s, selling at 6¼; Amerada-Hess November 30s, at 5¼; Digital Equipment October 40s, at 4½; American Telephone & Telegraph October 60s, at 4; General Electric October 55s, at 2; Texaco October 25s, at 2¹/₁₆; Corning Glassworks December 60s, at 6¾; Monsanto October 70s, at 4½; Bristol-Myers December 30s, at 1⅞.

By September 24, 1977, the discount on UFO had narrowed to 20.7 percent. The price of the stock had risen to 16⅝, in spite of a down market (the Dow Jones was at 839) and yet UFO's net asset value, after rising in August and September, was exactly where it had been in June—20.97. At that juncture the hedge could have been closed.

Proceeds from the sale of 4100 UFO shares at 16⅝ would have amounted to $68,162.50; the cost to cover the short positions in the calls would have been $2622.25. This would have meant a gain from the long position of $4787.50 and on the short position of $1096.50, for a total gain of $5844.

This, then, is the basic discipline of the Herzfeld Hedge—to go long a fund with an excessive discount from net asset value and to sell naked calls on the major stocks in that fund's portfolio. The Herzfeld Hedge is a continually revolving program. It is not limited to hedging one fund at a time. Rather, the program must be in a constant state of flux, rotating from overpriced funds into underpriced funds and covering underpriced options while establishing new positions in overpriced options. Occasionally, there will be an overlapping, when we still have short positions from a previous hedge while establishing a long position in a new hedge, or vice versa.

**TABLE 9.5**
**The Herzfeld Hedge: Going Long a Closed-End Fund at Discount
and Selling Short Calls on Major Positions in the Fund's Portfolio**

WEEK OF JUNE 4, 1977 (DJIA 912)

| Go long | | Sell following naked calls | | | | | | |
|---|---|---|---|---|---|---|---|---|
| 4100 UFO | @ 15.375 | 1 | IBM | Oct | 260 | @ | 6.25 | $625.00 |
| | | 1 | AHC | Nov | 30 | @ | 5.25 | 525.00 |
| | | 1 | DEC | Oct | 40 | @ | 4.50 | 450.00 |
| | | 1 | T | Oct | 60 | @ | 4.00 | 400.00 |
| NAV/UFO | 20.97 | 1 | GE | Oct | 55 | @ | 2.00 | 200.00 |
| | | 1 | TX | Oct | 25 | @ | 2.0625 | 206.25 |
| Discount/UFO | 26.7% | 1 | GLW | Dec | 60 | @ | 6.75 | 675.00 |
| | | 1 | MTC | Oct | 70 | @ | 4.50 | 450.00 |
| Cost | $63,375.00 | 1 | BMY | Dec | 30 | @ | 1.875 | 187.50 |
| | | Total proceeds | | | | | | $3,718.75 |
| | (Underlying Value of Options: $63,000) | | | | | | | |

WEEK OF SEPTEMBER 24, 1977 (BJIA 839)

| Sell | | Cover option positions (buy) | | | | | | |
|---|---|---|---|---|---|---|---|---|
| 4100 UFO | @ 16.625 | 1 | IBM | Oct | 260 | @ | 3.50 | $350.00 |
| | | 1 | AHC | Nov | 30 | @ | 1.875 | 187.50 |
| | | 1 | DEC | Oct | 40 | @ | 6.125 | 612.50 |
| | | 1 | T | Oct | 60 | @ | 2.75 | 275.00 |
| NAV/UFO | 20.97 | 1 | GE | Oct | 55 | @ | .25 | 25.00 |
| | | 1 | TX | Oct | 25 | @ | 3.125 | 312.50 |
| Discount/UFO | 20.7% | 1 | GLW | Dec | 60 | @ | 3.75 | 375.00 |
| | | 1 | MTC | Oct | 70 | @ | .0625 | 6.25 |
| | | 1 | BMY | Dec | 30 | @ | 4.875 | 487.50 |
| Proceeds | $68,162.50 | | | | | | | |
| | | Total cost | | | | | | $2,622.25 |
| Long position gain | $4,787.50 | Short position gain | | | | | | $1,096.50 |
| | Total gain = $5,884.00* | | | | | | | |

*Not adjusted for dividends received or trading expenses incurred.

Simultaneously, short positions can be established in overpriced funds, meaning funds trading at narrow discounts or at premiums, and naked puts can be sold on stocks in the funds' portfolios. Or, we can go long calls on stocks in overpriced funds and short the funds. Those are the basic ingredients of the Herzfeld Hedge.

To expand on this process of continual rotation, if U.S. & Foreign had made a sharp rally in the example cited above, we could have sold the stock and remained short on the options. Or as a substitute for UFO, we could have gone long a fund at a sharp discount that had a portfolio similar to UFO's. Or, if there was a sharp decline in some of the options, we could have covered some of them, by staying short in others and rotating into some with richer premiums. Thus, on one side we are constantly rotating in the fund position—by going long in excessively discounted issues, selling them when they become over-priced; then going short in other funds and covering them when they become undervalued—all of this while at the same time establishing short positions in calls or puts and covering them as they become prof-itable and then rotating into the sale of options which by then have moved to excessive premiums.

For another example of the Herzfeld Hedge, let's examine Figure 9.3 on Adams Express (ADX). At the end of January 1977, ADX was selling in the 11½–12 area with an excessive discount of 20.3 percent from its NAV of 14.75 (Point A). A purchase of 6500 shares of ADX would have cost $76,375. At the same time, the following naked calls could have been sold on January 28, 1977, against the major—or sim-ilar—positions in ADX's portfolio: Exxon July 50s, at 4; IBM July 260s, at 27⅛; AT&T July 60s, at 3⅞; General Electric July 50s, at 5¼; Stan-dard Oil of California July 40s, at 3; Schlumberger Ltd., August 60s, at 3; General Motors, July 70s, at 6½; Caterpillar August 50s, at 4; and Beatrice Foods, July 25s, at 2⅝. The proceeds from this sale would have been $5937.50. [It should be noted that since ADX at that time owned a large position in another closed-end fund, Petroleum & Resources (PEO), which primarily holds oil stocks, Exxon was substi-tuted for PEO on which to sell a naked call against. Because ADX held British Petroleum, on which no calls were available, Standard Oil of California was substituted.]

This hedge could have been closed at Point B on April 29, 1977. Then ADX could have been sold at 12⅞, bringing proceeds of $83,-687.50 and a profit on the 6500-share long position of $7312.50.

If the naked calls had been covered at the same time, the cost would have been $2937.50, based on the following prices: Exxon, 1¹⁵⁄₁₆; IBM, 7½; AT&T, 3; General Electric, 4¼; Standard Oil of California, 1³⁄₁₆; Schlumberger, 4; General Motors, 1⅜; Caterpillar, 5⅝; and Beatrice Foods, ½. The profit on the short positions would have been $3000, and the total profit on the Herzfeld Hedge, applied to ADX, would have been $10,312.50.

FIGURE 9.3
Adams Express

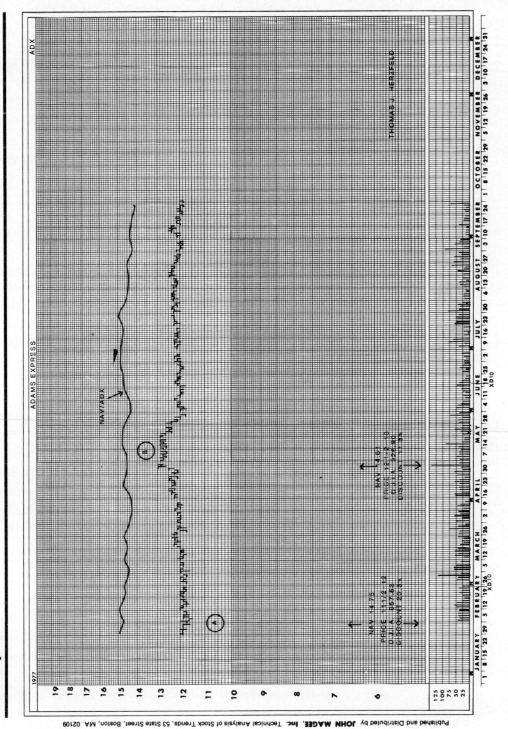

**TEKNIPLAT Chart Paper**

**165**

Before we leave this subject, let's review why this hedge would have been so successful.

1. The stock market declined between Points A and B, with the Dow moving from 957 to 926.

2. The NAV of ADX declined in the weak market from 14.75 to 14.61.

3. The discount of ADX narrowed from 20.3 percent to 11.3 percent, and, therefore, its price actually rose in a declining market.

4. Most of the stocks in the ADX portfolio declined along with the general stock market. As a result, the naked calls written against these stocks became profitable.

The key ingredient to success should be obvious here. It is, of course, the correct evaluation of the discount. Profitability can be increased by using sophisticated option selling analysis, but for purposes of simpler illustration I have avoided it. Many worthwhile books are available on option writing, and I suggest that the trader familiarize himself with a few of them before applying the Herzfeld Hedge.

## BOND FUND HEDGES AND CROSS HEDGES

The profit objective in bond fund hedging is usually smaller than in other forms of hedging. It is, quite frankly, a strategy better suited to the professional trader—one who manages money for a brokerage firm—than it is for a retail customer who must pay full commissions. For the record, a cross hedge involves the buying and selling of investment entities which are not identical but which historically have similar patterns.

By way of illustration, Figure 9.4 shows the net asset value and price movements of two bond funds, USLIFE Income Fund (UIF) and INA Investment Securities (IIS), from the end of 1977 through the beginning of 1978.

At Point A, the week of January 7, 1978, IIS was selling at an excessive discount, and UIF was at a premium. This was a situation calling for a simultaneous hedge by purchasing IIS in the 17¼–17⅜ area and selling UIF short at around 12. By the second week in February 1978 (Point B), the discount on IIS had narrowed in a declining bond market to where its price was 18½; at the same time, UIF had dropped to

**FIGURE 9.4**
**USLIFE Income Fund and INA Investment Securities**

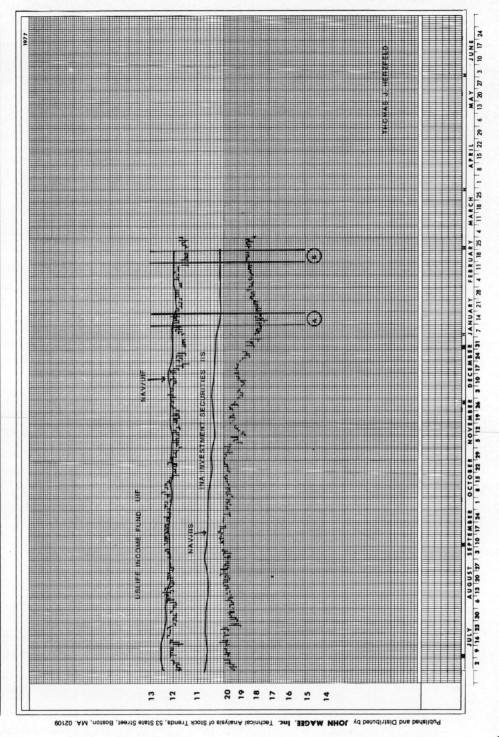

167

the $11\frac{3}{8}$–$11\frac{1}{2}$ area. The investor who had initiated the above positions at Point A and closed them at Point B would have realized a profit on both the long position and the short position in this bond fund hedge.

Another example of a bond fund hedge is shown in Figure 9.5. It could have been initiated at Point A on April 28, 1978, by selling John Hancock Income Securities (JHS) short at $17\frac{3}{8}$, with the NAV at 17.50, and going long USLIFE Income Fund (UIF) at $10\frac{3}{4}$, with the NAV at 12. The hedge could have been closed at Point B on May 10, 1978, by covering the short position in JHS at $16\frac{1}{2}$ (NAV unchanged at 17.50) for a profit of $\frac{7}{8}$ of a point and selling UIF at $11\frac{3}{4}$ (NAV unchanged at 12) for a 1-point profit.

Our next hedge involves going long bond funds at excessive discounts and short Treasury bond futures. A typical hedge of this sort is detailed in Table 9.6.

As viewed by the Chicago Board of Trade, this hedge is intended to result in a profit on only one side of the transaction. For instance, if the investor had a long position in bonds and a short position in bond futures and the market rose, the loss from the short position in the futures should be offset by the gain in the bonds. Conversely, if the bond market declined, the profit from the futures would be offset by a loss in the bond position.

However, in its publications the Chicago Board of Trade does not discuss the setting up of the hedge by using bond funds as opposed to bonds. This approach, employing the bond funds, creates the additional possibility of achieving a profit not merely on one side but rather on both sides—on the long and the short positions.

Treasury bond futures are traded on the Chicago Board of Trade in units with a face value at maturity of $100,000 and a coupon rate of 8 percent. They are quoted in $\frac{1}{32}$s. For example, a price of 100.18 is 100 $\frac{18}{32}$, in the same way as government bonds are quoted.

A typical closed-end bond fund hedge involving Treasury bond futures would have looked something like this on December 2, 1977, with the Dow Jones bond average at 91.91. The following long positions could have been established: 2000 shares of John Hancock Income Securities (JHS) with a net asset value of 18.34, a discount of 8 percent, and a per share price of $16\frac{7}{8}$ for a cost of $33,750; 2100 Drexel Bond Fund (DBF) with a net asset value of 20.29, a discount of 18.7 percent, and a per share price of $16\frac{1}{2}$ for a cost of $34,650; and 2300 shares of Pacific American Income Shares (PAI) with a net asset value of 15.73, a discount of 13.4 percent, and a per share price of $16\frac{5}{8}$

# FIGURE 9.5
## USLIFE Income Fund and John Hancock Income Securities

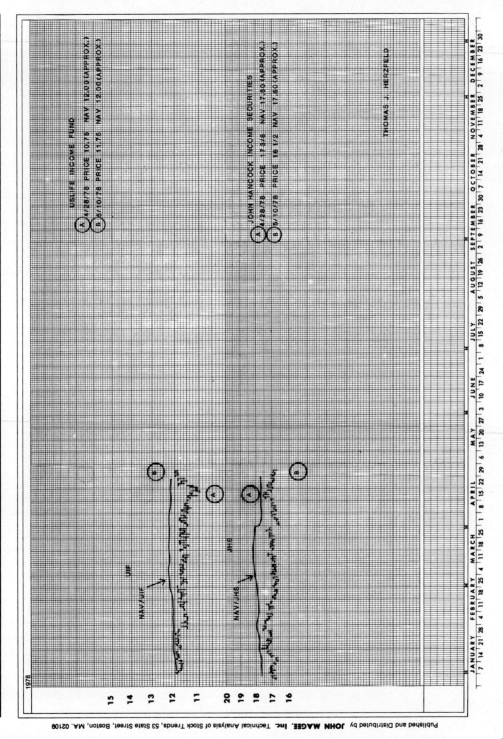

**TABLE 9.6**

**Going Long Bond Funds at Excessive Discounts and Short Treasury Bond Futures**

DECEMBER 2, 1977 (DJ BOND AVG. 91.91)

| Go long | | | Sell short |
|---|---|---|---|
| 2000 JHS | @ 16.875 | | September U.S. |
| NAV/JHS | 18.34 | | Treasury bond |
| Discount/JHS | 8% | | futures contract @ |
| Cost | | $ 33,750.00 | 100.18 (Yield 7.943) |
| 2100 DBF | @ 16.50 | | |
| NAV/DBF | 20.29 | | (Current market for |
| Discount/DBF | 18.7% | | TSY 8s—2001:101.15- |
| Cost | | 34,650.00 | 23) |
| 2300 PAI | @ 13.625 | | |
| NAV/PAI | 15.73 | | |
| Discount/PAI | 13.4% | | |
| Cost | | 31,337.50 | |
| Total cost | | $ 99,737.50 | |

FEBRUARY 10, 1978 (DJ BOND AVG. 89.79)

| Sell | | | Buy to cover | |
|---|---|---|---|---|
| 2000 JHS | @ 17.375 | | September U.S. | |
| NAV/JHS | 17.76 | | Treasury bond | |
| Discount/JHS | 2.2% | | futures contract @ | |
| Proceeds | | $ 34,750.00 | 96.12 (Yield 8.377) | |
| 2100 DBF | @ 16.625 | | | |
| NAV/DBF | 19.50 | | | |
| Discount/DBF | 14.7% | | (Current market for | |
| Proceeds | | 34,912.50 | TSY 8s—2001:97.18-26) | |
| 2300 PAI | @ 13.75 | | | |
| NAV/PAI | 15.63 | | | |
| Discount/PAI | 12% | | | |
| Proceeds | | 31,625.00 | | |
| Total Proceeds | | $ 101,287.50 | | |
| Long position gain | | $ 1,550 | Short position gain | $5,187.50 |
| | Total gain = $6,737.50* | | | |

*Not adjusted for dividends received or trading expenses incurred.

for a cost of $31,337.50. The combination of these purchases amounted to a long position investment of $99,737.50.

Two things must be kept in mind when establishing a long position in this kind of hedge. First, since Treasury bond futures contracts represent face value of $100,000 worth of Treasury bonds, the investor will want to go long approximately $100,000 worth of closed-end bond funds. When it comes to trading closed-end bond funds, I do not recommend buying more than 2000 or 3000 shares of a single fund for a short-term trade. That is why we would go long three different closed-end funds, representing positions of from $31,000 to $34,000 and amounting to approximately $100,000. That $100,000 long position offset the short position of 1 September U.S. Treasury bond futures contract at 100.18, priced at a 7.943 yield.

On February 10, 1978, with the Dow Jones bond average down to 89.79, two significant changes had taken place since we established our theoretical long and short positions: the long positions in the bond funds had become profitable, and so had the short position in the Treasury bond futures contract. For example, JHS was selling at $17\frac{3}{8}$, up from $16\frac{7}{8}$; DBF was up to $16\frac{5}{8}$ from $16\frac{1}{2}$; and PAI had gone from $13\frac{5}{8}$ to $13\frac{3}{4}$. The net asset values of all three funds had declined but the discounts, as predicted, narrowed more than the decline in net asset values, resulting in the profits.

The proceeds from the sale of the long positions on February 10 would have been $101,287.50, resulting in a gain of $1550. Covering the short position in the Treasury bond futures contract would have been at 96.12, resulting in a profit of $5187.50 and a total gain on the long and short transactions of $6737.50.

It should be pointed out that the type of hedge we have just described is primarily directed to the institutional investor. At the same time, it is designed to demonstrate to all investors some of the key advantages obtainable in trading bond funds as opposed to dealing strictly in straight corporate bonds.

Now let's turn to the sort of hedges which can be achieved with specialty funds.

## SPECIALTY FUND HEDGES

In this area, utility funds offer several interesting possibilities for profit, and especially when it comes to going long a utility fund and selling short utility stocks in which the fund holds major positions. This strategy is presented in Table 9.7 and is based on American Utility Shares (AU).

At the end of March 1977, AU was selling in the $11-11\frac{1}{4}$ range with a net asset value of $14.50 and a discount of 23 percent. The cost of 2300 shares would have been $25,587.50.

Among the fund's leading holdings were AT&T, Delmarva Power,

**TABLE 9.7**
**Going Long a Utility Fund and Selling Short the Fund's Major Positions**

### END OF MARCH 1977

| Go long | | Sell short | | | |
|---|---|---|---|---|---|
| | | Quantity | Stock | Price | Proceeds |
| 2300 AU @ | 11.00–11.25 | 100 | T | 62.75 | $ 6,275.00 |
| NAV/AU | 14.50 | 100 | GTE | 29.625 | 2,962.50 |
| Discount/AU | 23% | 100 | DEW | 13.25 | 1,325.00 |
| Cost | 25,587.50 | 100 | GTU | 13.00 | 1,300.00 |
| | | 100 | SCE | 23.50 | 2,350.00 |
| | | 100 | SO | 16.50 | 1,650.00 |
| | | 100 | ALG | 29.75 | 2,975.00 |
| | | 100 | CPL | 22.375 | 2,375.50 |
| | | 100 | CMS | 21.75 | 2,175.00 |
| | | 100 | IPL | 23.50 | 2,350.00 |
| Total proceeds | | | | | $25,600.00 |

### END OF JULY 1977

| Sell | | Buy to cover | | | |
|---|---|---|---|---|---|
| | | Quantity | Stock | Price | Cost |
| 2300 AU @ | 13.25 | 100 | T | 62.75 | $ 6,275.00 |
| NAV/AU | 15.90 | 100 | GTE | 32.625 | 3,262.50 |
| Discount/AU | 17% | 100 | DEW | 14.25 | 1,425.00 |
| Proceeds | $30,475.00 | 100 | GTU | 13.75 | 1,375.00 |
| | | 100 | SCE | 26.25 | 2,625.00 |
| | | 100 | SO | 17.125 | 1,712.50 |
| | | 100 | ALG | 33.50 | 3,350.00 |
| | | 100 | CPL | 24.625 | 2,462.50 |
| | | 100 | CMS | 24.00 | 2,400.00 |
| | | 100 | IPL | 26.25 | 2,625.00 |
| | | Total cost | | | $27,512.50 |
| Long position gain | $4,887.50 | Short position | loss | | $ 1,912.50 |
| | Net gain = $2,975.00* | | | | |

*Not counting trading expenses.

Gulf States Utilities, Southern California Edison, Southern Company, Arkansas Louisiana Gas, Carolina Power and Light, Consumers Power, and Indianapolis Power and Light. A 100-share short sale in each of these stocks would have resulted in proceeds of $25,600.

By the end of July 1977, AU's discount had narrowed to 17 percent, its net asset value was 15.90, and its per share price had increased to 13¼. Selling the 2300 shares would have brought $30,475, for a gain on the long position of \$4887.50. However, the cost to cover the short positions on the utility stocks would have been \$27,512.50, or a loss of \$1,912.50. This transaction is a perfect example of the fact that hedges do not and will not necessarily work profitably on both sides. At the same time—and of primary importance—is that the hedge did accomplish its original goals, protection and profit, in this case a profit of \$2975, despite the loss in covering the short stocks.

But let's wind up this chapter on an all-around positive note, and let's do it with that variety of funds that have an appeal all their own—closed-end gold funds.

As we have already pointed out, Anglo-American Gold Investment (AAGIY) and ASA Limited (ASA) have portfolios which are quite similar. They both hold substantial positions in West Driefontein Gold Mining, East Driefontein Gold Mining, Vaal Reefs Exploration & Mining, President Brand Gold Mining, Western Deep Levels, St. Helena Gold Mines, and Elandsrand.

However, there were differences which had to be considered. As Table 9.8 shows, at the end of 1976 AAGIY was selling at a discount of about 12.3 percent with a net asset value of 19.25. The cost of 5000

**TABLE 9.8**
**Going Long Anglo-American Gold Investment (AAGIY) and Short ASA (or ASA Calls)**

YEAR-END 1976

| | Go long | | | Sell short | | |
|---|---|---|---|---|---|---|
| 5000 AAGIY | @ 16.875 (net) | | | 4000 ASA @ 21.125 | | |
| NAV/AAGIY | 19.25 | | | NAV/ASA | 15.91 | |
| Discount/AAGIY | 12.3% | | | Premium/ASA | 33 % | |
| Cost | | $ 84,375 | | Proceeds | | $84,500 |

YEAR-END 1977

| | Sell | | | Buy to cover | | |
|---|---|---|---|---|---|---|
| 5000 AAGIY | @ 21.50 (net) | | | 4000 ASA @ 20.50 | | |
| NAV/AAGIY | 25.02 (approx.) | | | NAV/ASA | 19.90 | |
| Discount/AAGIY | 14.1 (approx.) | | | Premium/ASA | 3 % | |
| Proceeds | | $107,500 | | Cost | | $82,000 |
| Long position gain | | $ 23,125 | Short position gain | | | $ 2,500 |
| | | Total gain = $25,625* | | | | |

*Not counting commissions (1976–1977, NAV/AAGIY + approx. 30%; NAV/ASA + 25.1%).

shares of the fund at 16⅞ (net) would have been $84,375. At the same time, one could have bought stocks like West Driefontein, Vaal Reefs, and Elandsrand at a discount through purchasing AAGIY, or one could have bought them at a premium, or, as we shall show, sold them short at a premium—as we would have done using ASA as our vehicle.

The strategically correct move was to sell short 4000 shares of ASA at 21⅛. The proceeds from the sale would have been $84,500, with the fund at a 33 percent premium and a net asset value at the time of 15.91.

A year later, AAGIY, selling at a discount which had not changed considerably, had a per share price that had risen to 21.50. At that price, the proceeds from the sale of the 5000 shares would have been $107,500, for a gain of $23,125.

While AAGIY's net asset value had risen in the year to about 25.02 and while it had a discount of approximately 14.1 percent, the premium on its "sister" fund, ASA, had been almost wiped out. ASA's net asset value had risen to $19.90 and its price had dropped to 20.50, leaving it with a premium of but 3 percent. The cost to cover the 4000 shares of ASA was $82,000, producing a gain from the short sale of $2500. This meant that the total gain from both the long and short positions would have been $25,625.

It is hoped that this chapter has taken much of the mystery out of hedging and arbitrage. Our aim has been to prove that hedging and arbitrage are not conducted by an elitist band of super mathematicians, but that they are essentially straightforward strategies involving simple mathematics.

## NOTES

[1] *The Language of Investing*, published by The New York Stock Exchange.

[2] Frank G. Zarb and Gabriel T. Kerekes, *The Stock Market Handbook: A Reference Manual for the Securities Industry*, Dow Jones-Irwin, Homewood, Ill., 1970.

[3] Ibid.

[4] *Hedging Interest Rate Risks*, published by The Chicago Board of Trade, p. 41

[5] Zarb, op. cit.

# Open Ending, Takeovers, and Reorganizations

# 10

Since Wall Street appears to have an insatiable appetite for takeover and reorganization candidates, it was virtually inevitable that the closed-end fund group would become an item on the menu. It should be kept in mind, however, that the usual closed-end fund reorganization attempt or procedure is unlike the takeover of an industrial company in at least one very important respect: a closed-end fund reorganization is usually not attempted by an outsider group or a rival company, but rather by the shareholders of the closed-end fund itself through the process called open ending.

To understand what is behind open ending, one must remember the basic difference between a CEIT and a mutual fund, which we discussed in depth in Chapter 1. That difference, which bears repeating here, lies in the fact that a mutual fund continually issues and redeems shares at a price based on its current net asset value, while a CEIT, on the other hand, has a fixed capitalization whose per share price is determined by supply and demand in the open market.

It also bears repeating that almost all closed-end funds trade at discounts from their net asset value. Given a hypothetical closed-end fund with a NAV of $10 a share and a market price of $5—that is, selling at a 50 percent discount—the shareholders could eliminate the painful discount by voting to convert the closed-end fund into an open-end fund, that is, a mutual fund. After the conversion is completed, the shares of the fund could be redeemed at their NAV, thus completely erasing the discount.

Many highly qualified observers believe that the open-ending concept may very well be the finish of closed-end funds as a group. I, most definitely, am not one of them. Here, in addition to discussing the concept of open ending in depth, I intend to show why some funds will probably be vulnerable to open ending, and why most others may not. The result, therefore, will be that the group will remain substantially intact.

One of the first questions asked by most novices in the CEIT field is usually, "Why don't the shareholders of all CEITS trading at discounts vote to convert them into open-ended mutual funds?" The fact is that since 1966 many have: in the past 13 years, 12 closed-end funds have been open-ended, liquidated, or reorganized. The primary obstacle to conversion is, more often than not, a fund's management. Quite obviously, since the management fee is based on a percentage of a fund's assets, open ending is fraught with danger for management, because it could very well be followed by large-scale redemptions which would shrink the asset base on which the management fee is based. It should be noted that some funds such as Adams Express, Madison Fund, and U.S. & Foreign Securities are internally managed whereas most funds as a rule are externally managed under advisory contracts. The concept, nevertheless, of management compensation bearing directly on the size of the fund is essentially the same.

When a reorganization proposal is initiated not by management but by an outside stockholder, the odds are heavily against the adoption of the proposal on the first attempt. Thus far, the managements of the following funds have successfully resisted reorganization efforts: U.S. & Foreign Securities (twice), TriContinental (four times), Lehman (four times), and Central Securities (three times). Of the 12 funds which have been reorganized since 1966, 5 heeded the urgings of stockholders, promoting the change without obstruction. They are M. A. Hanna, Surveyor, Griesedick, Keystone OTC Fund, and Boston Personal Property Trust, the first closed-end fund formed in the United States.

One fund, Consolidated Investment Trust, open-ended for the sole purpose of avoiding a takeover by Madison Fund. United Corporation partially liquidated and partially merged with D. H. Baldwin Company for a number of reasons, including "threatened and rumored takeovers by foreign and other interests," according to the fund's proxy statement of December 19, 1977.

Five funds were open-ended at the initiative of outside shareholders and against the will of the directors. They are Dominick, International Holdings, Advance Investors, American Utility Shares and National Aviation.

(A personal note is necessary. With enthusiasm for open ending seeming to be at a high in recent years, I have been approached by individuals and institutions encouraging me to take one of two roles: to invest for them, on a passive basis, in closed-end funds I believed were candidates for open ending or to take an active role in forcing such funds to go open-end. I concede I have been involved in both situations.)

Now it is time to look at six different aspects of open ending and takeovers: the usual shareholder positions; the typical management responses to open-ending proposals; my opinions on both of the above; various approaches to open ending; an examination of successes and failures in open ending, including charts to demonstrate the effect when a fund open-ends; and, finally, a look at other forms of closed-end fund reorganizations.

## SHAREHOLDER POSITIONS

Of course, the most significant and cogent shareholder argument in favor of open ending a fund is that the changeover would immediately eliminate the discount. This is because, quite simply, shares would be redeemable at NAV. I have estimated that in recent years the aggregate discount of closed-end funds as a group represents a figure approaching 1 billion dollars. In a similar vein, other proponents of open ending argue that when a CEIT's shares are selling at a substantial discount from NAV, the fund is susceptible to what they themselves might be planning—a raid, only this time by "outsiders," whose goal is the management contract of the fund, not elimination of the discount. Open ending, these individuals say, could prevent such an incursion.

Advocates of conversion to the open-end form assert that it provides not only increased values for stockholders, but also greatly increases liquidity, since shares are readily redeemable at NAV in unlimited quantity. They also assert that the directors of closed-end funds have a fiduciary duty to promote the interests of stockholders, in good faith, without regard to their own selfish interests. Here, they insist, the interests of stockholders cannot but be enhanced by the elimination of the discount and cannot but be damaged when they are unable to realize the full NAV of their investment.

In this regard, a fascinating point of view was expressed by a holder of shares in a closed-end fund whose management performed the same functions for an open-end fund. He questioned why shareholders of the open-end fund were able to receive the full net asset value of their shares, while those owning the closed-end fund—operated by the same management—had to sell those shares at a discount. For him there was a bitter irony in the fact that in the case of these two funds, the quality of research and advice was the same for both the open-end fund and the CEIT.

## MANAGEMENT POSITIONS

The management positions in regard to open ending are much lengthier and more comprehensive than those of shareholders. CEIT managements in the early 1940s formed what is now known as the Association of Publicly Traded Funds to deal with the open ending and other industry matters. From most of the shareholder proposals to open-end that I have studied in proxy statements, it appears that individual managements use virtually the same standard arguments to defend against open-ending attempts. The arguments or positions are essentially:

1. That open ending would reduce a closed-end fund's income. By this, management usually means that redemptions would cause a shrinkage of a fund's asset base and therefore increase its expense ratio, resulting in a reduction of income to shareholders.

2. That large cash reserves for possible redemptions would have to be maintained. Such reserves, management claims, could prevent a fund from making prudent investments.

3. That it would be difficult for a fund to invest in less liquid securities, because in the event of large-scale redemptions, it might have trouble selling such securities at fair prices to raise cash to meet those redemptions.

4. That it would be more difficult for an open-end fund to borrow money than it would be for a CEIT.

5. That transfer costs would increase. This is because shares in closed-end funds are often held by brokers in "street name," while those in open-end funds are generally registered in the owners' names. Additional arguments regarding expenses are that conversion from closed-end to open-end status is a costly procedure, involving prospectuses and other expenditures which would have to be borne by shareholders, and that if a closed-end fund were open-ended, the cost of the fund would have to be divided among fewer shareholders.

6. That a CEIT's yield would be less attractive if it were open-ended. For example, a CEIT selling at $10 with a NAV of 12 paying an 80-cent dividend is yielding 8 percent. If that fund were open-ended and

selling at $12 a share, the 80-cent dividend would result in a yield of only 6.7 percent.

7. That the flow of funds in and out of mutual funds is very unpredictable. As a result, large redemptions could force sales of stock at inopportune times, and investments in smaller companies would also have to be reduced.

8. That sales efforts for open-end funds are costly.

9. That it would not be eligible for margin and that it would be disqualified for holdings by some institutional investors.

10. That a closed-end structure makes it easier to attract and keep good personnel.

11. That liquidation of a fund, as opposed to open ending, is costly. Here managements say that forced selling drives down the price of stocks and that the fund will incur such expenses as brokerage commissions and transfer taxes.

12. That a closed-end structure has been a significant element in the past success of a fund and therefore, by implication, would continue to be one in the future.

***Additional Key Management Arguments.*** There are three other key arguments made by closed-end fund managements in favor of keeping the status quo and against open ending.

The first of these, in a broad sense, has to do with the "attitude" of shareholders of a closed-end fund. Some closed-end fund managements claim that open-end attempts are the work of a minority of individuals who acquire stock solely with the goal of making a quick profit. Such shareholders are acting against the best interests of long-term shareholders, it is argued. In the same vein, managements have charged that open-ending is detrimental to individuals participating in a CEIT's dividend reinvestment plan, because if a fund were open-ended, they would no longer be able to buy their share at a discount. (On the lighter side, there was the surprising claim of one CEIT's management which stated it was advising against conversion to an open-end fund because such a switch might make it difficult for investors to find another suitable investment.)

The next key management argument concerns the discount. When opposing an open-ending attempt, most CEIT managements point out that the discount has been steady over recent years and that most investors who buy shares in CEITs do so at discounts and are not disappointed when they continue to trade at less than net asset value.

This argument is often supported by managements' claim that if shareholders wanted to invest in an open-end fund, they could have bought stock in one at net asset value.

Some managements also defend the discount by saying it is merely a result of lack of information concerning closed-end funds. Here they seem to be implying that if the investing public were better informed on CEITs, their shares would no longer sell at discounts. Carrying this argument a step farther, managements have attempted to stop efforts to open-end by saying that their funds may sell at premiums in the future, as some have in various periods in the past. This argument is, of course, at odds with another management point—that the discount is an advantage to investors who wish to purchase more stock in a CEIT.

Then there is a kind of middle ground, with managements saying that over the long haul the discounts in their funds have decreased.

(Lehman's management, trying to work its way out of the discount dilemma, at one time attributed part of their discount to European selling of shares caused by devaluation of the dollar.)

In one form or another, I've seen the following statement issued by several CEIT managements attempting to ward off an open-ending attempt: "All closed-end funds trade at discounts. Our fund is no exception." Then the managements will go on to cite any or all of the arguments against open ending which I have listed above, giving great emphasis to the fact that open-end funds are plagued by redemptions and why invite this sort of trouble? Besides, managements will frequently state in their final defense that it is their *belief* that most shareholders rightly want to preserve the closed-end status anyway.

The third key management argument against open ending is probably the most important. That argument holds that open ending could cause adverse tax consequences. It is an argument worth dwelling on.

There are two tax considerations to bear in mind in a possible open-ending situation. The first concerns a closed-end fund that holds stocks in which there are large, unrealized capital gains. If those stocks are sold, the capital gains must be distributed to shareholders in order for the fund to continue to be eligible for favored tax treatment. Such a distribution creates a capital gains tax liability for all shareholders. If a fund were dissolved or liquidated, such a capital gains tax liability would very likely occur in funds which are very old or have been very successful.

The second aspect of the tax consideration appears when a CEIT is open-ended and some shareholders want to redeem their holdings. This could force the fund to sell stocks in which it would realize large capital gains, thereby subjecting all shareholders of the fund to the capital gains tax liability.

## ASSESSMENT OF THE SHAREHOLDER POSITIONS

Now I would like to give my personal views on some of the open-ending and takeover views of dissatisfied holders of shares in closed-end funds. What strikes me immediately after reading the management views, which on the surface appear to be convincing, is that one would think that with such lengthy and numerous objections to the open-end fund one would assume that most funds are closed-end. As we have discussed previously this is not the case; quite the contrary, the overwhelming majority of funds since the Depression are in fact open-end.

When it comes to the subject of eliminating the discount in CEITs, perhaps the best comment I have seen was in Benjamin Graham's *The Intelligent Investor*. There he says: "The price discount of these companies may be viewed as an expensive monument erected to the inertia and stupidity of the stockholders. It has cost the owners of these businesses countless millions of dollars, yet it has been totally unnecessary. It could have been terminated at any time by the mere passing of a resolution at a stockholders' meeting. Yet the matter never seems to have been brought up for discussion."[1]

I also can say that I can find no argument with the following shareholder positions on open ending: that it would increase the market value and liquidity of the stock; that the directors have a fiduciary responsibility to promote the interest of shareholders; that investors are hurt because they can't realize the full net asset value of their shares; that there is something essentially wrong when the same management provides the same advice to an open-end fund and a closed-end fund and yet investors in the latter cannot realize the full value of their shares.

On the other hand, as this entire book should demonstrate, I do not agree with shareholders who claim that the CEIT structure is outmoded. I am convinced that there is a place and a role for such structures, particularly if they can operate to sustain a low discount factor and further, that they do not have to hold cash reserves for redemptions—as is the case with mutual funds.

## ASSESSMENT OF THE MANAGEMENT POSITIONS

Now I would like to give my views on some of the key positions taken by managements in regard to open ending.

1. That it would reduce the fund's income. I would say that is a faulty argument because it is a question of losing pennies but gaining dollars. If a CEIT is selling at a $2 or $3 discount from NAV and that discount is eliminated, it really does not matter, even if the dividend is decreased by a few cents a share.

2. That large cash reserves would have to be maintained. I disagree with this, because when necessary funds can borrow money to meet redemptions.

3. That a CEIT can invest in less liquid securities. I do not believe that most funds, unless specifically created for that purpose (such as Value Line), whether they are open-end or closed-end, would invest substantial amounts of money in less liquid securities.

4. That open ending would make it more difficult for a fund to borrow. In my opinion, open-end funds should not encounter significantly more difficulty borrowing money than closed-end funds.

5. That transfer costs would increase. Here again we have another question of spending a small fraction of a penny in the process of restoring dollars in realizable values. The same holds true for other management positions on open-end fund expenses, such as the cost of prospectuses.

6. That the yield of any open-end fund will be less attractive. Even if a $1 dividend should go down a penny to 99 cents, that reduction would be abundantly compensated for by a price rise of several dollars to the NAV.

7. That the flow of money in and out of mutual funds is highly unpredictable. For me, that's essentially managements' problem; it should not be a problem for shareholders.

8. That sales campaigns of mutual funds are costly. Shouldn't this too be the problem of management and not of the shareholder?

9. That an open-end fund could not be listed on the New York Stock Exchange or other exchanges and that it would not be eligible for margin. These are valid points of view. However, mutual funds may be used as collateral for bank loans.

10. That a closed-end structure helps attract and keep good personnel. This is a realistic point of view. Certainly, skilled individuals would be reluctant to join a fund which looks like it might go open end and

thus offer less job security. On the other hand, there is more job security at an established open-end fund than at a vulnerable closed-end one.

11. That a closed-end corporate structure is a major element in the success of a fund. This argument could probably be better—and more honestly—stated by rephrasing it to read: a closed-end corporate structure is a major element contributing to management's receiving the maximum of perquisites related as they are to the size of the fund which it runs or advises. I don't believe that, as a group, closed-end funds do any better or any worse than open-end ones. In the top 10 performers year after year there are usually representatives of both closed-end and open-end funds.

12. That open-ending advocates are a minority of shareholders seeking a short-term profit at the expense of long-term investors in a CEIT. My answer is that there is nothing whatsoever wrong with investing for short-term profits. Indeed, does this management argument mean that if a CEIT buys a stock for its portfolio at $25 per share and it goes to $30 quickly, the CEIT should not take the profit because it's a short-term one? Is it ungentlemanly to take short-term profits? What in the world is wrong with taking a profit, long-term or short? How would managements opposed to short-term profits for their stockholders feel about a resolution passed by shareholders forbidding funds from cashing in on the funds' short-term gains in their own portfolios?

13. That discounts of CEITs are a result of lack of information. I believe this position essentially reflects the views of the "Wharton Study," sponsored by the Association of Publicly Traded Funds, with which I am in almost total disagreement. In my opinion, that study is unrealistic and does not address itself to the real problems. Furthermore, the study is quite inconclusive.

14. That closed-end funds may sell at premiums in the future. This management position is quite possible and could very well happen in bull markets. For part of 1961, for instance, a few of the group did sell at premiums. An interesting paradox is that it can become tempting for the management of a closed-end fund selling at a premium to recommend that the fund be open-ended. Management's appraisal in this situation is that if a fund is selling at a premium, there probably would be more buyers of the fund than redeeming shareholders, thus creating an increase in the fund's asset base.

15. That management could not invest in special situations. I can't agree with that point of view, simply because management of a diver-

sified CEIT would not take a truly large position in a special situation. If a special situation attractive to management should come along, they could reduce some of their blue chip holdings in order to take a position, but they certainly would not be inclined to put the bulk of their fund's money into a special situation.

16. That large redemptions can force sales at inopportune times and that greater liquidity would have to be maintained. There is a good deal of validity to both of these positions. They are both quite possible. However, provisions could be made for redemptions in kind as opposed to traditional cash redemptions.

17. That investments in small companies would have to be reduced. Here I do not agree that there would have to be any basic change in a specific fund's investment methods or strategies.

18. That over the long-term the discount has decreased. It is true that discounts in CEITs have been decreasing in recent years, but this is most likely because of speculative purchases of CEIT shares by investors who feel that some of the funds may be open-ended. In cases where funds are not vulnerable to open ending the discounts tend to remain wide.

19. That most closed-end funds sell at discounts because of the capital gains liability. This, as I have noted, is one of the key reasons cited by management against open ending—because it would force sales of stocks in which there are unrealized capital gains, creating a capital gains tax liability for all shareholders, even those who did not want to redeem but remain shareholders of the fund.

Boston Personal Property Trust, the oldest investment company in the United States, found a solution to this problem in 1967. Frankly, I never could understand why it has been overlooked by both the managements and shareholders of other CEITs from the time Boston Personal Property Trust was open-ended.

In a letter dated July 19, 1966, to shareholders of Boston Personal Property Trust, the fund's trustees outlined their solution to open ending the fund without incurring the tax consequences which are generally voiced by most fund managements. That letter said in part:

> The proposal is to amend the Trust so that a shareholder who wishes to dispose of his shares would be able to turn them in for redemption, and the Trust would redeem them by delivering to him in exchange marketable securities, to be selected by the Trust-

## FIGURE 10.1
## General American Investors

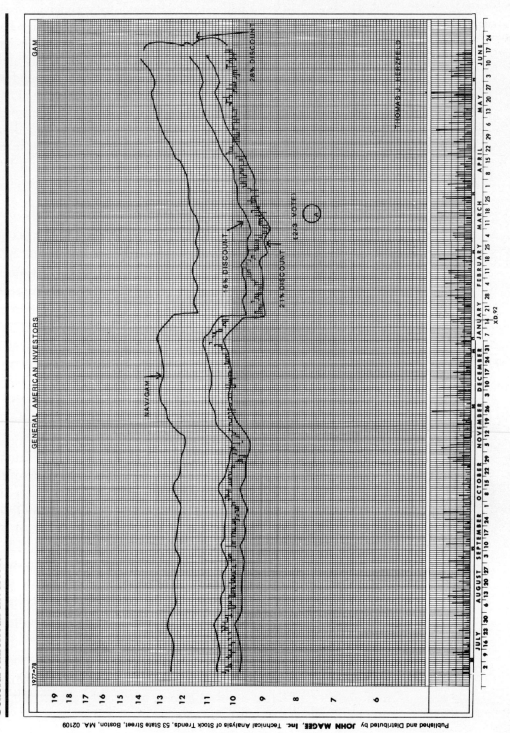

**TEKNIPLAT Chart Paper**

185

ees from the Trust's investments, substantially equal in market value to the net asset value of his Boston Personal Property Trust shares. . . . Counsel for the Trust have advised that on the basis of a preliminary investigation they are of the opinion that under present law the proposal developed by the Trustees is sound and that Federal income tax consequences of such a redemption of shares of the Trust would be that the Trust would not realize taxable gain or loss upon delivery of securities held by it to a redeeming shareholder, and that a redeeming shareholder would realize capital gain or loss measured by the difference between the basis for his shares of the Trust that are redeemed and the value of the securities delivered to him in exchange.

So here we have what I believe to be the solution to the tax question arising when converting a CEIT to an open-end fund: This appears to be confirmed by section 11 (d)(2)(F) of the Internal Revenue Code. According to this section, there is no recognized gain where there is no distribution by a regulated investment company if made in redemption of its stock upon the specific demand of the stockholder of the fund. The particular stock owned by the open-end mutual fund is exchanged for a particular amount of stock of the fund, and on a flow-through basis the fund is not taxed while the stockholder will have a capital gain on the difference between the value of the shares redeemed and his cost basis. (On matters such as the above, I advise that investors seek professional guidance from tax counsel.)

To make the strategy of the Boston Personal Property Trust's management as clear as possible, let's use a hypothetical example. If I own 1000 shares of a closed-end fund with a NAV of $10 that is converted to an open-end fund and I wish to redeem, the fund would not issue me $10,000 in cash. Rather, it would give me $10,000 worth of stock from its portfolio which I could sell in the open market to obtain my cash. As a result, the tax consequences would be mine, not the fund's.

Having given my opinions on most of the management arguments against open ending, I would like to offer one which I have never seen mentioned by advocates of CEITs. It is an argument which is really at the heart of this book, and it is this: closed-end funds are trading vehicles and in open-ending them, you are eliminating nine out of ten advantages in trading them. If an investor could make a single point in trading a CEIT five times in a year, what is the difference to him if that fund sells at a 2-point discount?

Now here is my capsulized appraisal of open ending. If a fund is selling at a 20 to 30 percent discount from its NAV, then in many cases it would be advantageous for its shareholders to convert it to an open-end fund. Furthermore, it is especially desirable to open-end funds which have poor track records, high expense ratios, and liquid portfolios. The big loser in this case would be the fund's management, not its shareholders, but the welfare of management should not be an overwhelming concern of shareholders. It is the shareholders' welfare which should be the primary concern of management.

## VARIOUS APPROACHES TO OPEN ENDING

The most common way to convert a CEIT to an open-end fund is by proxy solicitation. It should be pointed out, however, that in most states, shareholders cannot vote directly to open-end a fund; they can only vote to recommend that the directors reorganize the fund. But even though a vote to open-end is a recommendation which directors are not legally bound to follow, I do not believe a fund's directors could morally ignore it.

Another way to open-end a fund is through a tender offer. A group can make an offer for over 50 percent of a CEIT and once it has effective control, it can take the necessary steps to open-end the fund.

Management, on its side, has ways to prevent or forestall open ending. General American Investors' management succeeded in putting through a proposal changing the vote required to open-end the fund from one-half to two-thirds of all shares outstanding. This may have caused the discount of the fund to widen (see Figure 10.1). Before the vote, which took place in March 1978, the fund had been selling at a discount of between 15 and 21 percent. After the vote, Point A, the discount widened to 28 percent. GAM's management, to the best of my knowledge, was the first to initiate the two-thirds proposal. In light of the widening of the fund's discount after the vote, I consider it surprising that other funds have followed this strategy.

## SOME FUNDS WHICH WERE OPEN-ENDED

For the record, let's take a brief look at some of the more interesting funds which were open-ended or reorganized in recent years.

In 1966, the M. A. Hanna Company, a very large CEIT, was liquidated. At the time, Hanna was selling at about $40 a share, approximately a 25 percent discount from its NAV of $51. Hanna, a Cleveland-based company formed in 1885, owned a large minority interest in Hanna Mining. It also had principal investments in National Steel, Consolidation Coal, Standard Oil of New Jersey, and Texaco. The company said the decision to liquidate stemmed partly from potentially heavy capital gains that would make it impossible to diversify the holdings of the company without incurring major tax liabilities. Management also cited the 25 to 30 percent discount from NAV as a factor in its decision to liquidate.

Before it was open-ended in 1967, Boston Personal Property Trust, a diversified, nonleveraged closed-end fund, had been trading on the Boston Stock Exchange at a discount of more than 20 percent from its NAV.

When it was open-ended in 1967, Consolidated Investment Trust had a portfolio which was concentrated in common stocks and was traded over the counter. Its discount at the time of conversion was slightly above 20 percent.

In 1973, the closed-end Surveyor Fund merged with Eberstadt Fund, an open-end fund. The surviving company was Surveyor Fund which operated on an open-end basis. Before the merger, Surveyor, which was internally managed, had a net asset value of about 25.60 and had about 5 million shares outstanding. Eberstadt's NAV was about 9.84, with about 2.8 million shares outstanding.

The Dominick Fund was the next CEIT to be open-ended—in 1974. This fund, which had been traded on the New York Stock Exchange, was about 90 percent invested in common stocks. In 1962 it was selling at a 4 percent premium, but that disappeared by 1965, and like most of the other closed-end funds was selling at a substantial discount of 22 percent.

The discount of International Holdings Corporation had hit 40 percent in the beginning of 1975. This prompted the management in March of 1975 to form a committee to explore reorganization possibilities, which included merger, liquidation, or conversion of the company into an open-end fund. Later that year, International Holdings agreed to merge with Chesapeake Dollar Fund Limited, which would operate as an open-end fund.

Originally, the management of Advance Investors opposed openending the fund. However, a shareholder vote in 1976 was 25 percent in favor of conversion. Three days after that vote management decided to abandon the battle and recommended the change to open-end status.

An interesting change took place in 1978, when United Corporation was merged with D. H. Baldwin Company to form Baldwin United. At the time, United's shareholders were given the opportunity to take shares in the newly formed company or to receive the adjusted net asset value of United.

***Charts of Funds Which Were Open-Ended.*** Figure 10.2 on American Utility Shares (AU) provides us with a good example of what the effect of an open-end vote will be on the discount of a CEIT. AU usually traded at a discount ranging between 26 and 18 percent before the open-end vote. The vote came in November 1977 (Point A). The discount immediately narrowed to between 8 and 10 percent after the vote.

Compare this narrowing of the discount after a successful open-ending vote to the widening of the discount in GAM (Figure 10.1) after the passage of the management proposal which changed the requirement to open-end from a one-half to a two-thirds vote.

Note that, until the last day of trading in AU, which was July 28, 1978 (see Figure 10.3, Point A), the fund sold at a discount. Shares bought at 14.50 on July 28 could have been converted into 4.534 shares of Lord Abbett Income Fund (LAIF) the following week and redeemed at $3.33 or the equivalent of 15.10 in old shares of AU. The net asset value of LAIF (Point B) rose. In addition, record-breaking volume in Wall Street caused back office delays in redemptions. Such delays added an unexpected bonus to the AU trade.

During the period between the vote and the eventual open ending (in this case a merger with an open-end fund) the fund traded at a discount because of three factors:

1. The market risk that the NAV could decline before the eventual merger.

2. The time factor. An arbitrageur would have had his money tied up for almost a year before he could redeem at net asset value.

3. Possible snags in the reorganization. The shareholders had to approve the final merger, or the SEC could have questioned the reorganization plan.

**FIGURE 10.2**
**American Utility Shares after Open-End Vote**

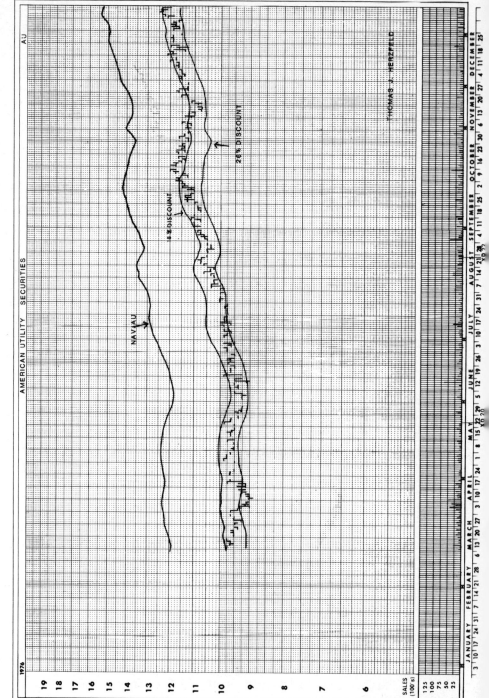

**TEKNIPLAT Chart Paper**

190

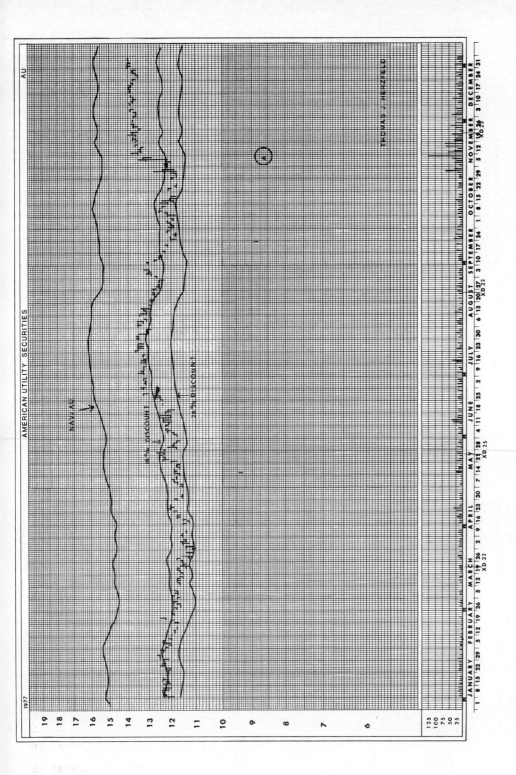

AMERICAN UTILITY SECURITIES

THOMAS J. HERZFELD

191

**FIGURE 10.2**
**American Utility Shares after Open-End Vote** *(Cont.)*

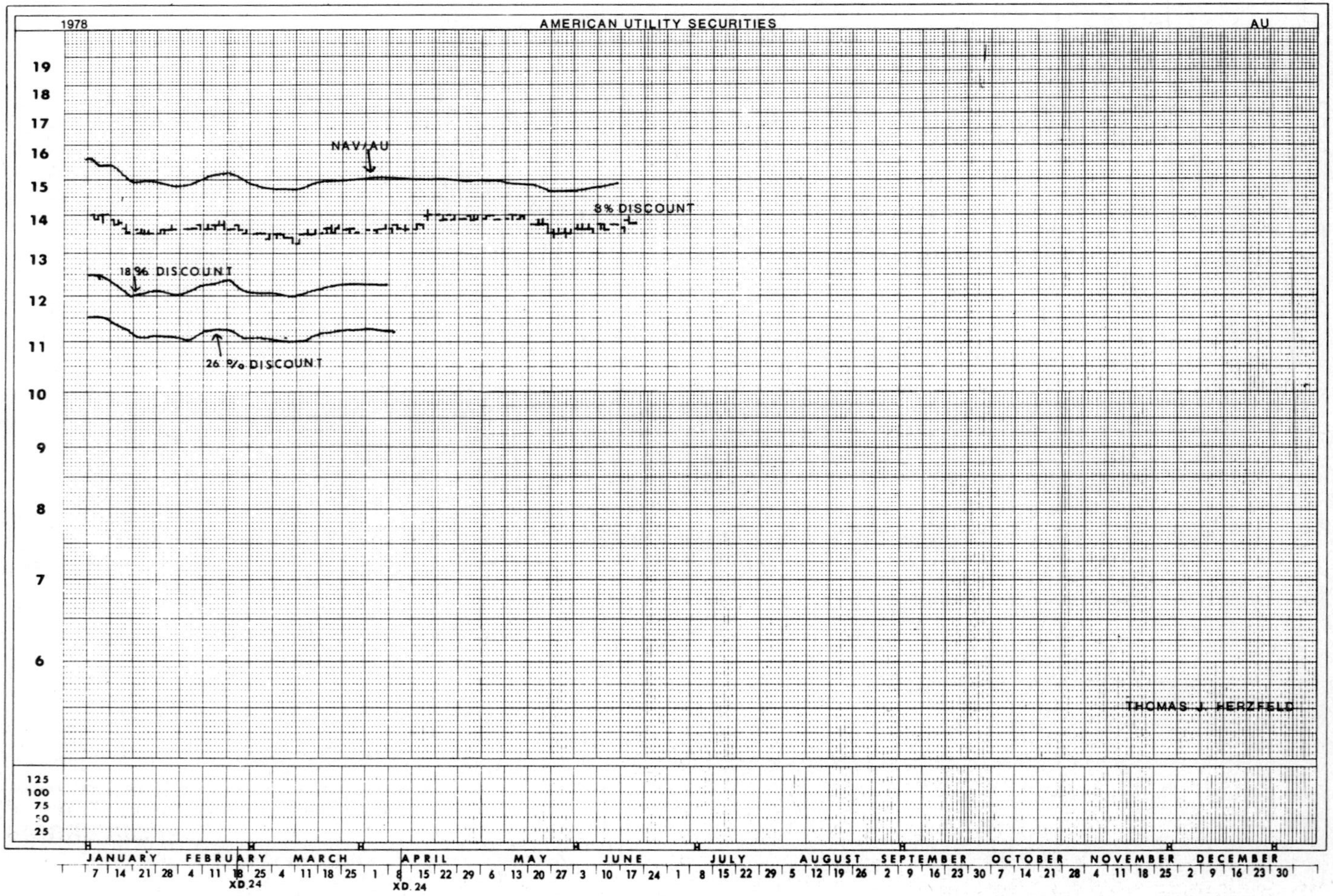

AMERICAN UTILITY SECURITIES

**FIGURE 10.3**
**American Utility Shares (Final Days)**

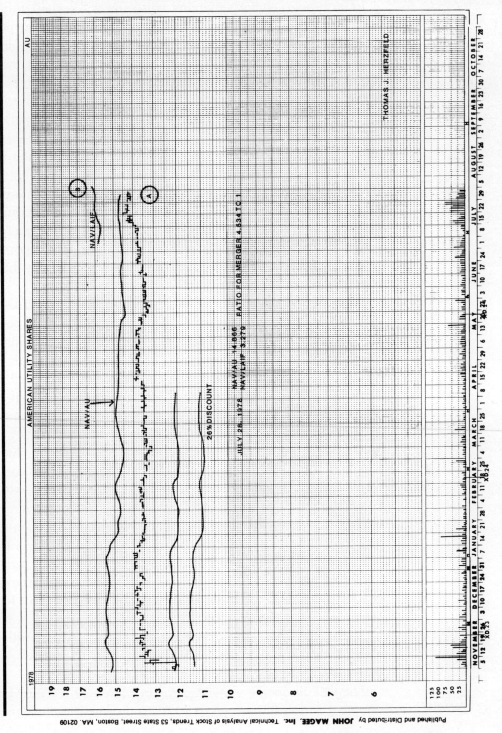

**TEKNIPLAT Chart Paper**

In most open-ending situations a discount will remain until the final day. Figure 10.4 shows the price of United Corporation prior to its merger with D. H. Baldwin Company. United traded at a discount as large as 17 percent in 1977 even though the merger was announced (Point A). It was not until the day before the merger was effective that the discount disappeared (Point B). The United merger, however, had several other variables causing the discount in the final period before the merger besides the three mentioned earlier. There were adjustments in the NAV for tax liabilities as well as the sale of a subsidiary before the redemption could be made. Also, only a percentage of the shareholders could redeem their shares. In the event of more redemptions than the percentage allowed by the merger, the remaining shareholders would have been forced to take shares in the merged company. The investing public realized that United Corporation was selling at too large a discount in the final weeks before the merger. Notice the high volume during that period (Point C).

In the period before August 1977 National Aviation and Technology (NTA) was trading in a range between approximately a 35 percent and a 21 percent discount. I had been recommending and buying NTA on the theory that it was an open-end candidate because of its large discount and liquid portfolio. I was, therefore, not surprised when on August 10, 1977, Neuberger and Berman announced that they had acquired over 5 percent of NTA's stock. The net asset value of NTA at the time was 23.80, and the price was about 18 (Point A in Figure 10.5). NTA's management then announced that it was studying the possibility of open-ending the fund, and the game was on. The discount narrowed to 15 percent after that announcement, as shown at Point A-1. In December 1977 (Point B) Neuberger and Berman offered to merge NTA into their Partners Fund—an open-end fund. The discount on this announcement narrowed to 13 percent.

In January 1978 (Point C) the management of NTA said it would hope to make a tender for some of its shares, and it recommended against the merger proposal of Neuberger and Berman. This was a good try by management, but it did not work.

A few days later Hobart Associates announced that with another group it had acquired over 130,000 shares of NTA and would make a shareholder proposal to open-end the fund.

The vote to open-end NTA came in March 1978 (Point D). It took one week to count the votes, a good sign for the shareholders, because

**FIGURE 10.4**
**United Corporation Shortly before Open Ending**

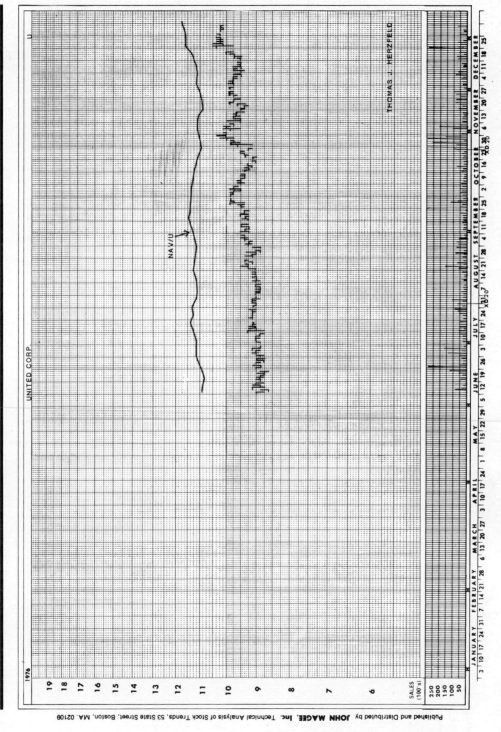

**FIGURE 10.4**
United Corporation Shortly before Open Ending   (Cont.)

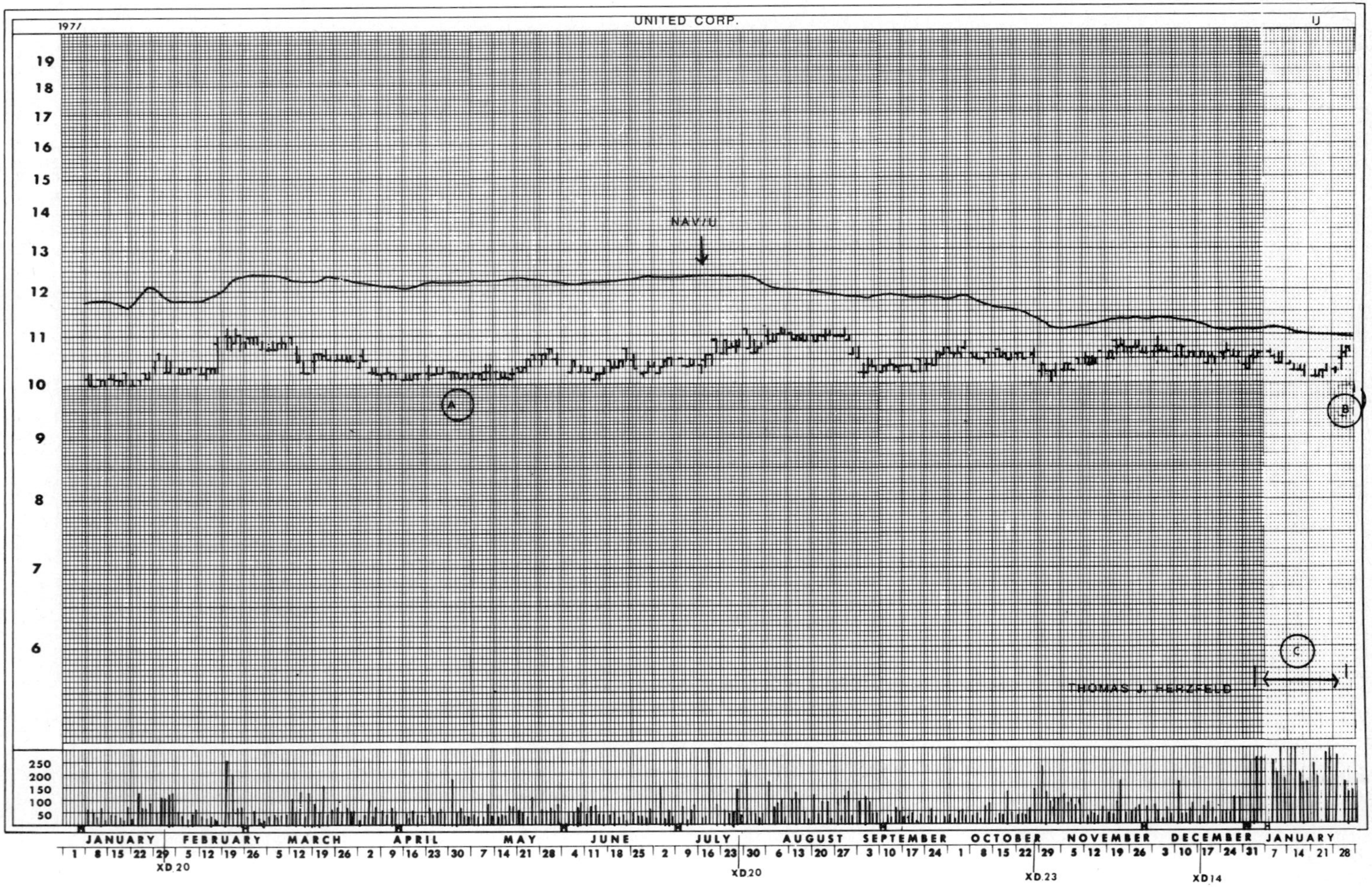

FIGURE 10.5
National Aviation and Technology Shortly before Open Ending

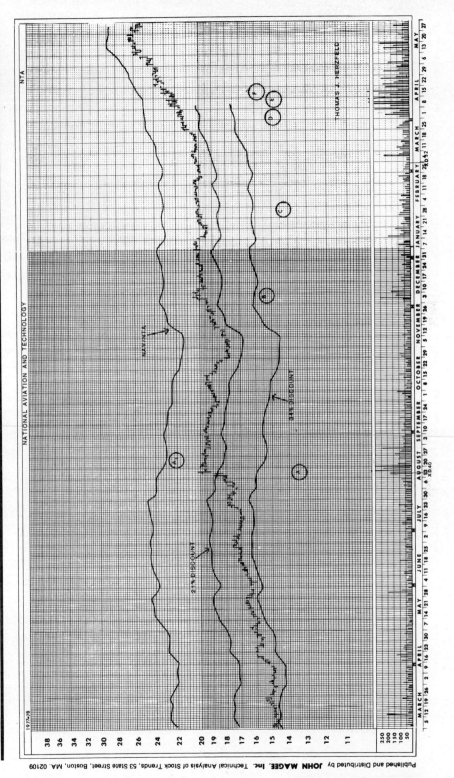

Published and Distributed by JOHN MAGEE, Inc. Technical Analysis of Stock Trends, 53 State Street, Boston, MA. 02109

when management wins there is usually a fast announcement. The results of the vote were announced on April 5, 1978 (Point *E*). The vote passed narrowly, despite the strong management opposition. This vote was, however, a *recommendation* to directors to open-end the fund. The management still had to accept the recommendation, formulate a plan, and submit it to stockholders for fund approval.

On April 13, 1978, the management announced it would take steps necessary to change NTA to an open-end fund (Point *F*).

During this entire episode the net asset value of NTA was rising very impressively. By August 1978 it was over 35, while a year earlier it had been approximately 23. Not only had the vote caused the discount to narrow, but combined with the rise in net asset value, the price of NTA moved from 15 in the beginning of 1977 to 32 by August 1978.

Reasons for the remaining 13 percent discount in the middle of 1978 were listed previously but, to repeat, they were (1) the market risk of a declining NAV, (2) the time lag before reorganization is completed, (3) the conversion is subject to a final vote and possible regulatory snags. The NTA episode was indeed one of the more exciting and, of course, more profitable ones.

## SOME FINAL THOUGHTS ON OPEN ENDING

***Odds in Open-Ending Attempts.*** When it comes to open-ending attempts, the odds are basically in favor of management. Here's a biting example: shareholders are limited as to how much they can say in a proxy statement in support of their recommendations. For instance, they are allowed only 200 words. However, there is no such damper on management. It has unlimited space to give its point of view.

Furthermore, management has the opportunity to see the shareholder proposal, examine it thoroughly and review it with attorneys, etc., and then make a response. The shareholder has no such advance opportunity to see the management response.

Management is spending the company's money to fight the proposal whereas the shareholder who makes an independent solicitation is spending his own money.

When it comes to a vote, most shareholders will tend to follow management's recommendations out of habit. They do not even have to mark their ballots for or against any of the proposals on the proxy statement. The proxy instrument can be so worded as to permit management to vote every unmarked ballot the way it wants to. The rules of the Securities and Exchange Commission permit this.

***Open-Ending Attempts on Bond Funds.*** At this writing, no open-ending attempt has been made on any of the bond funds. In my opinion, it is the bond fund group which should receive the attention of those interested in forcing open-ending attempts. While open-ending attempts have already been made on most of the comparatively vulnerable closed-end stock funds, such is not the case with the bond group. The bond funds, particularly those which sell at a discount of more than 15 percent, are in my opinion ripe for open ending or a takeover.

***Outlook for the Future.*** In 1978 California passed Amendment Article 13A, sections 1 and 2 (the so-called Jarvis Amendment), starting what has been called a taxpayers' revolt. I feel such a revolt is brewing among shareholders of CEITs. To prevent this revolt, managements must strive to keep expense ratios down and performance up, or they will be increasingly vulnerable.

## NOTE

[1]Benjamin Graham, *The Intelligent Investor: A Book of Practical Counsel*, 4th rev. ed., Harper & Row, Publishers, New York, 1973.

# Conclusion

One can never write a definitive or complete book on closed-end funds. They are an ever changing subject with a special dynamism all their own. Charts represent a good example of this. They must be continually updated to ensure that they reflect new developments which are taking place. What held true for a particular fund 6 months ago might be grossly inaccurate and misleading today.

Or consider the subject of open ending. Since I began writing this book, several shareholder proposals on open-ending various funds have been made but they have been either changed or withdrawn. Some of the funds which I believed would be open-ended in early 1978 are still closed-end vehicles as this book goes to press. On the other hand, funds which I was virtually convinced would not be open-ended in the foreseeable future are now well on their way to being converted.

The entire concept of discounts also has changed during the period in which this book was written. For example, the year 1978 saw a widening of discounts in bond funds, causing me to be less aggressive in my trading than I would have thought possible when I first drafted the chapter on such funds.

Of course, if Wall Street should get into a rip-roaring bull market in the 1980s, fund discounts are going to narrow considerably. In my opinion, the best way for the investor to participate in such a bull market—after so many bearish ones—would be through investing in CEITs selling at discounts. Not only should the net asset values increase substantially in a long-term bull market, but in many cases discounts would also disappear, and I think we would see many CEITs trading at premiums.

If funds should start selling at premiums, one of the major reasons for open ending—the elimination of the discount—would no longer exist for most investors. On the other hand, premiums could very well find individual fund managements reversing themselves and advocating open ending. This would be a result of their belief that while the premiums last, there is a heavy demand for the funds' shares. Open ending would enable managements to sell more shares than are redeemed and to increase their funds' capitalization. Such an increase would, of course, result in higher management fees.

## A WORD ABOUT INSTITUTIONS

In writing this book, I hope I have demonstrated that institutions as well as individuals should be actively interested in investing in closed-end funds. Let's consider a pension fund seeking income. Such a fund, without any doubt on my part, would be better off if it invested in bond funds or stock funds trading at a discount than if it invested in straight bonds or stocks selling at full face value in the open market.

One of the principal problems of institutional investors with closed-end funds has been psychological in nature. An example of this can often be found in bank trust departments which receive fees for managing individual accounts. As a result, the bank trust officers very often cannot justify investing in a closed-end fund because the fund, for its part, is paying a management fee to an investment advisor. There is a sound rebuttal to this fear or reluctance to pay two management fees. It is this: investing in a portfolio of stocks or bonds at discounts from their net asset values more than compensates for paying a double management fee.

Once bank trust officers forget their own egos, they should not have any problem buying a portfolio of stocks through a fund, especially if they are buying the portfolio at a discount. They might even discover that many of the stocks in that portfolio are already on their banks' buy lists.

I am convinced that if institutions such as banks, insurance companies, pension funds, and mutual funds followed the guidelines and trading rules for CEITs which I have outlined in this book, they would, to say the least, significantly outperform the overall stock market. They would also produce results which are superior to those they achieve by buying and selling individual stocks and bonds in the open market.

The frustrating fact is, however, that few institutional investors have recognized the advantages of closed-end funds. It took several years of continuous effort before I received my first closed-end fund order from an institution. Gradually, this sort of business has shown some solid increases. However, I estimate that at present less than 1 percent of the institutions investing in the stock market are buying and selling closed-end funds.

## THE "MUNICIPAL BOND TRAP"

I would like to spend a few moments discussing what I call the "municipal bond trap." If institutional investors are difficult to convert to closed-end fund enthusiasts, wealthy high-income investors were nearly impossible. Gradually, however, such investors are seeing the positive sides of CEITs for several reasons.

The singularly compelling avenue of investment for well-to-do individuals in Wall Street is bordered on one side by tax shelters and on the other by municipal bonds. (Tax shelters have their own serious drawbacks but that's a discussion for another time.)

Let's consider municipal bonds versus closed-end bond funds. Quite obviously, the key attraction of a municipal bond is tax-free income, ranging in recent years from 5 to 6 percent for AAA government guaranteed bonds to 7 or 8 percent on lower-rated issues.

The primary and considerable drawbacks of investing in municipal bonds, especially as compared to a closed-end bond fund are:

1. Interest rates which, when they are rising, force down bond prices

2. The possibility of a default on the payment of interest or principal

3. A relatively illiquid dealer market plagued with large spreads between bid and asked prices

At best, in a neutral interest rate situation, the holder of a muncipal bond can expect to receive tax-free income of about 6 to 8 percent. On the other hand, as pointed out in Chapter 5 on bond funds, a program of bond fund trading, even in a neutral interest rate situation, may produce total returns of 15 to 20 percent and also provide a cushion, should interest rates rise. Furthermore, the funds hold investment grade bonds and have the liquidity of shares traded on the New York Stock Exchange.

Even when subject to taxes at the highest rates, a 15-to-20 percent return in a bond fund program compares highly favorably with the 6 to 8 percent tax-free income of a municipal bond program. This is especially so when one considers the three disadvantages cited above which are inherent in a municipal bond situation.

## A CLOSED-END FUND OF FUNDS

Over the years, some investment bankers as well as some of my accounts have been urging me to form a closed-end fund to trade exclusively in closed-end funds. Frankly, the concept of a closed-end fund of funds intrigues me. Such a fund could employ all of the concepts and trading strategies which I have discussed in this book, plus a few others which are beyond the scope of this book. It could trade in stock and bond funds, do hedging and write options, etc. If the investing public becomes increasingly aware of the opportunities and advantages of both closed-end funds and the fund of funds itself, one of these days this fund may be born.

## SOME CLOSED-END FUND TRADING RULES

Now I would like to offer some trading rules for anyone considering closed-end funds.

• **Rule 1**   Never buy common stocks as long as you trade closed-end funds. To put it bluntly I regard common stocks as a fool's game, primarily because the odds are stacked against the individual investor, beginning with poor research and ending with commission expenses. If half of an investor's trades are profitable and half are not, commissions are bound to cause him to lose money.

In addition, and more importantly, a closed-end fund trader is very likely to become bored and dissatisfied with his profits, if he is simultaneously trading common stocks. This trader might make 10 or even 20 percent a year in closed-end funds, picking up a point here and a point there. And yet, if he makes a killing of 20 or 30 points in a single glamour stock, he'll very likely resent the time and effort he's putting into closed-end fund trading. Of course that killing is a thing of beauty, but a problem arises when the common stock trader inevitably picks a loser which wipes out all of his previous profits.

Closed-end fund traders have all the advantages to be derived from common stocks with a lot less risk, essentially because a CEIT provides a diversified portfolio. The investor in a CEIT enjoys a professionally managed portfolio purchased at an all-important discount from its net asset value. The trader in common stocks, on the other hand, is virtually on his own and besides, he's playing the full market value for his investments.

• **Rule 2**   Don't trade in CEITs unless you are prepared to devote substantial time to the project. CEITs must be continually monitored for changes in their prices, net asset values, changes in their portfolios, and for any and all developments which affect an individual fund as well as its group.

• **Rule 3**   Only trade with a broker who thoroughly understands your investment objectives and, most definitely, the intricacies of closed-end funds and the strategies essential to trading them properly. It must be recognized that only a handful of brokers are qualified to manage closed-end fund trading programs, and they must be carefully sought out. No investor should even consider relying on a broker who barely knows the proper names of the closed-end funds and who dismisses them by mumbling: "Oh, sure, closed-end funds are good buys. They're selling at discounts." CEITs, as this book should have made abundantly clear, are a highly sophisticated subject, requiring careful study and guidance.

• **Rule 4**   If you want to gamble, don't attempt to do so in closed-end funds or in the general market for that matter. It would be better to take whatever money you can safely afford to lose and head for Las Vegas, Atlantic City, or some race track.

Closed-end funds are not for those wanting to take a "flyer." Rather, they require an often tedious and always disciplined trading strategy which over the long haul can add up to substantial gains for the serious investor. In my opinion, such gains from closed-end funds can be achieved with less risk than in any other approach to the stock market.

# Index

**208**